User Privacy

PRACTICAL GUIDES FOR LIBRARIANS

About the Series

This innovative series written and edited for librarians by librarians provides authoritative, practical information and guidance on a wide spectrum of library processes and operations.

Books in the series are focused, describing practical and innovative solutions to a problem facing today's librarian and delivering step-by-step guidance for planning, creating, implementing, managing, and evaluating a wide range of services and programs.

The books are aimed at beginning and intermediate librarians needing basic instruction/guidance in a specific subject and at experienced librarians who need to gain knowledge in a new area or guidance in implementing a new program/service.

About the Series Editor

The Practical Guides for Librarians series was conceived by and is edited by M. Sandra Wood, MLS, MBA, AHIP, FMLA, Librarian Emerita, Penn State University Libraries.

M. Sandra Wood was a librarian at the George T. Harrell Library, the Milton S. Hershey Medical Center, College of Medicine, Pennsylvania State University, Hershey, PA, for over thirty-five years, specializing in reference, educational, and database services. Ms. Wood worked for several years as a development editor for Neal-Schuman Publishers.

Ms. Wood received an MLS from Indiana University and an MBA from the University of Maryland. She is a fellow of the Medical Library Association and served as a member of MLA's Board of Directors from 1991 to 1995. Ms. Wood is founding and current editor of *Medical Reference Services Quarterly*, now in its thirty-fifth volume. She also was founding editor of the *Journal of Consumer Health on the Internet* and the *Journal of Electronic Resources in Medical Libraries* and served as editor/coeditor of both journals through 2011.

Titles in the Series

1. *How to Teach: A Practical Guide for Librarians* by Beverley E. Crane
2. *Implementing an Inclusive Staffing Model for Today's Reference Services* by Julia K. Nims, Paula Storm, and Robert Stevens
3. *Managing Digital Audiovisual Resources: A Practical Guide for Librarians* by Matthew C. Mariner
4. *Outsourcing Technology: A Practical Guide for Librarians* by Robin Hastings
5. *Making the Library Accessible for All: A Practical Guide for Librarians* by Jane Vincent
6. *Discovering and Using Historical Geographic Resources on the Web: A Practical Guide for Librarians* by Eva H. Dodsworth and L. W. Laliberté

7. *Digitization and Digital Archiving: A Practical Guide for Librarians* by Elizabeth R. Leggett
8. *Makerspaces: A Practical Guide for Librarians* by John J. Burke
9. *Implementing Web-Scale Discovery Services: A Practical Guide for Librarians* by JoLinda Thompson
10. *Using iPhones and iPads: A Practical Guide for Librarians* by Matthew Connolly and Tony Cosgrave
11. *Usability Testing: A Practical Guide for Librarians* by Rebecca Blakiston
12. *Mobile Devices: A Practical Guide for Librarians* by Ben Rawlins
13. *Going Beyond Loaning Books to Loaning Technologies: A Practical Guide for Librarians* by Janelle Sander, Lori S. Mestre, and Eric Kurt
14. *Children's Services Today: A Practical Guide for Librarians* by Jeanette Larson
15. *Genealogy: A Practical Guide for Librarians* by Katherine Pennavaria
16. *Collection Evaluation in Academic Libraries: A Practical Guide for Librarians* by Karen C. Kohn
17. *Creating Online Tutorials: A Practical Guide for Librarians* by Hannah Gascho Rempel and Maribeth Slebodnik
18. *Using Google Earth in Libraries: A Practical Guide for Librarians* by Eva Dodsworth and Andrew Nicholson
19. *Integrating the Web into Everyday Library Services: A Practical Guide for Librarians* by Elizabeth R. Leggett
20. *Infographics: A Practical Guide for Librarians* by Beverley E. Crane
21. *Meeting Community Needs: A Practical Guide for Librarians* by Pamela H. MacKellar
22. *3D Printing: A Practical Guide for Librarians* by Sara Russell Gonzalez and Denise Beaubien Bennett
23. *Patron-Driven Acquisitions in Academic and Special Libraries: A Practical Guide for Librarians* by Steven Carrico, Michelle Leonard, and Erin Gallagher
24. *Collaborative Grant-Seeking: A Practical Guide for Librarians* by Bess G. de Farber
25. *Story-Time Success: A Practical Guide for Librarians* by Katie Fitzgerald
26. *Teaching Google Scholar: A Practical Guide for Librarians* by Paige Alfonzo
27. *Teen Services Today: A Practical Guide for Librarians* by Sara K. Joiner & Geri Swanzy
28. *Data Management: A Practical Guide for Librarians* by Margaret E. Henderson
29. *Online Teaching and Learning: A Practical Guide for Librarians* by Beverley E. Crane
30. *Writing Effectively in Print and on the Web: A Practical Guide for Librarians* by Rebecca Blakiston
31. *Gamification: A Practical Guide for Librarians* by Elizabeth McMunn-Tetangco
32. *Providing Reference Services: A Practical Guide for Librarians* by John Gottfried and Katherine Pennavaria
33. *Video Marketing for Libraries: A Practical Guide for Librarians* by Heather A. Dalal, Robin O'Hanlan, and Karen Yacobucci
34. *Understanding How Students Develop: A Practical Guide for Librarians* by Hanah Gascho Rempel, Laurie M. Bridges, and Kelly McElroy
35. *How to Teach: A Practical Guide for Librarians, Second Edition* by Beverley E. Crane
36. *Managing and Improving Electronic Thesis and Dissertation Programs: A Practical Guide for Librarians* by Matthew C. Mariner
37. *User Privacy: A Practical Guide for Librarians* by Matthew Connolly

User Privacy
A Practical Guide for Librarians

Matthew Connolly

PRACTICAL GUIDES FOR LIBRARIANS, NO. 37

ROWMAN & LITTLEFIELD
Lanham • Boulder • New York • London

Published by Rowman & Littlefield
A wholly owned subsidiary of The Rowman & Littlefield Publishing Group, Inc.
4501 Forbes Boulevard, Suite 200, Lanham, Maryland 20706
www.rowman.com

Unit A, Whitacre Mews, 26-34 Stannary Street, London SE11 4AB

British Library Cataloguing in Publication Information Available

Library of Congress Cataloging-in-Publication Data Available

ISBN: 978-1-4422-7632-1 (pbk : alk. paper)
ISBN: 978-1-4422-7633-8 (electronic)

∞™ The paper used in this publication meets the minimum requirements of American National Standard for Information Sciences—Permanence of Paper for Printed Library Materials, ANSI/NISO Z39.48-1992.

Printed in the United States of America

Contents

List of Figures

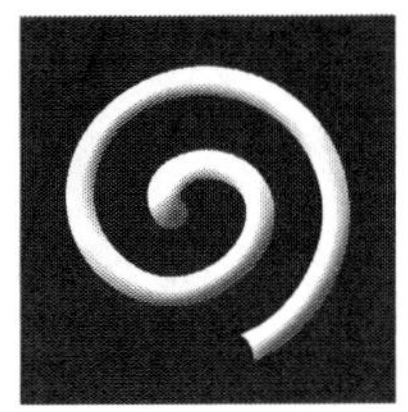

List of Textboxes

Preface

You might have noticed that online privacy and digital security are big topics of discussion these days. They're in the news everywhere, with reports of criminals breaking into online databases and stealing private data from millions of users, concerns over terrorists using modern communications and Internet technologies to keep strategy and planning safe from the eyes of the militaries opposing them, and revelations by whistleblowers like Edward Snowden detailing how governments are spying on the online lives of their citizens. Personal computing has changed drastically from a couple of decades ago, when for most people "going online" meant tying up a phone line with a painfully slow modem to interact with a primitive Internet sans World Wide Web for a few hours at a time. Today, being "offline" is inconceivable for many, especially younger users who have grown up in a world where there's always a network, always a connection for their smartphones and laptops.

The many benefits that this always-on networking confers on users and societies comes at a certain cost, however. In a very real way, computers (meaning a mobile phones and tablets as well as traditional laptops and desktops) become targets as soon as they're connected to the Internet. Being always online means that you have to be always vigilant against attack from criminals who want to defraud you, government agencies that want to monitor you, and advertisers who want to track and profile you. Unfortunately, many Internet users lack the knowledge of how to guard themselves against even basic online threats let alone the increasingly sophisticated tools modern hackers use to breach security and privacy protections.

User Privacy: A Practical Guide for Librarians was written to help librarians and library workers buttress their own privacy protections and help their users to do the same. Libraries have a special relationship with privacy protection: traditionally, they have been swift to assert the right to privacy of their users and to enforce that right within their walls. The people who work in libraries have had a long time to figure out how to do that. In the modern library, however, walls don't count for all that much. Library servers, public computers, wi-fi networks, digital books and journals, social networks, online catalogs, Google searches—all of them are networked, and all of them rely on technologies that advance so swiftly that keeping track of them all can be a full-time job. Ideally, a library should never begin using a new technology without thoroughly understanding how it will affect the library's existing security and privacy safeguards. In reality, it's hard to live up to that standard.

That's where this book comes in. Protecting patron privacy entails understanding the risks, resolving to defend privacy at the policy level, and then making technical changes and improvements to uphold that privacy. As you work your way through this book, you'll find plenty of information and suggestions to help you with each stage. Wherever possible, step-by-step instructions are provided to walk you through assessing your existing privacy tools and setting up new ones.

The intended audience for *User Privacy* is library professionals—librarians and library staff, particularly IT staff—who are concerned about online privacy and want to take concrete steps to shore up the defense of privacy at their libraries. The background material and instructions should be helpful to libraries of all types and sizes. It is hoped, however, that there is enough general information about privacy threats and countermeasures in this book to serve a wider audience that wants to stay knowledgeable about this rapidly changing field.

Assumptions and Conventions

The terms "privacy" and "security" are used somewhat loosely in this book. They're not really the same thing. Online *security* refers to safeguards implemented (or the field concerned with the implementation thereof) in a computer or network—e.g., firewalls, authentication systems, and antivirus software—to prevent unauthorized access or incursion. Online *privacy* more specifically focuses on preventing the loss or theft of personal data or information about one's online activities. Online privacy is protected by online security. Since the terms are so commonly united in purpose, this book may at times use them interchangeably when discussing the cause or effect of a particular online practice or tool.

Privacy protection is a field that is changing at dizzying speed, often on a daily basis. It would be impossible to address the entire problem space exhaustively in a book of this size—and even if it were possible, the manuscript would be out of date before it was published. The strategy taken to prepare this book has been to talk about general principles of a particular privacy practice first, then to discuss specific tools that ought to have a fairly long shelf life, and finally to list exact steps for implementation. The hope is that even if a particular step changes (in an app update, for example), the larger principles should still apply and be adaptable to the new circumstances.

Discussing the specifics of technology used by library patrons is challenging because of the range of devices available to users these days. Even to talk about "mobile devices" covers a complex landscape of smartphones, tablets, Apple products, Microsoft products, Android, Google, different operating systems, and different apps. Many discussions in this book use Apple devices—iPhones, iPads, and Macs—as exemplars. Generally, there are equivalent settings or functions available on other platforms, often found in more or less the same places as in their Apple cousins. Whenever possible, differences in features, functionality, or app availability have been noted. Some specific instructions assume that you have a basic working knowledge of how to use a computer and a smartphone; and there are a few cases where the text may refer you to an IT worker or developer in your library, if needed, to implement special tools on your website or server. No special technical knowledge is needed to benefit from this book, however.

How This Book Is Organized

User Privacy: A Practical Guide for Librarians can be thematically divided into three sections. The first part, consisting of chapter 1, "The Privacy Landscape," and chapter 2, "Policy and Privacy," prepares you conceptually to deal with privacy protection in libraries. After chapter 1 surveys the major threats to online privacy in today's Internet, chapter 2 will help you to marshal your principles into a cogent and coherent privacy policy.

Chapters 3 through 8 comprise the second part of the book, in which you'll learn the technical details involved in strengthening your library's technical infrastructure to support the policy you've chosen. Each chapter in this section focuses on a particular aspect of library technology or personal tech that your users might bring into the library. Each chapter also provides a threat assessment that attempts to highlight the worst implications of a breach of security or privacy protection in that area. Chapter 3 looks at networks and infrastructure, which provide the outer line of defense for most of your library's systems. You'll learn about methods of snooping on network traffic and how to secure networks against them. The following chapter examines the implications of offering public computers to your users. Public computers are a frequent point of interface between library patrons and library networks so they pose unique challenges to a privacy protection program. Of course, one of the primary uses of public computers is browsing the web, and chapter 5, "Web Browsers and Websites," delves into the details. It also discusses good password hygiene. Using strong passwords is one of the most basic privacy protection tools people have, yet it's often ignored.

Although public computers are still heavily used, more and more network activity comes from smartphones and tablets. Chapter 6, "Mobile Devices," begins to look at the implications of this shift. The next two chapters build upon this discussion by analyzing privacy issues for the apps that run on mobile devices (chapter 7) and for the "cloud" that commonly serves as a back-end storage and syncing solution for many mobile apps today (chapter 8). The enormous number of apps, app developers, and cloud providers makes this area of privacy protection especially complex. Each chapter describes the special concerns involved and best practices for securing your library and patrons against attack.

Finally, chapter 9 attempts to provide you with the weapons you'll need to keep patron privacy moving forward. It teaches you the basics of using the Tor system, a powerful modern defense against third-party monitoring of online activity, then wraps up the book by assessing the probable future of online security and privacy as it pertains to the library community—with an emphasis on the need for outreach and advocacy to better train your users to take responsibility for their own privacy protection.

Online privacy and security can be a labyrinthine area of study. It's the author's hope that *User Privacy* will help to simplify the complexity and guide you through the process of establishing strong privacy protection in your library. With that, it's time to start with a threat analysis of the privacy landscape.

CHAPTER 1

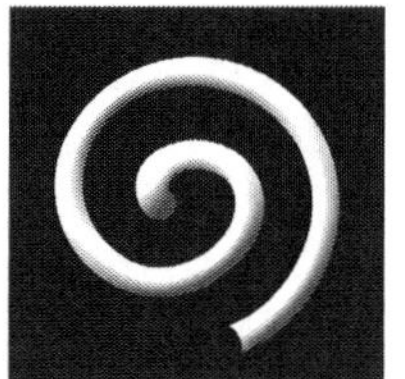

The Privacy Landscape

IN THIS CHAPTER

- ▷ Understanding the major threats to online privacy today
- ▷ Considering malware and malicious hacking
- ▷ Learning about the privacy implications of data collection by government and law enforcement agencies
- ▷ Understanding the risks of online advertising and tracking
- ▷ Determining threats to mobile devices and the Internet of Things
- ▷ Assessing the impact of social media and user habits

ONCE UPON A TIME, IT WAS PRETTY EASY to safeguard the privacy of library patrons. Before the arrival of the Internet, ubiquitous computers, smartphones, and social media, it was almost a no-brainer. Librarians and library staffers merely had to keep patrons' personal records confidential and locked away, purge records of loans and checkouts once they were complete, and maintain a zipped-lip discretion about reference sessions and other interactions with library users. But those days are long gone, and they're not coming back.

Instead, library workers of today are faced with an overwhelming number of technological threats to online privacy and security. Even recognizing and classifying different types of threats—as this chapter will attempt to do—is a Sisyphean task: new threats emerge over time, and they are protean, constantly changing in nature and number. This chapter might well have been titled "The Privacy *Minefield.*" Attempting to write a book on the subject is even worse; literally several times a week a fresh article appears in the news heralding a new privacy-curtailing technology, corporate data breach, malware scheme, legal challenge, or state-sponsored hacking scheme. It would be impossible to write about all of them, and there will undoubtedly be new, unanticipated revelations about this field before this book is published.

The world today seems to be awakening to the true scope and breadth of this privacy minefield. Online privacy has been a source of contention among technologists for as long as there's been an "online," but somehow, during the past few years, it has mushroomed into an issue large enough to draw the attention of the general public. That's not to say that everyone is taking measures to protect their privacy or that they understand the threats or even that they value privacy in the same way—but at least privacy is being talked about, thought about, and sometimes even protected. This book is about protecting privacy. Before you can start implementing protection for your library's users, though, you have to know the enemy. That's what this chapter is about: understanding the major sources of threats to privacy in today's world. Broadly speaking, those sources are *malicious hackers*, *government and legal agencies*, *advertisers and marketers*, *networked devices*, and *user behavior*.

Malicious Hackers

Another metaphor for characterizing the battle over privacy is an arms race. The arms race between innocent computer programmers and hackers who just want to get things done with their machine and malicious hackers who are out to steal, invade, or just sow chaos online—the "white hats" and the "black hats," in hacker parlance—has continued apace since the very beginning of networked computing. An example in microcosm concerns email spam (and later variants like blog comment spam and website form submission spam). As soon as spammers started abusing a perfectly good tool for online communication by mass-emailing unwanted ads to millions of people, programmers fought back. They implemented whitelists and blacklists for email clients (Internet domains or ranges of IP addresses that would automatically be allowed or disallowed as a sender of email to your account); the spammers figured out ways to defeat them. The white hats then came up with email "rules" that would let you match subjects, senders, or email content and treat them as spam; the spammers circumvented those protections. Programmers went on to develop heuristic techniques that let email programs "learn" what was spam themselves, CAPTCHAs, simple tests in online forms to prove that the sender is a real person, and so on. Each time, the spammers developed countermeasures and just kept on posting.

Spam by itself is a major annoyance, but of course there are much worse things you can encounter online. *Malware*, a general term for malicious software including viruses, trojans, worms, and scripts embedded in websites or files that do various nasty things to the computers that allow them entry, is another long-running epidemic. In bygone days, malware was transmitted relatively slowly, often needing to infect physical media—like a floppy disk—in order to propagate from computer to computer. Today, of course, there are no more floppies out there (and even their modern-day successors, USB flash drives, have probably passed their zenith), and malware can happily spread through the Internet in the blink of an eye. And malware is no longer the sole purview of skilled albeit misguided programmers; with a trivial online search, you can easily find malware kits that you can download and install to create and spread your own malicious software. Often scorned by more skilled hackers as "script kiddies," the people who do this can nonetheless inflict great harm on computers and servers that haven't been properly secured against attack.

Malware can be used in a variety of ways. Deployed on a large scale, it can create *botnets*—sets of hundreds or thousands of computers that have all been infected with the same software that places them at the hacker's disposal. Usually they continue to function normally under their owners' control, but they will also respond to commands sent to them from a remote system. Botnets can be used to collect personal information from victims' machines (such as passwords, credit card numbers, or anything else stored on the hard drives) or send spam (circumventing some of those aforementioned email protections). With all of its infected computers used collectively, a botnet can also be deployed as a weapon against websites by coordinating a *denial of service attack*—bombarding the site with enough simultaneous requests that its server breaks down under the load.

Another popular malware trick these days involves *phishing*—sending email or linking to websites designed to look like email from or the site of a legitimate sender. The intent is generally to trick the victim into attempting to log in to his or her account on the site—whereupon the malicious hacker takes the login credentials that were entered and uses them on the actual website to break into the victim's account. You may well have seen examples of phishing emails sent to users that purported to be from your own institution. Unfortunately, many people still fall for these schemes. "Social engineering" is often successful in bypassing security when an online system's direct countermeasures are strong enough to deflect a direct attack. Humans are often the weakest link in an online security system, and nothing but user education will prevent them from falling for phishing schemes.

Malware attacks can be directed against individuals, large groups of people, or larger entities (organizations, businesses, and governments). Attacks focused on a single person are usually aimed at high-profile targets: celebrities, politicians, wealthy elites, troublesome activists. The intent can vary. Attackers might be trying to obtain embarrassing or compromising media for purposes of extorting, blackmailing, or discrediting the victim (when such material is released publicly, the practice is known as *doxing*); to steal personally identifying information to use in identity theft or fraud; or simply to make money by accessing bank accounts and other financial materials. Attacks against groups of people (e.g., a phishing attempt sent via email to hundreds of thousands of user accounts) usually focus on personal gain. An attacker can try to obtain credit card numbers, bank accounts, and so forth for his or her direct use—but a more frequent approach, especially for lower-level, amateur criminals, is to collect the personal information of their victims, compile it into lists of tens or hundreds of thousands, and then sell it on shady websites to other criminals who want to make use of it.

Building those marketable lists of user account details, Social Security numbers, or credit card information is one of the major motivations for the third category of malware targets: larger entities, particularly web service providers. Popular web services, where in some cases tens or hundreds of *millions* of users store sensitive personal data, make extremely tempting targets for criminal hackers. And the stakes are only growing as people's lives become more and more enmeshed with technology. To take but one example, a person who goes all-in on Apple might own and use an iPhone, iPad, Macintosh, Apple Watch, and Apple TV. Most of those devices are constantly accumulating information about a user's online activities, movements and locations, daily behavior, and now even health. You can now even use an iPhone or Watch as a secure payment terminal. While Apple is one of the strongest advocates of user privacy in the tech world today and much of this personal data is only stored locally on each device or is heavily protected and encrypted, there's still one critical vulnerability in the system: iCloud, Apple's cloud storage and syncing solution. You can be sure that cyber-criminals would *love* to break into iCloud and its nearly one billion user accounts. You can also bet that Apple protects its iCloud servers like they're Fort Knox. Thus far, there have been no confirmed breaches of iCloud security (although there have been instances of iCloud accounts being hacked, they can all be traced to social engineering and user error). Other comparably sized companies haven't fared as well, though. Yahoo! in particular has been rocked by a series of major data breaches and (for now) holds the dubious honor of being the victim of the largest breach in Internet history, with more than one billion user accounts compromised in a single attack (Goel and Perlroth, 2016).

What's new(ish) in the malware arms race? *Ransomware*—a form of extortion in which an attacker gains access to a vulnerable computer, encrypts all the files on its hard drive so that they become unusable, and then demands a ransom from the victim in exchange for decrypting the data. What makes this technique particularly despicable is that it has been deployed not just against individuals and corporations but even against hospitals and nonprofit organizations—groups whose websites and servers often lack the necessary technical protection to guard against such attacks.

Libraries often provide public-facing technical services like public computers, which is comparable to going out and shaking hands with a hundred strangers. If you don't wash your hands afterward, there's a fair chance that you'll catch a cold. Upcoming chapters—chapters 3, 4, and 5 in particular—will help you understand and implement the technical equivalent of a good hand-washing for a public computing environment.

Government and Law Enforcement

Typically, law enforcement is perceived as the antithesis of shady criminals and purveyors of malware. Unfortunately, governments and law enforcement agencies in today's world are just as much a threat to online privacy as the cyber-criminals.

The laws governing online activities and surveillance are tangled and confusing. In many instances, they have been slow to keep pace with technological innovations, especially those relating to the implications of a globe-spanning, always-available Internet. As you'll see in chapter 8, which covers legal issues in more detail, the legal justifications for online monitoring and data collection by government agencies often cite laws that predate the Internet—or even modern computers. To complicate matters further, some of those same laws have been amended or superseded by legislation hastily passed in a post–9/11 atmosphere of panic. The USA PATRIOT Act, which enabled controversial, far-reaching online surveillance by the U.S. government in the name of preventing terrorism, is a classic example—but by no means the only one. The fear of terrorism plays a significant role in the erosion of online privacy protection; people will often give up out of fear a right to privacy that they would otherwise guard jealously.

Just how much has been done and justified as "preventing terror" was revealed by the classified documents released by Edward Snowden beginning in 2013. They disclosed information about secret data-collection programs operated by the CIA (Central Intelligence Agency), NSA (National Security Agency), and other government agencies not only in the United States, but in Canada, Australia, and Great Britain as well. They show evidence of indiscriminate online data collection on an unprecedented scale, collecting email, contacts, instant messages, phone calls, and much more. While the Snowden revelations triggered public outrage and pushback and some of the more egregious practices involved were officially rolled back, it's not unreasonable to believe that the NSA and similar organizations are still stealthily collecting whatever information they think will be useful. In fact, a good rule of thumb for your own online activity is to assume that anything you do on the Internet—i.e., anything that requires your computer or mobile device to be connected to a wi-fi hub or Ethernet jack—is being monitored by a third party. That may sound paranoid, but if paranoia impels you to do more to protect your privacy online, that's not such a bad thing.

The temptation to overreach also affects legitimate criminal investigations by law enforcement at a lower level. As more and more of people's lives and interactions move online, it's perfectly natural that policing would move there as well. Just as there are legitimate uses for online surveillance and subpoenaing of personal information from online service providers for anti-terrorism investigations, it's understood and expected that law enforcement will use similar techniques to track down criminals at a lower level.

However, the tools for online snooping that are available now are so powerful that the temptation to deploy them a little more liberally than they ought to be can be hard to resist; and the relentless drive of technological advances means that the very availability of these tools almost guarantees that they will fall into the hands of people or groups that should not have access to them and can't be relied on to use them ethically. Devices like the StingRay, which can be used to eavesdrop on cell phone traffic in a particular area (see chapter 6), are now small, compact, and inexpensive enough to be purchased not only by a low-budget police force but even by individuals. Other tools act as aggregators of data from different sources, combining public information—including social media—to compute an individual threat level for persons or locations that the police are investigating (Jouvenal, 2016). As you'll learn in this book, data aggregation can be an insidious pursuit: even with the best of intentions and a genuine attempt to anonymize the collected information, combining fragments of personal data from different sources can lead to unexpectedly precise identification of individuals in places where they should not be identified.

A particularly heated debate stemming from the tension between valid uses of online surveillance for law enforcement and the desire to protect people's right to privacy concerns the use of encryption by individuals. Encrypted data on computers is nothing new, but personal computers and even smartphones boast enough processing power today that they can support strong encryption techniques that—if properly implemented—can't be broken by third parties within a feasible timescale (unless they have an incredible amount of time and computing resources to devote to the decryption). As public awareness of online privacy issues grows, more and more tech companies and app developers are providing strong encryption for their users.

While adoption of encryption is not quite mainstream yet, a conscientious computer user can make the right choices to ensure that most of his or her data and online activities are shielded from prying eyes. It's not surprising that these developments are viewed with apprehension by law enforcement and government agencies like the NSA, which imagine powerful networks of criminals and terrorists communicating with impunity over encrypted channels. They have responded to this perceived threat in different ways. There is, of course, the war of words: politicians and officials have attempted to play on fear of terrorism to turn public opinion against encryption. For example, Senator Dianne Feinstein, member of the Senate's Select Committee on Intelligence, has stated that "if you create a product that allows evil monsters to communicate [using encryption], to behead children, to strike innocents . . . that's a big problem" (Zakrzewski and Wilhelm, 2015). More alarmingly, among the Snowden revelations is evidence that the NSA has attempted to influence worldwide standard encryption techniques in order to make them more accessible (Buchanan, 2017). Tech companies have also been pressured to introduce "backdoors" into their systems to allow law enforcement to bypass encryption when "necessary."

This last issue came to a head in early 2016 when the FBI discovered that an iPhone owned by San Bernardino terrorist attacker Syed Rizwan Farook was encrypted. Unable to access its contents, the FBI approached Apple and asked them for help. More specifically, they wanted Apple to provide them with a specially modified version of iOS (the operating system that runs on iPhones and iPads) that would let them bypass the encryption on the phone.

Apple, which had been publicly stating their commitment to customer privacy for years, had already arranged their encryption schemes in such a way that Apple itself couldn't access a user's encrypted data on a phone or iPad. Now the company's directors put their money where their mouth was, refusing to comply with the FBI's request even in the face of a court order compelling them to do so. Although the FBI claimed that this was a one-time deal, to be used only to access Farook's iPhone, Apple and pundits were skeptical. In a message to Apple customers published in February of that year, CEO Tim Cook outlined their justifications for the stance they took against the FBI: complying with the order would set a dangerous precedent that would *not* end with a single case and would fundamentally weaken Apple's encryption (Cook, 2016).

It appeared that the government and Apple were at an impasse and headed for a court battle—until the FBI abruptly backed down. Supposedly a third-party company had offered them a way to access the phone by exploiting an unpatched vulnerability in the operating system. However, there was speculation at the time that the government was more interested in setting a precedent for legally defeating encryption and had changed course when public opinion seemed to be favoring Apple's position.

Since the fight with the FBI, Apple has continued to improve and expand its use of encryption across devices—and so have many other companies, particularly those that provide messaging apps like iMessage, WhatsApp, Signal, and more. For the time being, this encryption seems to be secure. You can be sure, though, that the NSA would love to change that.

Libraries have a traditional role in proactively guarding the privacy of their users. When it comes to interference from government and law enforcement, that will sometimes mean adopting a stance similar to Apple's. Libraries have to familiarize themselves with the legal landscape that governs their records and databases; they must know when to accede to a legitimate request for information in pursuit of real justice, and when to resist a demand that goes too far.

Advertisers and Marketers

A third category of privacy threats comes from the proliferation of online advertising and marketing. Many people feel that the Internet, particularly the web, should be free to use for the most part. But that's not realistic! Merely maintaining a website costs money, either to run a server or to pay for a service provider to do it for you; and the more successful a website is, the more visitors it gets. More visitors means more bandwidth and network traffic, and more of that usually translates into higher costs.

Websites need some kind of income, and the obvious solution for a lot of them is to incorporate advertising into their pages. Even Google does it. And that's fine—legitimate advertising is a time-honored means of funding content or ventures. The problem is that over time, web ads have become more and more intrusive. A lot of people don't like *any* ads; if ads are implemented on a webpage tastefully and considerately, they'll just be ignored by a large swath of the visitors to the site. After a while, some users don't even see the ads—they've successfully trained their brains to just ignore the areas on the page where the ads appear! So the advertisers have fought back. At one time, an ad that was considered intrusive might be a rectangular banner ad with a colorful, eye-catching illustration or perhaps some blinking text or animation—a bit distracting, but acceptable. In recent years, though, advertisers have really started to concentrate their efforts on the growing field of targeted advertising. "If we can deliver ads that are personally relevant to the specific individual viewing a page," the thinking goes, "then we'll have much higher click-through and conversion rates than we do with generic ads."

This is where advertising collides with personal privacy. In order to deliver targeted ads to you when you visit a site, the ad agency has to know something about you. More often than not, this is accomplished by tracking your online activities: the websites you visit, the pages you click on, the things you search for, the products you view in an online store, and how much time you spend doing all of that. They accomplish this by dropping cookies into your browser that identify you to the system, or by using JavaScript or other embedded scripts on the page to monitor activity. If the same source maintains scripts or reads cookies across a number of different websites, then you can be personally identified on each one you visit. This can be demonstrated in the common scenario where you view a couple of products on a shopping website and then start to see ads for that same product embedded on pages of completely different sites that you subsequently visit.

It's bad enough when advertisers track you in this sort of way for the purpose of selling things to you. Much worse, though, is the practice of advertisers selling you to other businesses. Like a criminal hacker selling lists of personal login credentials amassed through deployed malware, some advertisers will sell collections of the personal data they've built up about the visitors they track to other parties. And beyond the problem of having absolutely no idea what part of your personal data is being sold, who is buying it, or for what purpose, there's the same old problem of data triangulation to be concerned about: the possibility that this data, combined with a disparate data set collected from somewhere else, could perhaps expose or identify you in unexpected ways.

Of course, there are technological countermeasures that can be deployed against overzealous advertisers. The use of ad blockers (or more generally, content blockers) as extensions for desktop and mobile web browsers has picked up in recent years. Most blockers can be configured to reject content from certain IP addresses or domains, certain ad content providers, or certain types of ads. There is a downside to using them, though. When configured to indiscriminately block all or most advertising content, ad blockers can hurt legitimate sites that depend on non-intrusive advertising for revenue to keep their content up. For that reason, the use of ad blockers is still controversial. Some websites have begun fighting back against them by preventing you from viewing their content if they notice that you're using an ad blocker in your browser.

Libraries are unlikely to deploy their own online advertising or trackers, but you should remain on guard against ads that might sneak in from outside—for example, in embeddable widgets that you might incorporate on your library website from a third-party vendor. Likewise, if you maintain public computers in the library, there's a pretty good chance that using them to browse the web will accumulate a number of different tracking cookies in the browser. Of course, you should already be resetting the entire computer environment when a user's session is finished, but this is just one more reason for ensuring that "dirty" data isn't left behind on a machine (see chapters 4 and 5 for more information on public computers and web browsers).

Networked Devices

The privacy dangers discussed thus far—malware authors and hackers, government and law enforcement, and online advertisers—can all be classified as outside threats. They're not the only sources of concern, though. Personal device technology is advancing at such a rapid pace that it's easy to get swept up in the excitement of the latest features and apps that connect you to the world and other people. Sometimes though, those new features can have unanticipated side effects that are detrimental to your privacy.

As privacy concerns grow, device manufacturers have become more careful about allowing access to personal information and device features that could compromise privacy. Apple famously—or infamously—keeps its iPhones and iPads in what critics describe as a "walled garden." Generally speaking, the only apps that can run on Apple devices are ones that have been approved by Apple and made available on the company's own App Store. While the Android device market is more fragmented, the Google Play Store offers a comparable system. Acting as gatekeepers, the companies using this approach are able to screen out malware and privacy-violating apps before users can download them. And apps that do get the thumbs-up from Apple or Google must then be approved by individual users for each type of hardware or data that each app wants to make use of: access to the camera, health data, location tracking, etc.

However, this still entails a certain amount of trust on the part of users. Even though an app may not be implementing obvious malware, granting it access to personal data may mean that the developers or the company providing the app will also have access to your data—and you have to determine whether or not you're comfortable with that. It's very easy to overlook the possibilities that a clever hacker might use to violate your privacy. For example, many apps, like websites, are supported by third-party, in-app ads that may be personally targeted. In one somewhat arcane experiment, researchers at the Georgia Institute of Technology determined that a bad-faith app developer could analyze the content of those ads delivered through his or her app and use them to put together a profile with personal details about the user the ads were customized for (Georgia Institute of Technology, 2016).

Even if your device manufacturer, app developer, and you take as many precautions as possible, bugs and poorly designed app code and infrastructure can lead to inadvertent exposure of your personal data. Properly securing websites, databases, and app logins is nontrivial, and not every developer that builds an app handles those crucial pieces correctly. If you trust an app with personal information that is then routed through the developer's servers (e.g., to sync it with the same app on your other devices), then it becomes vulnerable to attacks against the server, which is often less secure than the app running on the actual device.

A new, burgeoning source of insecurity involves the so-called Internet of Things (IoT), the practice of making more and more gadgets Internet-connected: security cameras, DVRs, light bulbs, thermostats, home automation devices, "intelligent assistants" like Amazon's Echo, fitness trackers and wearable computers, even espresso machines. This is the new wild frontier; businesses are scrambling to put an Internet connection into every type of device that can feasibly accommodate one. Quite apart from the dubious utility of some of these new offerings, many of them pose a significant security threat.

Like any networked computer, an IoT device is vulnerable to outside attack if the proper safeguards aren't put in place. And in the rush to get new devices to market, it seems that many of them lack proper safeguards. Most egregiously, some items are shipped out with default usernames and passwords that are easily discoverable if the manufacturer and model is known. Malicious hackers continuously scan the Internet, trying to locate web servers that are unprotected and to infect them with malware. Now, they can add IoT devices to the list of potential targets. There have already been incidents in which large numbers of compromised IoT appliances have been formed into botnets (Leyden, 2017). With no real oversight in place to provide standards for protection, it's likely that it will happen again.

A final category of inner threats, and one that hits closer to home for many libraries, involves the use of third-party services as extensions of your own provided library services. The issue of ads embedded in outside widgets has already been touched upon, but there is more to consider. Every time your library utilizes a third-party service that makes use of patron information—e.g., an ebook and ejournal provider that offers its own login system and accounts to users—you have to consider the implications of how that service views and respects personal privacy. Those views may not match your library's standards when laid out and compared, but—again—the rate of innovation in library services can sometimes outpace the careful determination of how new features and services may impact privacy. When a service adds a lot of value and is trivial to implement, library staff may not stop to think about the details.

A classic example is Google Analytics, a popular tool for assessing how a website is used by its visitors. Unlike more traditional web analysis systems that analyze web logs stored on your own servers, Google Analytics uses JavaScript to pass information about user activity on a page back to Google's own servers, where the data is stored indefinitely. There's a fair bit of potentially identifying information that can be gleaned from web logs, and entrusting it to a service provider like Google, which has not been especially good about respecting user privacy in the past, may not be the best idea. But it's very easy to overlook that when library administrators are ooh-ing and ahh-ing over the reports they can get about site activity!

User Behaviors

Before turning to the practical details of implementing privacy protections, there is one more source of threats to user privacy that should be considered: the actions and behavior of users themselves. As mentioned earlier, a popular technique for gaining access to a user's personal data or online accounts involves social engineering: tricking the user into revealing his or her account information to the attacker. That should communicate just how much users can be a risk to themselves!

User error also plays a role in the privacy failures outlined in the previous section, where poorly secured apps or Internet-connected devices can be vectors to theft of personal data or a loss of privacy. Many users are uneducated about the intricacies of online security and privacy, and services and apps often do a poor job of warning them of the risks involved in using their products (it's poor marketing to dissuade your potential customers from signing up, after all). Furthermore, even when the risks *are* obvious and well-known, human nature dictates that a fairly large percentage of people won't bother to protect against themselves out of laziness or indifference. Everyone who uses a computer these days ought to know the risks of using an easily-guessed password like "password" or "123456." But one of the few silver linings to the massive data breaches that have plagued Internet companies in recent years is that some of that stolen data, posted to shady sites on the web, can be used to analyze interesting things like the most commonly used passwords today. And guess what—the most popular password in a set of 10 million entries from 2016 was "123456" (Guccione, 2017; the good news, if it can be called that, is this password was number eight on the list). Chapter 5 goes into the details of why passwords like that are a bad thing. For the moment, just note that many people don't bother to use even basic online security practices. That failure leads to loss of personal data, malware infections, identity theft, and more. As part of an overall privacy protection strategy, libraries should consider educating users about these dangers in outreach sessions or workshops.

One anti-privacy user behavior that would be particularly challenging to eradicate is the use of social media. Everyone's doing it these days (a statement so obvious in today's world that it's hardly worth mentioning). The sharing of personal news, photos, videos, travels, and more is so commonplace that entire generations of younger users are growing up with the never-questioned assumption that it's just what you do. But sharing so much personal information, potentially with the entire world, carries obvious privacy implications that older users are at least somewhat more sensitive to. A Facebook account that isn't restricted to a well-defined circle of friends is a great source of personal data for anyone interested in identity theft or fraud. Posting about your vacation while you're away from home can give observant burglars a wide-open window to loot your house. And as facial recognition technology improves, having a massive online database of photos tagged with the names of their subjects can lead to all sorts of potential abuse. Clearly, the balance between what personal details are kept private and what users are willing to cede to a service in exchange for useful or fun experiences has shifted. Social media isn't going anywhere, but its use in a library should be carefully weighed against the risks to patron privacy.

Key Points

The major sources of threats to privacy include malicious hackers and malware; online data collection and surveillance by government and law enforcement agencies; tracking and monitoring by online advertisers; rapid technological innovations outpacing security protection in mobile devices, apps, and Internet-connected devices; and user psychology and behaviors. As you continue, keep these points in mind:

- *Malware*, a blanket term for different types of malicious software, can be used to target individuals, groups, or large-scale entities for purposes of intimidation or personal exposure, fraud, identity theft, or direct financial gain.
- Personal data gleaned through malware or hacking is often sold online as a commodity.
- Phishing schemes and ransomware have become popular forms of attack by online criminals, often using social engineering to trick victims into revealing their passwords or account information.
- Governments and law enforcement have used the threat of terrorism as an excuse to execute large-scale online surveillance and collection of personal data. You

should assume that agencies like the NSA still have the ability to spy on any online activities that you conduct.

- The use of encryption by private individuals is a controversial subject supported by tech companies and opposed by government and law enforcement. This is best exemplified by the fight between Apple and the FBI over decryption of a phone in a terrorism investigation.
- Online advertisers attempt to track users of websites by monitoring their browsing, searching, and viewing behaviors and linking that data with activities on other sites. This behavior can sometimes be defeated by using ad blockers.
- The popularity of mobile devices and the growth of the "app economy" leaves users vulnerable to developers and businesses that don't properly protect their servers and systems from outside attack.
- Devices in the Internet of Things are often vulnerable to malware attack because they are not properly secured by the manufacturer.
- Despite heightened awareness of privacy issues, many users still ignore basic privacy protections like using strong passwords.
- Social media is one of the biggest sources of shared private data, but many users are willing to accept a loss of privacy in order to use them.

Now that you have these cautionary points firmly in mind, it's time to start addressing them. Chapter 2 will start you off at the policy level, where you can evaluate how your library intends to protect your users' privacy and ensure that your official policy reflects those intentions. Subsequent chapters will focus on the technical details.

References

Buchanan, Ben. 2017. "Bypassing Encryption: 'Lawful Hacking' Is the Next Frontier of Law Enforcement Technology." *The Conversation*. March 16. http://theconversation.com/bypassing-encryption-lawful-hacking-is-the-next-frontier-of-law-enforcement-technology-74122.

Cook, Tim. 2016. "A Message to Our Customers." Apple. February 16. www.apple.com/customer-letter.

Georgia Institute of Technology. 2016. "Georgia Tech Discovers How Mobile Ads Leak Personal Data." *EurekaAlert!* February 23. www.eurekalert.org/pub_releases/2016-02/giot-gtd022316.php.

Goel, Vindu, and Nicole Perlroth. 2016. "Yahoo Says 1 Billion User Accounts Were Hacked." *New York Times*. December 14. www.nytimes.com/2016/12/14/technology/yahoo-hack.html.

Guccione, Darren. 2017. "The Most Common Passwords of 2016." *Keeper*. January 13. https://blog.keepersecurity.com/2017/01/13/most-common-passwords-of-2016-research-study.

Jouvenal, Justin. 2016. "The New Way Police Are Surveilling You: Calculating Your 'Threat' Score." *Washington Post*. January 10. www.washingtonpost.com/local/public-safety/the-new-way-police-are-surveilling-you-calculating-your-threat-score/2016/01/10/e42bccac-8e15-11e5-baf4-bdf37355da0c_story.html.

Leyden, John. 2017. "Mysterious Hajime Botnet Has Pwned 300,000 IoT Devices." *Register*. April 27. www.theregister.co.uk/2017/04/27/hajime_iot_botnet.

Zakrzewski, Cat, and Alex Wilhelm. 2015. "Our National Encryption Debate, in Quotes." *TechCrunch*. November 18. https://techcrunch.com/2015/11/18/our-national-encryption-debate-in-quotes.

CHAPTER 2

Policy and Privacy

IN THIS CHAPTER

- ▷ Understanding the American Library Association's principles of privacy and confidentiality as library fundamentals
- ▷ Crafting a privacy policy for your library
- ▷ Considering special policy issues for libraries

"The right to privacy . . . is the bedrock foundation for intellectual freedom."

—AMERICAN LIBRARY ASSOCIATION, 2008

AS YOU PROGRESS THROUGH THIS BOOK, you will begin to see that protecting privacy is a matter of awareness and questioning—*awareness* of the points of the library where patron privacy and personal information may be at risk, and *questioning* how your library deals with those risks (if it does) and why things are done the way they're done. Many of the new threats to privacy are technological in nature; what was previously a comprehensible problem space—guarding sensitive records, keeping interactions with library users confidential, and dealing with occasional legal demands for data—has become an ongoing fight with a hydra. For each new security hole that you discover and patch in your network, your data retention, or your public computers, two more will spring up as you find other problems you overlooked or as previously unknown software flaws suddenly make your website vulnerable to attack.

In addition, the lines around the edge of the library have been blurred. No longer just a physical location where users go to read or borrow physical items, today's library is better pictured as a node in a network. Extending out from the library are numerous connections to the outside world via online catalogs; subscriptions to online journals and periodicals; ebooks; websites; links to social media; mobile devices and apps; and much more. Each of these connections that your library employs represents one more piece of uncertainty about how the library's privacy protection is working in reality. If you subscribe to an ejournal package provided by a third-party vendor, for example, do you know what sort of information about your users is being collected by that vendor when they connect to the service? How it is used? How long it is kept? Of course, it's possible to find the answers to those questions—but each connection is a potential rabbit hole, and many libraries these days have plenty of connections to worry about.

Basically, you can't be too careful about user privacy and online security. In fact, it's best to resign yourself to the idea that you're never going to be able to provide 100 percent complete, foolproof privacy protections in the library. You just have to do the best you can. Subsequent chapters in this book will take a systematic look at different technological threats to library privacy and solutions you can implement to protect against them. Before delving into that material, however, this chapter will help you to plan your approach to privacy.

Without a plan and a vision of how users of your library will have their privacy enforced and valued, you'll end up with a hodgepodge of unevenly implemented protections. That's why comprehensive privacy protection begins at the policy level. In some cases, privacy standards are brought into existence then appended or amended as circumstances warrant—with the advent of a new technology, perhaps, that requires new guidelines for use. Naturally, it's all too easy for this to result in a set of policies that are fragmented, contradictory, redundant, or just plain confusing, and perhaps even living on different websites or invisible to users. That's not what you want. Instead, you have to start by understanding the problem space (the different facets or dimensions of privacy threat in the library) then attempting to make a *comprehensive* plan for how your library is going to handle these threats. This may sound like an intimidating task. Don't worry, though—you're not starting from scratch. Plenty of thought has gone into the privacy problem already, and there are good resources you can rely on for help. A great place to start is your nearest library association.

Library Associations and Privacy Policy

One of the best resources for library privacy policy is the American Library Association (ALA; http://ala.org). In numerous documents and policy statements, the ALA has reiterated the importance of privacy and confidentiality as not just desirable characteristics in a library but fundamental principles of librarianship and intellectual freedom. Among other assertions, the ALA has stated the following:

- "Confidentiality of library records is a core value of librarianship." (ALA, 2014a)
- "We protect each library user's right to privacy and confidentiality with respect to information sought or received and resources consulted, borrowed, acquired or transmitted." (ALA, 2006a)
- "Users have the right to be informed what policies and procedures govern the amount and retention of personally identifiable information, why that information is necessary for the library, and what the user can do to maintain his or her privacy." (ALA, 2006b)

In its Code of Ethics, Library Bill of Rights, Privacy Tool Kit, and policies, the ALA vigorously defends the necessity of user privacy in libraries. Consequently, the ALA website is loaded with information about how this plays out in practice: where the friction points are between the convenience of technology and the desire to keep users' browsing and research sessions confidential; how to determine the compatibility of an external vendor's privacy policies with your own library's policies; and the impact, effects, and legal validity of various types of government or law enforcement requests for information about your users' activities.

The ALA distinguishes between privacy and confidentiality. "Privacy," or rather the right to privacy, is defined as "the right to open inquiry without having the subject of one's interest examined or scrutinized by others" (Privacy Toolkit). "Confidentiality" transpires when a library possesses personally identifiable information about a user and keeps it private. The definition of "personally identifiable information" is also important. It refers not only to specific facts about a person's identity, such as their name or Social Security number, but also to activity information, such as a history of checked-out materials, web browsing sessions, reference sessions with librarians, and connections from a personal smartphone to the library's wi-fi network.

The ALA provides a useful set of guidelines for crafting a comprehensive library privacy policy. These will be referred to throughout the rest of this chapter.

Crafting a Privacy Policy for Your Library

Initial Steps

Before diving into the details of writing a privacy protection policy for your library, there are a few basic steps you should take first to make sure things are lined up at a high-level.

1. The ALA recommends beginning the process with a privacy audit. Given the complexities of modern-day library systems, as discussed above, this may not be a very quick or straightforward task—but it's a necessary one. Essentially, you want to do a complete review of every point or process in your library's handling of patron data; all your connections to external systems, particularly third-party commercial vendors; and all your library's direct contact with patrons for research consultations or other potentially sensitive conversations. You may well find that your existing policies are not up to snuff ethically or legally—they might not even reflect what you thought they said! Don't worry, you'll take care of that soon enough.
2. Once you've inventoried everything, take a careful look at how you handle patron data. Ascertain how much of it is collected when a user checks out a book, searches your online catalog, browses the library website, uses online chat to talk to a librarian, applies for a library card, gets permission to use the rare books room, or even rents a locker in the library. How sensitive is the data? Is it all necessary to collect? How long is it kept—and are there consistent, known policies about data retention?
3. After you're done with your audit, it's time to think big. This is when you have to figure out what the guiding principles are going to be for the library's privacy protection policies going forward. You probably aren't in a position to do this on your own: it's a conversation that has to be held at the highest level of the library's policy makers, and you've got to sell them on the idea that privacy protection is as important as the ALA says it is. You'll also want to involve legal counsel to help disentangle the byzantine array of federal, state, and local laws impacting patron

confidentiality, electronic records, wiretapping, and subpoenas, not to mention the wild world of vendor contracts.

A General Principle

One general principle of privacy protection and personal data management should be remembered and applied to each part of the policy that you design: the anti-hoarding principle. A hoarder accumulates endless quantities of useless things and retains them forever. In dealing with user data, you want to be the exact opposite of a hoarder! Your library should take in the bare minimum of personally identifying information (PII) needed to provide a service and retain it for as short a time as possible. This might require making changes to a lot of your services and procedures. One obvious candidate for scrutiny is any web server that a user might access. As you might know, web servers almost always keep a log file of requests made to them, often including information such as a visitor's IP address, computer operating system, and type of web browser (see chapter 5 for more information). If you're running your own library web server, consider ways to minimize this type of data collection or the length of time the log files are kept before deletion.

Now you might be tempted to argue that some of this collected information, such as the type of web browser being used to connect to a server, doesn't really matter that much. Who cares about your web browser? But that's missing the point and ignoring the reality of today's data environment. Data collection and analysis is taking place throughout the Internet on a staggering scale, and the businesses (and government agencies) that mine that collected data for patterns have become quite adept at piecing together frighteningly accurate pictures of individual users from fragments of such information scattered across different places: an IP address here, a Facebook profile there, visits to certain websites, types of merchandise searched for or bought on Google and Amazon, and so forth. Each little piece of information about an individual retained in a web log or database somewhere online is one more piece of the puzzle that can be used to connect the dots about someone's lifestyle, habits, interests, or political views.

Going back to the web log example—a popular approach to handling the PII issue is to try to anonymize the log entries rather than throw the whole log out. It's very tempting; after all, even if you don't care about identifying the visitors to your website, other data from the logs—search queries, pages visited, time spent on the site, etc.—can provide valuable data for efforts to improve your website and its user experience. The problem is that it's very difficult to determine if you've managed to anonymize things well. Maybe you decide to strip out the IP address and browser information and keep the rest. By itself, the remaining data might appear to be truly anonymous, only revealing what was done using your site—not who was doing it. But suppose that your web logs are subpoenaed for a criminal investigation. The investigators know that their suspect uses your library; they also have logs from his email provider that identify him and the times that he logged into his email account. By analyzing your log data and cross-referencing it with the other data set, they might be able to identify—or at least guess at the identity of—your user and start to make judgments about the materials he chose to look up in the library.

When it comes to privacy protection, less is more: less data collected, less time retained. Anonymizing logged data is good (maybe); not logging it at all is better. This will frequently entail a tradeoff between privacy and convenience. Many of the latest technological conveniences, such as "intelligent" assistants like Amazon's Alexa or Google's often dead-accurate search results, depend heavily on collecting, storing, and analyzing their customer's PII in order to understand what it is they're looking for. You and your library will have to decide how far to take that tradeoff. For most libraries, though, favoring individuals' privacy over fancy data mining seems like the way to go.

The ALA Model

In its document "Developing or Revising a Library Privacy Policy" (www.ala.org/advocacy/privacy/toolkit/policy), which in turn is part of the Privacy Tool Kit, the ALA proposes that a thorough privacy policy for libraries should address the following points:

- Notice and Openness
- Choice and Consent
- Access by Users
- Emerging Technologies
- Data Integrity and Security
- Enforcement and Redress
- Government Requests for Library Records

Each of these points will be considered in turn in the following sections. Note that the ALA document also provides links to specific libraries with privacy documents that exemplify the principles for each section, so you should consult it for more details. Your library's document doesn't need to follow this format exactly (although some libraries have done just that). Rather, these seven areas are aspects of policy that impinge on user privacy and confidentiality of personal data. The purpose of incorporating them all into a written policy, regardless of whether these aspects are named explicitly or not, is to make perfectly clear to library staff and library users alike

- what personal information a library user might have to entrust to the library
- why it's needed and what's done with it
- how it's safeguarded
- how long it's kept
- what control users have over the personal information they share with the library

As you go through the points of each of these subsections, you'll realize quickly that you're not going to be able to compose a perfect policy. There are many areas where the realities of technology or the practicalities of library services fall short of the ideal approach to privacy protection (comprehensive information, complete transparency, full personal control, and wholly time-limited retention of data). But you want to do the best that you can.

Notice and Openness

The notice and openness portion of a privacy statement serves as a sort of executive summary of your entire policy for the convenience of your users. A well-crafted privacy policy should be the antithesis of the secretive world of online surveillance that we live in today, and so you want to make it completely clear and obvious to your users when their personal information is being collected or used by the library. This first part of your statement should lay out the general principles of your policy. You want to inform your users

- that personal information may indeed be collected under certain circumstances (and name those circumstances)

TEXTBOX 2.1

"NOTICE AND OPENNESS" BY EXAMPLE

"You should be aware that information collected about you through any of the above means may be de-identified and aggregated with information collected about other users, visitors or donors. This de-identified and aggregated information cannot be used to reasonably identify you. This information helps us to administer services, analyze usage, provide security and identify new users of our Library services. In addition, it helps us to improve your user experience" (New York Public Library, www.nypl.org/help/about-nypl/legal-notices/privacy-policy).

"Staff or students working at the Dartmouth College Library will NOT disclose the following:

- The name of a patron who has a particular item checked out.
- The titles that are checked out to a particular patron.
- Personal information of any patron (address, phone number, email, etc.).
- Identify [*sic*] a patron who has checked out a particular item or describe them in any other way" (Dartmouth College, www.dartmouth.edu/~library/home/about/privacy.html).

- that the library strives to keep information collection to a minimum and takes the user's privacy and confidentiality very seriously
- why it's necessary to collect information about users, and what the collected data is used for
- how the library safeguards personal user information and how long it's kept

If necessary, you can go into greater detail here. If there are a lot of points in your system where different types of data are collected and used in different ways, though, this first section could get bogged down in unhelpful complexity. Depending on your needs and the length of your complete privacy document, you might consider creating subsections for each of these special cases and linking to them from your main document. See textbox 2.1 for an example.

Choice and Consent

There's nothing worse than a website that silently collects all the information about you that it can find, sticks it in a never-deleted database, and occasionally sells it as part of a collection of user profiles to an online advertising firm. Most libraries aren't like that, thank goodness—at least, they won't sell your data, although they could well be collecting more than they need and keeping it for longer than necessary. Keeping the anti-hoarding principle firmly in mind, you shouldn't be doing that anyway. Even if you do, though, you want to give your users some choice in the matter.

In an ideal world, library users (or users of any website or system, for that matter) would have complete control over the information that they shared with the library and could choose to decline to share it if they chose. And they could, of course, by not using the library at all. That's hardly ideal, though; and realistically, they may not have the option of *not* using the library if it's, say, required for student coursework. In practice, there are some situations where sharing personal information is unavoidable. If a user wants to borrow a book from the library, the library must have some way of identifying the user to track the loan and ensure that the item is eventually returned. However, once the item is returned, many libraries automatically erase any history of that loan: there's no point in retaining a piece of information that impacts the user's privacy. (In an extreme concession to privacy, a library could conceivably delete the user's entire record once the loan is concluded. Most people want to borrow on more than a single occasion, though, making that policy a little impractical!) Another example concerns libraries affiliated with schools, colleges, and universities. In many cases, personal information about students entering the institution is sent to the library automatically in order to generate a patron profile and set up borrowing privileges. The students themselves generally have no say in the matter—or know that it's happening. In cases where data collection is unavoidable (basic services), you should at least inform your users that it's taking place.

In addition to basic services, such as circulating items and website access, your library may offer a variety of enhanced services that require users to relinquish additional personal information in exchange for convenience or additional functionality. One example might be a bookmarking service on a library website or catalog enabling users to save their own sets of items or links and access them again on subsequent trips to the site. Obviously, in order for such a service to work, a user has to voluntarily allow the library to retain personal information—at the very least a list of bookmarks, and possibly a username and password as well—for an indefinite period. The circumstances under which that happens, the personal information needed, and how it will be used, should be clearly spelled out under choice and consent.

Access by Users

A user's ability to review, correct, or remove his or her stored personal information is an important right that relates to the philosophy of choice and consent discussed above. How this plays out in practice, though, will probably vary wildly. For some basic types of data, ensuring this right of access should be straightforward. Most websites that provide some sort of user account or registration also offer a way for users to access their accounts, check their personal information, and adjust relevant settings. Ideally, sites should also include a means of completely deleting an account and all its associated data if the user so chooses. (Unfortunately, some major social media sites make it difficult or impossible to erase every trace of your account. And if some of your personal information gets indexed

TEXTBOX 2.2

"CHOICE AND CONSENT" BY EXAMPLE

"Members [of the Kenyon Electronic Community] have the right to be informed about personal information collected about them, how it is to be used, and the right to review and correct that information.

"Members have the right to expect reasonable security against intrusion and damage to their electronically stored information" (Kenyon College, https://lbis.kenyon.edu/about-lbis/policies).

by Internet search engines, then all bets are off; it's almost impossible to contain data that's been leaked to the Internet at large.) Your library can provide the same functionality for a user's primary library account details. Another relevant data set for a library is a user's collection of currently loaned items. If possible, provide a way for users to review online the list of materials they have checked out, interlibrary loan requests, scans of articles, and other transient data. If, for some reason, it's not possible to provide that on the library's website, then patrons should be able to request a copy from staff at a service desk.

The ALA asserts that "the right of access covers all types of information gathered about a library user or about his or her use of the library, including mailing addresses, circulation records, computer use logs, etc." (ALA, 2014b). However, facilitating that right is going to be difficult or impossible in some cases. Getting an ejournal database vendor to provide access to personal usage logs is a tall order; even your own library server logs are probably not set up for easy review by users because that was not their original intended purpose. Implementing the principle of user access is probably going to remain an imperfect and incomplete project for the foreseeable future.

Emerging Technologies

The Emerging Technologies section of a library privacy policy is something of a catch-all category focused on trying to anticipate the constantly changing world of new tech that might find its way into libraries—particularly forward-thinking libraries that are eager to experiment with technological solutions to long-standing problems. Of course, each new

TEXTBOX 2.3

"ACCESS BY USERS" BY EXAMPLE

"You can manage most information within your registered user account or you can ask our staff to assist you by phone at 1-917-ASK-NYPL, by emailing us at gethelp@nypl.org, or by visiting a Library location and speaking to our staff. Our information storage systems are configured in a way that helps us to protect information from accidental or malicious destruction. To that purpose, the information we collect is also saved in backup storage systems. Therefore, any update, change or deletion you make to your information or preferences may not immediately be reflected in all copies of the information we have and may not be removed from our backup storage systems until overwritten" (New York Public Library, www.nypl.org/help/about-nypl/legal-notices/privacy-policy).

"In addition to the information that is available on the Toronto Public Library website, you have the right to request access to general records or personal information (information about yourself), or request a correction to personal information. Your identity will need to be confirmed before you are provided with access to your personal information. The Library reserves the right to charge fees for requests as outlined in the MFIPPA Regulations. Such fees may include search/retrieval time, photocopying charges, and time spent preparing records for disclosure" (Toronto Public Library, www.torontopubliclibrary.ca/terms-of-use/library-policies/online-privacy-access-to-Information.jsp).

TEXTBOX 2.4

"EMERGING TECHNOLOGIES" BY EXAMPLE

"We use Google Analytics to collect useful information about how visitors use our website. Google Analytics sets cookies on a visitor's computer to achieve this. All data collected by this method is anonymous, and a visitor's IP address is not reported to Google. All Google Analytics cookies start with 'utm'. This data will be used only by ourselves" (Cambridge University, www.lib.cam.ac.uk/privacy-policy).

technology that comes along carries with it its own set of challenges to user privacy (and library security), some of which may be new or unanticipated. The pace of technological innovation today is so rapid that it can be quite difficult to thoroughly review every aspect of privacy that it touches upon, and some threats to privacy may not be immediately visible. One telling example as noted earlier is the Internet of Things (IoT), which is composed of smart devices that are Internet-connected. Such devices can be found in countless product categories today: fitness trackers and wearable tech, thermostats, home security systems, cameras, televisions, "intelligent assistants," even light bulbs. From a security standpoint, IoT devices are effectively the same as a server, laptop, or smartphone connected to a network. No one today would expect traditional computers to be safe on the Internet without any kind of firewall, network filter, or antivirus protection—or a password, at the very least! Yet many IoT devices are sold and installed with gaping holes in their network security (if they have built-in security at all). The result is that there have been multiple, major security breaches in the IoT—and most customers who purchase them have no idea that that's even a possibility.

On the privacy front, the situation is equally opaque. The difficulties in managing user privacy in new technologies often relate to connections to third-party services, where policies about data retention and use are inconsistent and frequently inscrutable. It's challenging enough for library staff to keep themselves informed about such risks, let alone to inform their patrons. Yet for the sake of protecting your patrons' privacy, you must try. In the Emerging Technologies portion of your document, you should outline the types of special technology in use at the library (e.g., smartphones and apps, social media links or widgets on your website, use of iBeacons or RFID tags in the stacks or on items, etc.) and relevant information about how they affect user privacy.

Furthermore, in order to handle technology in a systematic manner going forward, you may want to consider establishing a Technology Review Committee for your library. This group would be responsible for receiving proposals for incorporating new tech into the library, assessing any threats to privacy that it may entail, weighing those threats against potential improvements to library services, and providing a recommendation to allow or disallow use of the technology. Once the committee is established, it would be good to describe its operation in this part of your privacy policy.

Data Integrity and Security

Data integrity and security—the protection given to personal user data that the library collects and uses—are a crucial component of a privacy policy. If you or someone at your library doesn't know what happens to user data once it enters the library system, then you can't honestly say that you have a privacy policy at all.

Integrity and security imply that the library is going to take responsibility for protecting user data and guarantee that it will be protected to the best of the library's ability. Responsible handling of data comes into play at all points in the library-user data lifecycle:

1. At the point of contact between a user and a library system, the responsible library is careful to only collect the minimum amount of information needed to fulfill the user's needs or provide the system's advertised service. It also ensures that the collection is implemented in such a way that the user's data won't be leaked or hijacked en route to the library in an online transaction (e.g., by requiring HTTPS/SSL connections on the web, as described in chapter 5). When registering a new library user, for example, don't collect extraneous demographic information just for the sake of having it; stick to the bare minimum needed in order to identify and contact the user.
2. Once collected, user data is stored in a secure way. When dealing with paper-based records, this might mean keeping all patron records in locked filing cabinets with restricted staff access. The electronic equivalent of a locked filing cabinet is a secure library server protected from electronic snooping or hacking, with server access limited to library staff with specific roles or identities. Whenever possible, patron data should also be stored using encryption.
3. The data is always used responsibly by the library. Collected user data should only be used for the purpose stated when it was first collected (and as stated in the library's privacy policy). Repurposing data for other library uses, even perfectly legitimate uses, is a potential violation of your users' trust and could also lead to unanticipated privacy violations. As mentioned above, anonymizing log data might leave you with a false sense of security; but added to a different data set, a combination of different types of metadata might triangulate and identify a particular individual. Eliminating such repurposing and recombination altogether is the best way to avoid such privacy traps, which could be very difficult to spot ahead of time.
4. Responsible curation of the data requires that library staff only retain it for as long as necessary. When it's no longer needed, it is destroyed securely (i.e., in such a way that it can't be recovered). If a student graduates from your library's university, or a patron announces that he's moving to a different state and won't be using your

TEXTBOX 2.5

"DATA INTEGRITY AND SECURITY" BY EXAMPLE

"OverDrive takes information security very seriously. We have implemented measures to protect against the loss, misuse, and alteration of your Personal Information. Any Personal Information that you choose to submit to us is protected by physical, electronic, and procedural safeguards to prevent unauthorized disclosure. We encrypt the transmission of sensitive data we collect from visitors of our Services using secure sockets layer (SSL) technology. We use computer safeguards such as firewalls and data encryption and physical access controls to our buildings and files. We authorize access to Personal Information only for those employees who require it to fulfill their job responsibilities" (Overdrive, http://company.overdrive.com/privacy-policy).

public library anymore, then their records should be purged once all loans have been settled and there are no outstanding fines on their accounts.

Enforcement and Redress

It's not enough to state what your policies are; the library has to have a means of ensuring that they are actually implemented properly. In this part of your privacy document, you should lay out the details of that assurance. The ALA recommends setting up a regular schedule of privacy audits to confirm that the actuality of your privacy implementation matches the plan laid out in the policy itself. This is especially important because of the rapid change of library technology, as described in the Emerging Technologies section above, and the difficulty in keeping track of the new potential privacy violations that new tech may bring to the library.

The other half of enforcement is redress—giving your users a mechanism for raising issues or concerns about how their private information is being handled by the library. In cases where a potential privacy violation may exist, the library should have procedures in place to investigate the claim and take whatever action is needed to correct the problem if it is substantiated. Throughout this process, library staff should do their best to communicate clearly with the user, answer his or her questions, and be open and honest about the library's policies and handling of data.

Government Requests for Data

Legal requests for private patron data held by a library constitute a thorny issue. The library is legally compelled to comply with a valid, legal order from a legitimate law enforcement agency. Most of the terms in that statement, however—"valid," "legal," "legitimate," "law enforcement agency," and even "comply"—are abstractions. What they really mean for any particular library is heavily dependent on the nested federal, state, and regional laws that govern its locality. Your library should ideally have legal counsel who can assist with interpretation of the applicable laws or, at the very least, trained staff and administrators who understand the general principles in play.

TEXTBOX 2.6

"ENFORCEMENT AND REDRESS" BY EXAMPLE

"Library users who have questions, concerns, or complaints about the Library's handling of their privacy and confidentiality rights may file written comments with the University Librarian. We will respond in a timely manner and may conduct a privacy investigation or review of policies and procedures. We authorize only the University Librarian and/or her designees to receive or comply with requests from law enforcement officers, as noted in formal policies and procedures. We will not make library records available to any agency of state, federal, or local government unless a subpoena, warrant, court order or other investigatory document is issued by a court of competent jurisdiction and is in proper form. We have trained all library staff and volunteers to refer any law enforcement inquiries to library administrators and managers" (Portland State University, http://library.pdx.edu/about/privacy).

TEXTBOX 2.7

"GOVERNMENT REQUESTS FOR DATA" BY EXAMPLE

"Under the USA PATRIOT Act, information about a person's library account and usage can be obtained by Federal Agents using a court order. The act prohibits library staff from informing the patron if such an order or search has been undertaken by means of a gag order. The FBI can retrieve any information about the patron that the library has. Information from the library may include, but is not limited to, books and other materials checked out; searches done on library computers, including places visited on the Internet; materials borrowed through interlibrary loan, use of library meeting rooms, and notes taken by librarians when assisting with questions" (Lanesboro Public Library, www.lanesboro.lib.mn.us/wp-content/uploads/2014/03/data-privacy.htm).

It's hard to deny that in many instances, law enforcement overreaches in its requests for information and casts a net that's too wide or deep. A library should have the tools and resources needed to evaluate the requests it receives concerning private patron information, and if a request is deemed valid, then the library should respond with *only* the relevant information required—no more, no less. If, on the other hand, after review of the request and legal consultation, the library concludes that the request is invalid or too vague to answer without compromising other patrons' confidentiality, then it should have the fortitude to resist the request (and any subsequent pressure to comply).

In the interest of openness, the library should inform users about the type and number of legal requests that it receives. Note that in some unfortunate cases, standing laws may prohibit you from disclosing information about a request, even to the point of not allowing you to state that you received a request at all. This concept is the antithesis of transparency and full disclosure, but you may be legally forced to comply with it. In such matters, there are workarounds that you can use to at least signal to your users that something is going on. See chapter 8, especially the section on "warrant canaries," for more information.

Special Policy Issues

By now, you should have at least a rough outline of what you want your privacy policy to look like. Before you fill in all the details, though, there are a few more points—special cases, really—that you should give some thought to.

Storing Sensitive Data

As stated in the policy section on data integrity, your library has a responsibility to make sure that any private information it possesses is kept safe and secure from prying eyes. In a sense, that's what this entire book is about, and you will find considerably more information about data security in subsequent chapters. But the more sensitive the information you're holding is, the more careful you have to be about protecting it. If you're trying to save your place in a crowded movie theater, you might feel comfortable leaving your jacket draped over your seat while you go out to the lobby to buy overpriced snacks.

You probably wouldn't leave your keys or smartphone, though. By the same principle, you want to keep sensitive user data close at hand in the library. The ideal is to keep it stored on in-house library servers (adequately protected from intrusion, of course). These days, though, a lot of servers are not maintained in-house. If your library is part of a school or college, there might well be a central IT department that handles servers for the entire campus. You might have to store your data there, but presumably the staff are knowledgeable enough to apply appropriate protection to your storage and keep things confidential for you. An increasingly popular alternative to local, physical server space is to turn to one of the many cloud-based storage platforms offered by businesses large and small. Chapter 8 delves in detail into the implications of using cloud storage; here, you should just remember that a third party may have a very different understanding of privacy and confidentiality than your library does, and the security of your data is only as good as the security practices of the hosting company.

Another common situation is for important data to be distributed in a haphazard fashion across different library computers. Bear in mind that the more fragmented or duplicated your data set becomes, the more difficult it will be to protect it against privacy violations. As much as possible, you want to consolidate confidential data in one place where you can focus your privacy control efforts. Any other computer used to store such data should at the very least be encrypted. This holds true especially for laptops, which are more vulnerable to theft, and most of all to personal laptops that store sensitive library data. The latter case should be considered a big no-no and forbidden by your privacy policies unless there's an extraordinary reason to make an exception. Directly attributable, sensitive user data, such as Social Security numbers or credit cards, should never be kept on personal machines. Ensuring that any laptop hard drive or flash drive is encrypted with a good passphrase ought to prevent thieves from accessing its contents—but in most cases, sensitive data should never be on the drive in the first place.

The very real threats to users posed by unsecured, sensitive data mean that you have to do your best to prevent such data from spreading and leaking to unauthorized machines. A scanning tool can help you by periodically doing a full-drive sweep on your library computers (and any personal machines used for library work) and identifying any personal or sensitive data that might be present. Old, unneeded, or unauthorized data should then be purged. You will find a number of such tools online, including Spirion (www.spirion.com) and the open-source CUSpider maintained by Columbia University (Windows only; www.columbia.edu/acis/security/spider). Running these scans on a regular basis should be part of your standard privacy audit.

Storing Circulation Data

Circulation data—charges, recalls, holds, and other patron requests for library materials—is one of the biggest library-specific data sets that impact user privacy and confidentiality. Many libraries have already recognized and dealt with the privacy threat posed by circulation data by proactively eliminating it when it's not needed. If for some reason your library does not, then you should consider changing your policy as soon as possible. Once a transaction is concluded, meaning that a loaned item has been returned or a request for a scanned article copy has been handed to the user, then any history of that transaction should be erased. To do otherwise has a limiting effect on your users' ability to browse and read library materials without fear of judgment or consequence, which runs contrary to a library's fundamental mission.

With all the goodwill in the world, though, a library might retain traces of old circulation data without realizing it. Web servers, databases, and apps/software programs all do, or at least can, maintain logs of their activity. In some cases, these logs can contain traces of personally identifying information. Depending on your library's IT policies, log files might be retained indefinitely. You should investigate how relevant log files are recording and storing user-sensitive data. How exactly you go about this will be unique to your library or institution, but you will have to enlist the help of a knowledgeable system administrator or DevOps staff member who can help you assess the logs and reconfigure them to remove unnecessary circulation information.

Third-Party Services

Third-party services are a major privacy friction point. Once you start connecting your library's online presence to outside vendors, apps, and cloud providers (and in all likelihood, your library is already so connected), then you step out from a curated environment with distinct boundaries into a chaotic grey area of confusing, conflicting, and inscrutable privacy policies. There's no easy solution for untangling this mess; it requires prudent selection of service providers (or rethinking of the ones you already have), determined negotiation of contracts with vendors, and careful reading of third parties' equivalents of your own privacy and data integrity policies.

Consider the type of business you're working with. While some vendors of library systems and services might appear dusty and technologically antiquated next to today's nimble, sleek, and flashy web companies, with library vendors you at least have the distinct advantage of knowing their straightforward business model: you give them money, they give you services or software or subscriptions. Things aren't always so clear when you're using a more generalized web service provider. Be especially wary of free services: the companies offering them have to be making money somehow, and if they're not taking your money, then they might be selling information about you to their advertisers. In all cases, make sure that the service providers that your library is using are respectful of their users' privacy and confidential data—in fact, they ought to have policy documents equivalent to the one that you're working on right now. Find them, read them, and make sure you understand them before committing your users to them. Many users aren't going to see a distinction between your library and the external services that your library might direct them to; to them, it's *all* "the library." It's up to you to make sure that their privacy is protected all along the way.

Usability Testing

One issue that might be overlooked in the library is the matter of usability testing. Testing library systems, software, and websites with real users is considered a best practice for any design project and has been steadily gaining traction in many libraries. Doing so, however, potentially puts users' privacy at risk. Most usability testing in a library is low-impact and has no deleterious effects on the users (or "testers") who participate in a study. Often, though, testing entails eliciting personal information from testers such as study habits, research topics, occupation or area of study, opinions about library systems, and so on. In some cases, the usability researchers may record audio or video of a tester's session and interactions with researchers and the system under test. All of these personal details and recordings should be treated as confidential.

If your library is part of a college or university, your school probably has an Institutional Review Board (IRB) that is responsible for giving a thumbs-up or thumbs-down to proposed research on human subjects. All potential usability studies should be planned in cooperation with the IRB. In many cases, proposed usability work may be exempt from IRB review; in others, the IRB might choose to grant a blanket approval to the usability team for ongoing studies that use the same test methodology. One of the key pieces of information that the IRB might request, however, is the usability team's approach to handling data collected from the tests. You should be able to give a good answer to that question.

Although usability testing is conceptually different from most of the other areas of library work where privacy protection comes into play, data gathered from a usability test should be afforded the same consideration and protection given to user data collected directly through library service transactions. Whether your library has its own in-house usability team, you bring in an outside group to conduct tests on your behalf, or individual library staff members conduct small-scale studies on their own, you should work to ensure that the group understands and agrees to the library's umbrella privacy policy before beginning a study.

Library Workers

If outside usability researchers should know and accept your library's privacy policies, then your own library staff definitely should as well. Information about users' right to privacy and confidentiality, what constitutes personally identifiable information, and the library's expectations for handling and retaining private user data should be a standard part of the library's staff training program.

Generally, a near-instinctive respect for privacy in at least the traditional roles of library interaction (e.g., doing research or checking out books) is drilled into librarians from the beginning of their education. This may not be the case for library support staff, though, and especially not for temporary workers like students. Nonetheless, students and other low-level library workers are often put to work at library reference or circulation desks, where they will regularly interact with library users. They may not realize that by overhearing the questions a user asks of a reference librarian, or by glancing at the titles of the books or DVDs a user is borrowing at the circulation desk, they are being entrusted with private and potentially sensitive information about that user. Supervisors should make sure that the privacy principles covering that situation are explained to all library staff, especially those who have a user-facing service role, so that they know what to do (nothing) with the private information they hear and see in such cases.

Informing Your Users About Your Policies

So you've worked through all the steps, had the tough conversations with administrators and staff, come up with some good governing principles to protect your users' data, and codified it all into a clear, comprehensive privacy document that the whole library can be proud of. Good for you! Now, how are you going to share it with your users? Remember, many of the tenets of your policy relate to a user's knowledge and understanding of how his or her rights are protected by the library when it comes to surrendering or sharing personally identifying information and content. The whole document becomes largely meaningless if your users are unaware of it.

The first and most obvious thing to do is to make sure that users can find your policy online. Depending on how you've crafted your privacy document, you may end up with a single webpage or a set of linked pages, each detailing one aspect of policy. On the library website, these pages should be featured prominently; ideally, you would link to them from the front page of your site. A best practice might be to take linking one step further and link to the privacy policy from *all* your webpages and websites. An easy way to do this is to incorporate a privacy link into a standard header or footer that appears on all your sites. If you have a multi-page privacy document, you can supplement the general links to it by special links to particular policy sections on relevant areas of your site. For example, a page about the library's new mobile app could include a link to the Emerging Technologies part of your privacy statement.

Don't depend entirely on electronic copies of the statement. You should also keep some printed copies of your policy handy for users who want one. Furthermore, make sure that public-facing staff are able to explain the salient points of the privacy policy and answer questions about it. Once your users catch on to the fact that the library takes their privacy seriously and doesn't want to spy on their activities or keep their transaction histories forever, they'll gain a greater appreciation for the library as a refuge from the crueler motives of the outside online world!

Key Points

Developing an all-encompassing privacy policy for your library can be challenging. While you're working on yours, recall these points:

- Libraries in general, and in particular as voiced by the ALA, have a long-standing practice of safeguarding private information about their users' identities and library activities.
- The ALA provides a number of online documents and resources to help you understand and implement robust privacy protections in libraries.
- The complexities of modern libraries, especially regarding their online systems and services, make protecting user privacy a nontrivial effort. Libraries need a comprehensive policy that clearly explains to staff and users alike what the library believes about privacy protection, how it collects and uses data from its users, and what rights and control users have over the data they give to the library.
- New technologies and connections to third-party vendors and services introduce uncertainty into privacy protections since they require libraries to venture beyond their own circle of control and consider others' policies that may differ greatly from their own.
- Storage of sensitive data, including circulation records and usability test records, requires careful consideration to avoid breaches of privacy. Ideally, sensitive data should be kept on an in-house library server, encrypted and accessible only by authorized library personnel.
- Every librarian, library staffer, and temporary worker in the library should be trained to understand, respect, and implement the library's privacy policies as part of their job.
- Libraries must make a good-faith effort to inform users about their privacy policy, including providing both online and physical copies of the library's policy as much as possible.

Now that you've worked out a good set of principles to guide your privacy protection implementation, it's time to get started on the more technical concepts that you'll need to be familiar with to carry out that implementation. You'll start at the network level in the next chapter.

References

American Library Association (ALA). 2006a. "Code of Ethics of the American Library Association." July 7. Document ID: 615b49c6-2ba0-1f64-f914-6bfb9b240357. Accessed May 6, 2017. www.ala.org/advocacy/proethics/codeofethics/codeethics.

———. 2006b. "Privacy." July 7. Document ID: 5c653c23-920b-b254-d94c-6dcf4ccd86c6. Accessed May 6, 2017. www.ala.org/advocacy/intfreedom/librarybill/interpretations/privacy.

———. 2008. "Privacy." June 13. Document ID: 1b8e7062-6f53-8e54-c9ce-87dff34d8008. Accessed May 6, 2017. www.ala.org/advocacy/privacy.

———. 2014a. "Developing or Revising a Library Privacy Policy." April 25. Document ID: 7cd349b3-3845-0ae4-e98d-d0c56c901041. Accessed May 8, 2017. www.ala.org/advocacy/privacy/toolkit/policy.

———. 2014b. "Privacy and Confidentiality: Library Core Values." April 25. Document ID: dde40983-ba20-94c4-0dd8-8989479de1da. Accessed May 6, 2017. www.ala.org/advocacy/privacy/toolkit/corevalues.

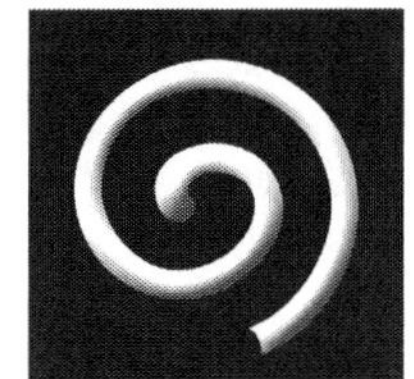

CHAPTER 3

Networks and Infrastructure

IN THIS CHAPTER

- ▷ Understanding network structure and packets
- ▷ Understanding packet sniffing and man-in-the-middle attacks
- ▷ Using VPNs and segregated networks
- ▷ Using firewalls and network filters
- ▷ Understanding the security of Internet communication protocols
- ▷ Hacking your router's firmware
- ▷ Using (or not using) log files

Threat Assessment

YOUR LOCAL NETWORK IS YOUR OWN PRIVATE (or your library's private) corner of the Internet. This is the small section of the networked world where you—or your network administrator—has direct control over what data comes in and what goes out. It behooves you to protect your corner, and the protections you place on your network represent the first line of defense that you have against malicious attacks, such as viruses, and intrusive snooping on private data.

Facebook has proven that people often don't give too much thought to what sort of personal information they're disseminating to the larger world. They probably think even less about how the information they pass along gets from one computer to another. A piece of data doesn't magically jump from your iPhone to a server in the cloud; it goes on a journey through connecting network links, and that journey makes it vulnerable to third-party monitoring. Such monitoring—properly known as *packet sniffing*—can be a serious concern if your network is not set up properly. But that's not the only consequence. Failing to secure a network can leave it open to computer viruses and other types of malware. (Malware can't do any harm by simply passing through your network, but it's far better to keep it out of your domain altogether than to let it find a laptop, server, or smartphone to target.)

Finally, even if your network configuration is doing a first-rate job of keeping data encrypted and private while blocking suspicious files that attempt to penetrate your defenses, you may not realize that there's a device *inside* the network that's dutifully recording personal information about everyone who passes through: your own web server. If your library or institution hosts its own websites or other online services, there's most likely one or more logs kept automatically with information about each request a visitor—whether internal or external to your network—makes to that server. An online catalog, for example, could be making a permanent record of every search term entered. (Such a record by itself can be an immensely useful source of data for improving and fine-tuning a library's search interface, of course. But your privacy alarm should start ringing if those search terms are attached to information about the users who entered them.)

If you work for a larger organization, chances are that the nuances of your network setup are out of your hands and attended to by professional IT staff. If so, you may not have much to do in this chapter!

Network Structure and Packets

Figure 3.1 is a diagram of a very simple, traditional network arrangement. The local network as depicted is your private realm, mostly isolated from the rest of the Internet. Although your users might not realize it, with wireless signals beaming from phones and tablets in every direction, if they're on your network then they're going through your doorway to the outside world. The gatekeeper to your network is a modem or router (which might connect to a larger local network if you're part of a large organization, or else to an ISP that represents the "whole Internet" for the purposes of this book). The router provides a firewall (depicted as a separate layer in the diagram) and controls for determining what traffic flows in and out of the network and where each message that's passed through should be sent.

The primary modem/router will often be connected to a wireless router to provide a wi-fi network for users to connect to. A network of any size much larger than a home setup will probably contain one or more hubs or switches, which take in the network messages passed to it from the router and redistribute them to smaller clusters of computers or other devices.

Messages are passed between computers on the network (and beyond it) in the form of *packets*. Packets are the primary unit of communication in the IP (Internet Protocol) system on which the Internet itself is based. Whenever you send an email, download an MP3, view a webpage, or do pretty much anything else on the Internet, your message, music, or JPEG is first broken up into packets. Each packet is individually addressed with a source and destination IP address, and each packet is sent individually through the network to its destination. (Since the Internet itself is made up of innumerable servers and computers that represent the nodes in the network, each packet can potentially travel along a different route to its destination. For IP communication, it's the destination, not the journey, that matters.) It's a bit like having a worker in the post office cut up the letters you mail into tiny fragments, stuff each one into an envelope of its own, and copy the address and return address onto each new envelope before dropping it into the mail chute. Packets vary in format and length, but here's a typical example:

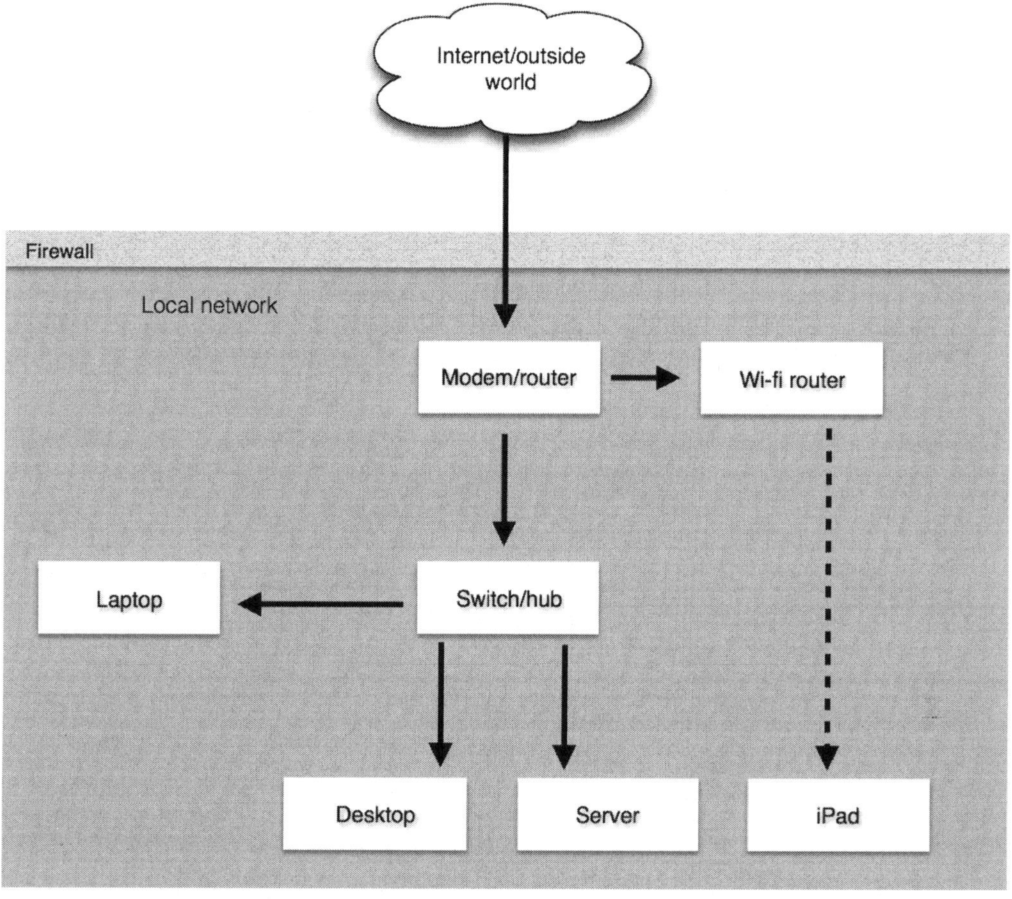

Figure 3.1. Simplified network diagram showing primary components and connections.

```
17.132.4.56.http > dhcp-gs-1090.eduroam.cornell.edu.62061:
Flags [S.], cksum 0x7101 (correct), seq 2064930574, ack
629282686, win 5792, options [mss 1382,sackOK,TS val 1307097387
ecr 483456607,nop,wscale 1], length 0 15:36:18.059016 IP (tos
0x0, ttl 64, id 30132, offset 0, flags [DF], proto TCP (6),
length 52)
```

Since packets are the basic unit of Internet messaging, it's important to ensure that they are carefully guarded from interception or interference as they travel to their destinations.

Packet Sniffing and Man-in-the-Middle Attacks

The biggest danger at the network level, be it a wired or wireless network, is a technique known as *packet sniffing*. The packet sniffer, as a tool, was originally developed for use by network administrators. It gives an administrator a way to peek at what can be thought of as the subatomic level of a network: the individual packets that make up all network traffic between devices. Recall that every packet is a small chunk of a message (in the broadest sense of the term): a portion of an image, a fragment of text from an email, an HTTP request to a website, or just about anything else your computer is doing that requires communication with another device. A packet sniffer sits in the stream of network traffic and looks at each individual packet that passes by. This is a perfectly legitimate thing to do if you have to debug a tricky network problem, which can leave behind clues at the packet level. Unfortunately, it's also a very easy thing to do if you're more interested in snooping than debugging. Sniffers are not exotic, expensive tools—they're often free and readily available. In fact, if you're using a Unix- or Linux-based computer (including Macs), then you probably have a couple of packet sniffers installed already as command-line tools or wi-fi diagnostic software (such as Apple's Wireless Diagnostics app).

Packet sniffing is the reason why you should never use an unsecured network if you have a choice—and certainly not if you're accessing sensitive information through the network. By default, packets on the Internet are sent as plain text. Let's say you're away from home, and your spouse needs to log in to your online bank account. You've given the account a great password, but it's long and complicated; rather than give it to him or her over the phone, you send an email from your hotel room. Unfortunately, you didn't set up your email client program to use secure communication, so your message goes out over the wire as plain text. And now not only does your spouse have the password to your bank account—the fellow down the hall, using a packet sniffer, has it as well.

Fortunately, more and more Internet traffic is being sent securely. (In a web browser, this is the difference between URLs that begin with "http"—which is insecure—and "https.") Although the "secure" protocols used are not *wholly* secure and may be vulnerable to a determined hacker with advanced technical skills, they are usually enough to deter more opportunistic snoopers. A packet sent as part of a secure (encrypted) protocol is mostly unintelligible to a packet sniffer, apart from some of the header information. This is an important consideration for protecting the privacy of patrons. Web browser requests made to a website using HTTPS will obscure the details of what those requests are (although they still may reveal that the site was visited). A site that uses HTTP, however, will reveal all. Thus, if you're secretly a fan of the movie *The Room*, you can search for information about it on Google to your heart's content: even if you try to go to http://google.com, you'll be redirected to https://google.com, and your search terms will be hidden at the packet level. On the other hand, if you expand your search to include IMDB (http://imdb.com), you risk leaking your secret to the world.

The technique of packet sniffing is related to a more dangerous network-level privacy assault known as a *man-in-the-middle attack* (MITM). In a MITM, the attacker actually modifies the behavior of a network by tricking it into believing that the attacker's computer is an integral part of the network—usually the server acting as a gateway to the outside world. It then sets itself up as a relay, intercepting the network traffic between the other computers and outside servers. The MITM computer's intervention is transparent to the other machines on the network, which may have no idea that their messages have been compromised, but the data being passed through is vulnerable to packet sniffing. At the same time, there is the added danger that the MITM operator will not only *look at* data but also *modify* data—changing the contents of the messages being passed through the fake server.

Ethernet and Wired Networks

When you're connected to a network by a physical wire—typically an Ethernet cable—then it's more difficult for an outsider to eavesdrop on the information being passed back and forth. They need to gain access to the physical network in order to do any harm. On the other hand, this may be small comfort in a library environment that may still be offering Ethernet jacks for users to plug into with their own laptops. And simply providing public access computers that aren't properly secured (see the next chapter) gives a knowledgeable user an entry point into your network that can be used for unsavory purposes.

There's no practical way of detecting that a packet sniffer or MITM is in operation. Short of preventing physical access to your network, you can't *guarantee* that someone isn't using a sniffer to look at network traffic. However, you can minimize the risk by building your network properly.

Recall that hubs and switches are both network components that distribute messages from one part of the network (generally a larger, outer section) to another (usually a smaller subsection or cluster of machines). The primary difference between them is that a hub is a "dumb" component and a switch is "smart." A hub doesn't know what it's connected to; its sole mission is to take whatever messages it receives on its incoming line and rebroadcast them to every outgoing line that is connected to something (a computer or another hub or switch, for example). This makes it a simpler piece of technology, but it's also a less efficient way of relaying data for a number of reasons.

A switch is like a hub that has better awareness of its place in the network: it knows the identity of the devices or other network segments that it's directly connected to. This means that it can rebroadcast incoming messages selectively, passing them directly and solely to the destination for which they are intended. A switch offers better efficiency—and somewhat better security. A packet sniffer operating on a hub-distributed cluster will be able to monitor traffic for all the machines it's connected to; but one plugged into a switch will only see the traffic for that particular machine. You should be aware, though, that switches only offer *improved* security. It's still possible to trick or circumvent their intended behavior with the right access and knowledge.

Wireless Networks

Wireless—wi-fi—networks are everywhere these days. They're quite a boon in this age of portable laptops, tablets, and smartphones; whether you're at home, in the office, at a coffee shop, in the gym, or even on a plane somewhere above the Atlantic, there's a good chance that there's at least one wi-fi network operating there. And since this is also the age of expensive, capped, cellular data plans, ubiquitous and freely available wi-fi networks present an almost irresistible temptation to the mobile user—a temptation that *should* be resisted at all costs! The preceding section should give you a hint as to why.

You've seen that Internet traffic is unencrypted by default and sent as plain-text messages. And there are numerous tools that are both free and easy to use to eavesdrop on that traffic if they're running on the same network. A wi-fi network presents the same risks of packet sniffing and MITM attacks that a wired network does—except that there's no physical boundary to the network! *Anyone* standing within wi-fi range could sign in to the same network you're on and start listening in. Moreover, malicious users will set up open networks in public spaces to tempt people to connect to them and then will use those connections for nefarious purposes. For these reasons alone, you should never use an unsecured wi-fi network (one that isn't protected by a password). You might think of connecting to one and just being careful: only using it to check the weather and the latest sports scores. But modern operating systems, be they on your laptop or your smartphone, are frequently running dozens of apps and background processes simultaneously; and many of those apps and processes will reach out as soon as an Internet connection becomes available to update their data from remote sources. Email is an obvious example, but by no

TEXTBOX 3.1

HOW TO AVOID PACKET SNIFFING

Since packet sniffers are passive elements in a network—assuming they aren't being used in a man-in-the-middle attack to alter the contents of a packet—it's difficult to detect that they're being used. Therefore, your best hope is to employ defensive practices to minimize the risk of encountering a sniffer. Three things to do include

- Trying to use switches instead of hubs if you're building your own network. This is a good general practice anyway since switches provide better efficiency and message routing, but they also reduce the amount of traffic a packet sniffer can pick up within the subsection of the network each switch governs.
- Avoiding unprotected wi-fi networks. If you do nothing else, do this! Using an insecure wi-fi network for anything beyond the most mundane and impersonal tasks is asking for trouble. And recall that many laptops and mobile devices may be silently using the network in the background, without you realizing it, the entire time that you're connected.
- Using secure communications and services regardless of the network you're on. The rest of this book contains more information about secure apps and tools, but it's good to get into the habit of questioning how communication works in any app that you use. Don't send personal data to a website that's not encrypted with SSL (HTTPS); set up your email clients to use secure traffic; and connect to a VPN if possible when you're on an unfamiliar or suspect network.

It's important to remember that none of these techniques will guarantee that your communications are sniffer-proof. Online security is an ongoing war between those who are trying to protect privacy and those who are trying to defeat it.

means the only one. Like it or not, your use of that insecure network will probably be far more extensive than you intend it to be.

Conversely, if you have a wi-fi network set up in your library, you should never leave it unprotected. When you configure your wi-fi router, be sure to use a good password or passphrase to protect it. Unfortunately, most routers require you to choose the method of encryption to use with that password, and not all of the available methods are good ones. Predominant encryption techniques include the following three.

Wired Equivalent Privacy (WEP): This was the first widely used wireless security protocol. However, it's also the weakest. Numerous holes in its security mean that it's basically worthless as a protective measure in today's world—and yet it continues to be used, largely because people don't understand its weaknesses (and because it usually appears first in the list of protocols!).

Wi-Fi Protected Access (WPA): WPA was developed as a replacement for WEP and offers considerable security improvements over its predecessor. However, vulnerabilities in WPA have been found over time, and it's no longer the preferred method of encryption.

Wi-Fi Protected Access II (WPA2): This is the current encryption leader for protection of wi-fi networks, so use it. There's no reason to even look at WEP or WPA unless, for some reason, WPA2 isn't available (in which case, you should probably just look for a different router).

As with many topics that will be covered in this book, the development of wi-fi security protocols reflects the ongoing cat-and-mouse game of trying to create—or crack—unbreakable, cryptographic algorithms. The exponential rise in computing power can reduce the time required to defeat an encrypted data source from years to days to hours, so it's no surprise that old protocols are superseded by newer developments and techniques.

DMZs and VPNs

By now, you may be feeling pretty discouraged about network security! You're learning that it's probably not possible to achieve complete protection against privacy intruders; the best you can hope to do is block the most common routes of attack and hope that nobody comes along to exploit the more exotic ones.

One simple thing you can do in your library to bolster security is to segregate your public network from your private (staff) network. This can be accomplished at the router level by using a DMZ (demilitarized zone). A DMZ, in the network world, is a specially created sub-network that is isolated from the rest of the network. Requests from outside the network—i.e., from the rest of the world—can only reach into the DMZ. Thus, public services like web servers can be placed in the DMZ, and more sensitive functions and data used by library staff can be kept out of harm's way.

Another option, and one of the best things you can do for your network-level security, is to use (or provide) a virtual private network. A VPN is like a layer of protection around your Internet connection, encrypting your communications even when you're on a public, unsecured network. As the name suggests, when you operate a VPN client, it acts as though your computer were physically connected to a remote, private network: safe and secure—even if you happen to be on the other side of the world from where the server you're connected to resides. All of your Internet traffic is then routed through this remote, trusted server, and the communications between the server and you are encrypted with, ideally, strong, secure algorithms. The setup is reminiscent of a man-in-the-middle attack server, except that you're connecting to the VPN server by choice! (In addition to their privacy benefits, VPNs are often used to alter one's apparent geographic location. If you connect to a VPN server in, say, France from the United States, you'll appear to be working from Europe.)

"VPN" is a loose term that encompasses a number of techniques (or protocols) for achieving the same goal. There are a number of different implementations of a VPN. If you are part of a larger institution, such as a college or university, you may already have a VPN that you can use for your own protection. For some VPNs, you may have to install and configure a client program such as Cisco AnyConnect. Mac, Windows, and Linux computers all come with VPN software installed (that can be used to create VPN servers as well as act as VPN clients), although it doesn't necessarily work with all of the various VPN protocols. There are also client apps available for iOS and Android mobile devices.

If you don't have an institutional VPN already and would like to provide a VPN for your users, you have a few options. One is to install client software onto an existing computer that can act as one end of a VPN connection. There are a number of client programs available, sometimes under the guise of more general-purpose communication software. One popular example is TeamViewer (www.teamviewer.com). TeamViewer offers VPN-based connections between two computers (Windows, Mac, Linux, Chrome OS, and a variety of mobile platforms) for file sharing, VoIP, chat, remote desktop sharing, and more.

A second option is to install a dedicated VPN router. VPN routers are physical devices sold by Cisco, Netgear, and other providers of more common routers. If you're short on funds and high on ambition, a variant of this approach is to start with a more run-of-the-mill router and install third-party firmware (see below) that provides VPN functionality.

If you're not quite ready to invest in creating your own VPN, consider investing in someone else's: buy a subscription to one of the many commercial VPN services out there. You can configure appropriate client software on your public computers and provide instructions for using the VPN service. This is an excellent way of protecting your users' privacy during their computing sessions in the library. Configuring client software for a VPN service is usually straightforward; the most difficult part of the process is choosing which service to use. A website called That One Privacy Site (https://thatoneprivacysite.net, run by That One Privacy Guy) provides a superlative set of resources for informing that decision. Charts on the site offer detailed information for well over a hundred different VPN services and include important considerations like business jurisdiction, ethics concerns, supported protocols, and logging practices.

Firewalls, Filters, and DNS

Another privacy protection that you can add at the network level is some measure of content filtering. It's all very well to make sure that your public computers are protected against viruses and adware by installing appropriate software, but why let malware into your neighborhood at all? There are a variety of ways to block it at the front gate.

Firewalls

You may already be familiar with the concept of a firewall. Firewalls take a variety of forms and can be implemented either in software or hardware. Most modern desktop-class (i.e., not mobile) operating systems provide a built-in firewall, although their exact capabilities vary quite a bit. For example, Apple's macOS (formerly OS X) firewall can be found by clicking on Security and Privacy in the System Preferences App and choosing the Firewall tab. There you can choose which of your apps and programs can accept incoming network traffic. It's not a very sophisticated implementation, however.

While it's good to make use of your computer's own firewall, a more comprehensive approach is to activate a firewall in your network router. Many, although not all, routers offer this option. A router firewall lets you set up a rule-based configuration that determines exactly what types of connections are allowed to enter your network from outside. The rules you set up are based on *software ports* (not to be confused with hardware ports, such as your computer's USB connectors). A software port can be thought of as a channel on a TV tuner: just as turning to a particular channel lets you watch content from a specific broadcaster, listening on a particular software port connects you to a specific type of network traffic. Computers can have thousands of active ports. While some ports are generally used for communication with a specific app (port 3724 is primarily used by the game World of Warcraft, for example), others are designated for particular communication protocols that can be implemented by any number of different programs. One of the most commonly used ports is port 80, which is reserved for HTTP traffic—that is, standard web traffic. Many application types use two or more ports: one for insecure and one for secure communication (e.g., port 20 for FTP—File Transfer Protocol—exchanges and 22 for SFTP—Secure FTP).

When configuring a firewall, the basic rule is to begin by closing off just about everything. Then you can open only the ports that you need. Most people these days don't have much need for (insecure) FTP or Telnet transactions, so there's no reason for ports 20 and 23 to be open; that's just inviting trouble. You will probably want to leave port 80 open, or else users won't be able to browse the web. Something like port 25—the SMTP protocol used for email—is a toss-up, dependent on your particular needs.

A good way of testing how open—and thus vulnerable—your network is is to visit the venerable ShieldsUP! website (www.grc.com/x/ne.dll?bh0bkyd2). ShieldsUP! provides several tools for checking the state of your software ports, reporting whether each one is open, closed, or in "stealth" mode (blocked before any requests reach your computer). Since you're testing your router firewall, any ports that you close in the configuration should be listed as stealth ports. Stealth mode is preferable to simply blocking ports because it minimizes the information that an aspiring attacker can learn about your system. Figure 3.2 shows a sample test report from ShieldsUP!

Each block in the grid represents a port on the computer, and its color indicates the result of the scan: blue for closed ports, red for open, and green for stealth. Hovering over any port will reveal information about its purpose. Note that in this case, ShieldsUP! gave this machine a failing grade because a single port (port 113, used for identification and authentication) revealed that it was closed—even though all other ports are in stealth mode!

Network Filters

Firewalls are perhaps the most common network-level filters, but there are other types as well. Many different filters exist to keep undesirable content from entering your network. One common application, used by both businesses and families, is to block access to pornographic websites and other child- and office-inappropriate material. At the home level, these are often referred to as "parental controls." As with firewalls, content filtering can be achieved through several different methods.

You can install content filtering software on individual computers or mobile devices, but that requires reduplication of effort (or cloning software). You can also buy routers that offer filtering based on content categories. Most routers provide at least basic whitelisting/blacklisting functionality that lets you block individual websites or domains—but it's difficult to create a comprehensive list of sites. One example of router-level filtering is the Linksys Smart Wi-Fi router and apps (www.linksys.com/us/smartwificenter). With the router installed, you can buy one or more accessory apps through your mobile store that let you control the router's filtering behavior. Its Block the Bad Stuff app, for instance, lets you choose different levels of content blocking, starting with basic malware and working up to adult content and materials about drugs, violence, and gambling.

A further alternative is to purchase a physical filter. These are devices that you attach to your existing network to add various filtering capabilities. These are often deployed

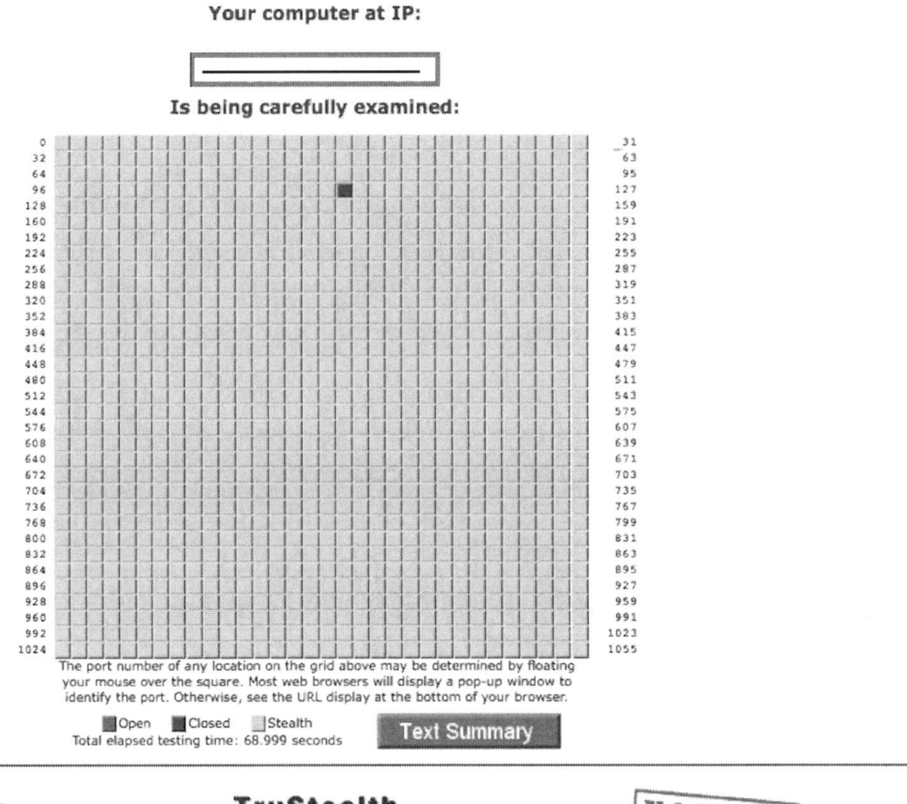

Solicited TCP Packets: RECEIVED (FAILED) — As detailed in the port report below, one or more of your system's ports actively responded to our deliberate attempts to establish a connection. It is generally possible to increase your system's security by hiding it from the probes of potentially hostile hackers. Please see the details presented by the specific port links below, as well as the various resources on this site, and in our extremely helpful and active user community.

Unsolicited Packets: PASSED — No Internet packets of any sort were received from your system as a side-effect of our attempts to elicit some response from any of the ports listed above. Some questionable personal security systems expose their users by attempting to "counter-probe the prober", thus revealing themselves. But your system remained wisely silent. (Except for the fact that not all of its ports are completely stealthed as shown below.)

Ping Echo: PASSED — Your system ignored and refused to reply to repeated Pings (ICMP Echo Requests) from our server.

Figure 3.2. Sample output from a port scan by ShieldsUP! of the author's laptop. Screenshot from ShieldsUP! website.

at the enterprise level—Barracuda (www.barracuda.com) is one such provider, offering many different models. If your needs are less sophisticated or your budget less extensive, a simpler implementation of the same idea is Disney's Circle (https://meetcircle.com).

DNS Servers

One approach to filtering that combines the ease of use of a software filter with the comprehensive blocking of a network-level hardware device is to use a special DNS server. The DNS (Domain Name System) is the Internet's tool for associating human-readable URLs (such as www.google.com) with actual machine IP addresses that enable your computer to properly address the packets it sends out into the world. DNS is a distributed system, with servers providing addressing at many different levels of the Internet's structure and exchanging information with one another to keep their address books synchronized. If you work for a college, university, or large business, your organization probably has its own DNS servers; so does your ISP if you're on a smaller or home network. Every computer has to be able to connect to one or more DNS servers in order to communicate with others. Quite often server IP addresses are configured automatically with the rest of your network settings, so you may never have looked at them. On a Mac, you can check your DNS settings by going to the System Preferences app, selecting the Network pane, selecting your Internet connection in the list, clicking Advanced, and selecting the DNS tab. (If you're comfortable working on the command line, you can also go to the Terminal app and type "scutil --dns".) In Windows, go to Control Panel > Network and Sharing Center; click Change Adapter settings; right-click on your network connection and select Properties; select Internet Protocol Version 4 in the list; and click Properties.

The DNS is a powerful system. If anything happens to it, confusion ensues—or in worse cases, a complete breakdown in communication. Even the largest online entities are vulnerable. Since the system's servers are distributed, it's possible for a subsection of the Internet to suffer DNS problems without affecting the whole. It's also possible for a malicious hacker to cause chaos by attacking one or more DNS servers. Someone could, for example, change the IP address associated with an online store and redirect traffic intended for that site to another server under the hacker's control. There, by creating a close copy of the original site, he or she could potentially trick visitors into revealing their login credentials or credit card information.

On the other hand, judicious use of DNS can be a valuable asset in privacy protection. A firewall configured with privacy-related rules can block unwanted content or visitors; using a privacy-sensitive DNS can give you many of the same benefits, while leaving the details of the implementation to professionals. Changing the DNS you're using is as simple as changing the IP addresses specified in your computer's network settings. But if you're protecting any significant number of devices, it's easier to make the same change in your router configuration. Businesses offering both free and paid DNS services are plentiful; shop around until you find one that you like. Most of them provide filtering of malware and unwanted content, and some allow you to create custom rules and blacklists/whitelists. Some also claim to provide faster DNS service than you would otherwise get. The world's largest public DNS service is Google Public DNS (https://developers.google.com/speed/public-dns). Since Google's commitment to user privacy has been questioned in recent years, though, Google might not be a preferred choice for privacy protection. One of the other most popular providers is OpenDNS (www.opendns.com), which provides a range of DNS solutions for both individuals and businesses.

How to Set Up a Router and Firewall

Every router has its own idiosyncrasies, so be sure to refer to the manual for details. These are some basic steps to take once you have the hardware set up (modem or WAN—wide-area network) source plugged into the input, wi-fi router or Ethernet cable plugged into the output, and power turned on).

1. Most router configuration systems are accessed through a web interface by going to a particular IP address once the router has been turned on and the default network has established itself. The address to use depends on the router (or at least on the router manufacturer). Netgear routers, for example, can usually be found at 192.168.1.1. Figure out which IP address to use, fire up a web browser on your computer or tablet (make sure it's connected to the network!), and browse over to that address. You should be greeted with the router's configuration page, protected with a login screen.
2. Like the IP address itself, the default login name and password offer little mystery: admin/password (yes, "password") or something along the same lines. Look it up,

enter it, and then *remember to change it once you're logged in!* Well-known router login credentials pose a significant security threat. If you don't change the defaults, then anyone with a basic knowledge of routers can log in (if they're on the network) and do bad things to your configuration.

3. Once you're in, you can start adjusting settings. Many routers provide a setup wizard for basic configuration, although you can always choose to do a manual setup if you want fine-grained control over it. For purposes of privacy protection and security, there are some settings to watch out for. (Note that the exact name given to each setting will vary from manufacturer to manufacturer.)
    a. DNS: if you want, you can switch the default DNS values provided by your ISP to something like OpenDNS.
    b. Wi-Fi: make sure that your wireless network is password-protected and encrypted using WPA2. If Wi-Fi Protected Setup is offered as an option, you should disable it unless you need it; there are some security concerns associated with it.
    c. Ping blocking: If your router gives you the option to block "pings" from the outside world, use it. Pings are a way for one computer to shout out to another, "Hey, are you there?" They can be misused by hackers looking for vulnerable computers on the Internet, so blocking pings—i.e., not responding when you receive them—will keep your machine off their list.
    d. Remote management: Remote management usually means the ability to access and change the router configuration page from anywhere on the Internet. This is not a good thing! Turn it off if you don't need it.
    e. Firewall: Turn the firewall on. At its most basic level, it may block known malware and attacks.
    f. Filters (or parental controls): If your router gives you the ability to filter out content types that are unwanted, this is where you'll configure that. This may also be the place where you can blacklist or whitelist certain websites and domains and where you can specify custom filtering rules.
4. There should be a button or link somewhere on the page to update the router's firmware. Give it a try. Updating your firmware is akin to downloading the latest security updates for your computer's operating system. It's a good idea.

Internet Communication Protocols

The World Wide Web is the one component of the Internet that most people are intimately acquainted with (the other contender, email, has arguably become a quaint antique for the newest generations of Internet users!). Nontechnical users may not even understand the distinction between "the web" and "the Internet." Nevertheless, the full Internet is a collection of many disparate forms of communication and network traffic. It's worth taking a look at some of the most common and considering their security implications.

- Telnet is an ancient protocol (by Internet standards) used to connect from a terminal on one computer to a second networked computer. It gives you command-line access to the remote machine, enabling you to work as if you were actually sitting in front of it. (It's a precursor to more modern tools known as "remote desktop" programs.) Telnet is not widely used these days because it is, by default, completely insecure. Data is exchanged in clear text without encryption and is thus vulnerable to eavesdropping in the form of packet sniffing. The Telnet protocol has been almost completely supplanted by SSH (see below), and it's unlikely that you'll encounter Telnet in mainstream Internet use.

- FTP (File Transfer Protocol) is another very early development in network communication. Its primary purpose is to facilitate the exchange of files between two machines over a network. In the days before the development of the web, a user might fire up an FTP client, connect to a public server, browse through a list of folders and files, and download the ones he or she was interested in. However, just like Telnet, the original FTP system has no true security features. It is possible to log in to an FTP server as an anonymous user, but only if the server allows anonymous connections. You can still find FTP offered as an option in some software—a website design app, perhaps, that has to upload the HTML files you create to a web server. Don't use it unless you have to; most modern servers ought to allow more secure transfer methods, such as SFTP (see below).
- SSH (Secure Shell) is a powerhouse of secure communication. It was designed from the start to use encryption to prevent snoopers from intercepting messages sent back and forth, and it's still the basis of many forms of encrypted communication today. At the most basic level, an SSH connection can be thought of as a secured Telnet connection, but it goes far beyond that. SSH can be used to create a protected channel between two computers even if the network between the two—such as an open wi-fi network—is not secure. Different apps and protocols can create one of these SSH "tunnels" and pass messages through it, letting them benefit from the same security. The basic SSH program is a tool that's still used every day by IT administrators, software developers, and web designers who have to do their work on remote servers. On its own, however, SSH doesn't appear in much mainstream software (although there's a good chance it's being used behind the scenes).
- SFTP (SSH File Transfer Protocol), as its name suggests, is a secure form of FTP communication based on the same principles as the original FTP protocol. It has widely supplanted FTP exchanges and is another common tool for tech developers. This is also a possible option you could select in your web builder app for uploading files to a server, and it's a much better choice than plain FTP. A related technology is FTPS (FTP-SSL), which uses the Secure Sockets Layer (SSL) protocol more commonly associated with secure web communication (think HTTPS).
- SMTP, POP, and IMAP: SMTP (Simple Mail Transfer Protocol), POP (Post Office Protocol), and IMAP (Internet Message Access Protocol) are all related to the use of email. SMTP is the mechanism used for sending messages from a client computer to an email server or for transferring messages between servers. POP (aka POP3, the most common version in use) and IMAP are both used by client apps or computers for retrieving mail from servers. POP is a fairly basic mechanism for downloading messages, and it usually deletes the downloaded messages from the server afterward. IMAP is more sophisticated and allows for the ongoing storage of messages on a server and synchronization between the server and one or more clients—obviously a much more desirable mechanism for today's world when many people are juggling at least two different email-capable devices at the same time. None of the three protocols is inherently secure, but they all *can* be secured. Unless you're running your own email server, that's the job of your email provider.

But you should do a check of your email configuration—for each provider that you use—and ensure that you're using the secure option whenever available. Remember that many email clients, whether on mobile devices or traditional computers, are set up to check for new email automatically at fixed intervals. If your client is not set up to use secure communication, and you happen to be on an unprotected network, then bad things could happen.

Key Cryptography and Email Encryption

There's a way to encrypt the text of your email messages so that even if a snooper manages to intercept an email intended for someone else, he won't be able to read it. It's an old technique, but very few email users employ it. Most have never heard of it.

Key-based cryptography is a system in which text is encrypted based on a mathematical algorithm that hinges on one or more keys—long strings of letters, numbers, and other characters. PGP (Pretty Good Privacy) is a variant of key-based cryptography that employs two keys: a *public key* and a *private key*. A sample public key appears in textbox 3.2.

A private key looks similar but is considerably longer so an example won't be printed here. There's no problem with publishing the above public key in a hopefully best-selling book because, well, it's a *public* key—it's meant to be shared with the world. The beauty of the PGP system is that messages are encrypted with a public key, but they can only be decrypted by using the corresponding private key. (This technique is referred to as *asymmetric* encryption.) Thus, it's perfectly safe to distribute your public key to others, but never, ever reveal your private key.

Using the public key in textbox 3.2, the sentence "Personal privacy protection is a terribly tricky topic" can be encrypted into the following:


```
Gtxz5NDZCThMG418TeC/DIyjGTSrbwpgugJKiKjXDbq3GSCalF0BEXT-
FtyyWJh5/1mwJA0Gb6JFY02GAZuldyVg7XGNpn6esGtCL7JzSWIc9xvB-
zBtqNtTx0h2lkHqsWY2uv4By3I1C1Oz7mCc3Y44yVLZTQG1dnG3v5NaD-
qYdA=
```


Now, that's obfuscation! If you'd like to try this yourself, there are public/private key generators online that you can use and test. There's a good one at the JSEncrypt code library site (http://travistidwell.com/jsencrypt/demo).

TEXTBOX 3.2

EXAMPLE OF A PUBLIC KEY


```
-----BEGIN PUBLIC KEY-----
=MIGfMA0GCSqGSIb3DQEBAQUAA4GNADCBiQKBgQDG9b76IjY81A+b-
WeNJnSV3DYvjFfvxfommS9bWOprsM0dwP6jZfWbcQ8EO0HPfA-
6jYExGpQZyiJ4E65hnsinGETp5CSn3jGL55YtJV5y3PwhCSZH0h-
fgN1r6oyTuu+kXv0wKoa2ZuKT3VC+cpgoxAF/3aOY2dTa3r6TYHX-
deKPvwIDAQAB
-----END PUBLIC KEY-----
```

Since the encryption keys that are generated are long and ungainly, you typically generate and store them on your computer, and there are a variety of apps and command-line utilities you can use to do this. Once you have your keys, you can use them for a variety of purposes—including encrypting your email messages. There are a couple of hurdles you have to cross, though. The first is that many email clients don't support encryption right out of the box (not even Google's GMail, possibly the most popular email provider out there). You'll have to install one or more tools to get the job done—either an extension for your web browser (such as Mailvelope, www.mailvelope.com), an email client app (e.g., GPG Suite, https://gpgtools.org, for Apple Mail), or an entirely new email client app built with encryption in mind (such as ProtonMail, available for iOS and Android mobile devices).

The other problem is that, as stated earlier, very few email users bother with encryption. And that's an issue because encryption is a two-step process: one party has to encrypt the message and the other has to decrypt it. Thus both parties have to have encryption set up and have access to the necessary keys to use it. In practice, this means that you'll only be able to exchange encrypted messages with other privacy-sensitive individuals who have the desire and technical know-how to jump through a few hoops for the sake of security—for now, at least. Some users publish their public keys as part of their email signatures; do that yourself, and you might just get someone curious enough to start asking what it's all about!

Hacking Router Firmware

As mentioned earlier, it's sometimes possible to modify how an existing router behaves by modifying its *firmware*—the built-in software that controls the operation of the device. Similar to jailbreaking your iPhone, installing third-party firmware on a router opens it up to behavior and abilities that go beyond the capabilities installed by its manufacturer. Also like jailbreaking, modifying router firmware operates in a somewhat shadowy space: the FCC allows it within reason (Hruska, 2015) and most router manufacturers don't block you from doing so, but there's no guarantee that that will remain the status quo. And regardless of whether or not they take active steps to prevent you from modifying their firmware, router manufacturers will most likely be happy to tell you that you've voided your warranty by doing so. Thus, firmware hacking isn't for everyone: it's relatively complicated, unsupported by the companies that would otherwise offer help for their products, and not the easiest path to better network protection. It's good to know that the option exists, however. As with many things in the world of Internet security, this ability can be used for good or for evil. Routers infected with malware have been detected in multiple countries (Kovacs, 2015), modified by attackers who gained access to the devices through remote connections.

There are numerous third-party firmware packages available to download and install. They vary in their capabilities and in which models of routers they support. The right firmware can speed up your network, enhance security, add specialized features like VPN serving, and even strengthen your wi-fi signal and range. One of the most comprehensive offerings in terms of both features and device support is OpenWRT (https://openwrt org), although it's not necessarily the easiest to use. Once it's installed, you can download hundreds of plugins to extend its abilities. A much simpler alternative is called Tomato (www.polarcloud.com/tomato). Although Tomato doesn't provide nearly as many utilities as OpenWRT and only runs on a handful of different router models, it's much more approachable for newcomers.

Servers and Logs

Most of the time, you leave virtual fingerprints behind as you make your way through the Internet. Most servers retain some type of activity log—at least for a certain period of time—that can provide very detailed information about visitors and what they do with the service in question. Even email servers can store information about the mail that passes through them. If you're using an external service, it behooves you to understand its policies for data retention: what data about you is being kept, and for how long. Beyond knowing this, there's probably not much you can do about external logging except avoid the services you don't trust.

Remember, though, that the same questions apply to your own services. If your library operates its own web servers or other online systems, you most likely have logs of your own with visitor information. It's up to you to decide how much of it you keep and what you do with it; but if you're reading this book, you're presumably concerned about respecting your visitors' privacy—and that means retaining as little server data about them as possible.

One of the most popular web servers in use is the Apache HTTP Server (https://httpd.apache.org), or Apache for short. This is the predominant server found on Unix- and Linux-based computers (which includes Macs). Apache is infinitely configurable, so the structure and appearance of its log files may vary. But this is a typical log entry:

```
24.58.233.70 - - [06/Oct/2013:15:55:41 -0600] "GET /indo_custom/index.php HTTP/1.1" 200 1025 "-" "Mozilla/5.0 (Macintosh; Intel Mac OS X 1085) AppleWebKit/537.71 (KHTML, like Gecko) Version/6.1 Safari/537.71"
```

The format may be a bit confusing, but the major pieces of information being collected are apparent: date and time of access, the particular file on the server being requested by the visitor, the type of computer or mobile device the visitor is using, and the type of web browser being used. And the very first series of numbers—24.58.233.70—is the user's IP address. This is the single most important piece of data in the log entry since it can be used in many cases to identify a specific computer on the Internet. In other cases, it can at least be tracked to a particular ISP or corporate entity controlling a particular domain of machines from which the request originated. The owner of the ISP or business usually retains similar records for network traffic within that subdomain that can be stolen, abused, or subpoenaed. Therefore, it's in your users' best interest for the IP address to be stripped from the log file as soon as possible.

Apache can be configured so that IP addresses aren't logged at all, and that's an option worth considering. However, there are legitimate reasons for retaining IP addresses, such as web analytics. Apart from identifying a unique user, the IP address can tell you what country, city, or geographic region a request originates from. It can be very useful to know that your online collection of Scottish pottery photos is being accessed primarily by visitors from Indonesia. The best compromise between privacy protection and utility may be to process the log file data into a different format, discarding the IP address but adding a field with the result of a geographic lookup. Then the original log can be deleted, and the modified file can be kept and used for analytics. This can be done easily by writing a simple processing script in Perl, Python, Ruby, or your script language of choice.

Be aware that your choice of analytics system can affect user privacy as well. A popular choice for web analytics today is Google Analytics (https://analytics.google.com), which offers ease of use (analytics can be added to a webpage by adding a couple of lines of JavaScript to the file) and extensive charts, graphs, and tracking tools. The downside to using Google Analytics is that your site's visitor data is being sent to Google and stored there, where you have no control over how it's being used. Other alternatives may offer better privacy protection (see chapter 5 for details).

You can also determine how long log files are kept on your server before they're deleted. This is usually handled by the operating system, which periodically cleans up and removes a variety of different log files, including the web server's logs. Configuring this cleanup process varies from system to system, but there should be a way to adjust the frequency of removal. If you aren't using the logs for analytics or other purposes, it's best not to keep them around for very long.

Key Points

Your network is your first line of defense against privacy threats. It's important to keep it secure using these key facts:

- The basic unit of communication in the Internet is the packet, a fragment of an actual message or file.
- Networks are vulnerable to packet sniffing and man-in-the-middle attacks, and the risk of these attacks can be mitigated but not eliminated entirely.
- VPNs, firewalls, and router configurations can be arranged to provide secure communications and to block malware or unwanted content from entering a network.
- Internet traffic consists of data being sent using numerous protocols. Each protocol has its own security considerations and may be more or less suited to protecting privacy.
- Most servers on the Internet retain logs of user activity, often containing identifying information about their visitors. You should understand the data retention policies of sites and services you use.
- Consider the data retention of your own web servers; if you don't need log data, don't collect or keep it.

The next chapter moves out of the concerns of low-level networking and the abstractions of remote servers and log files. Instead, it will consider privacy issues related to that most vulnerable piece of library technology: the public computer.

References

Hruska, Joel. 2015. "FCC Clarifies Third-Party Router Firmware Is Allowed—But with Restrictions." ExtremeTech.com. September 28. www.extremetech.com/internet/215012-fcc-clarifies-third-party-router-firmware-is-allowed-but-with-restrictions.

Kovacs, Eduard. 2015. "Malicious Firmware Found on Hundreds of Cisco Routers." Security Week. September 22. www.securityweek.com/malicious-firmware-found-hundreds-cisco-routers.

CHAPTER 4

Public Computers

IN THIS CHAPTER

- ▷ Selecting used machines to serve as public computers
- ▷ Deleting apps completely from a computer
- ▷ Keeping users' data private from other users
- ▷ Resetting a computer's configuration and storage after each user session
- ▷ Avoiding viruses, worms, ransomware, and other malware
- ▷ Keeping your public computers up to date with security patches and operating system updates
- ▷ Recognizing Mac- and Windows-specific security features
- ▷ Decommissioning public computers for reuse or recycling

Threat Assessment

THE SECURITY-CONSCIOUS HOMEOWNER WOULD PROBABLY not leave for a two-week vacation with his front door wide open and his house full of valuable, unguarded possessions. But a library that offers public computers for its patrons and visitors to use runs the risk of doing just that—metaphorically speaking, of course. If you don't take the proper steps to ensure that your public computers are secure and unable to affect (or *infect*) the rest of your network, then you'd better hope that a knowledgeable user with questionable ethics doesn't sit down at one of your keyboards. Here are a few possibilities to keep you awake at night:

- Your well-meaning library intern, tasked with setting up a public workstation, discovers an old machine collecting dust under the circulation desk. He wipes it off, sets it up, turns it on, and walks away. One week later, a user is idly poking around the files on that particular computer. She discovers a spreadsheet of past collected fines, complete with patrons' names and personal information.

- You have a group of three public computers that stay on all day; at closing time, they get turned off for the night. One afternoon, a user sits down at a machine, goes to the web, and pulls up Facebook—only to discover that he's logged in as somebody else. He takes the opportunity to post a series of embarrassing photos to the prior user's wall. The prior user blames the library for not protecting his privacy.
- A user accidentally downloads and opens a piece of malware on one of your public machines. Since you haven't properly configured your network or computer-level firewalls, a worm is able to spread to other machines on the network—staff computers as well as public machines—and infect the systems it finds there.
- Another piece of malicious code, another network configuration. This time, your network successfully keeps the malware confined within the computer that first downloaded it. But a user plugs in a flash drive to copy some files, and the virus infects it. She goes home blissfully unaware, and the next day spreads the virus to a friend's laptop when sharing her document.

These are the scenarios that you want to avoid! The good news is that it doesn't have to be this way. If you're careful about how you acquire, configure, and dispose of your public computers, you can minimize the risk of them being used as weapons against your library or your users.

Choosing Machines for Public Computing

There are different approaches to obtaining and setting up public computers in your library, but the worst thing you could do from a privacy standpoint would be to pull a couple of old machines out of storage that had previously been used by staff—or perhaps you can't remember what they were used for—and just set them out for patrons to use. At least some of the reasons this would be a privacy nightmare should be obvious: old data has a way of sticking around on computers. Even if you made a careful sweep of the machine's hard drive or drives and removed any files that users shouldn't be able to access, there's always the possibility that you could have overlooked something. Also, it's often possible to retrieve files even after they've been deleted. Most computer file systems don't actually destroy a file when you delete it; they merely delete their references to the file. The computer "forgets" about the file, but the actual data can linger for days, months, or even years until another file happens to be saved to the same drive location that the old one occupied. (For more information about truly deleting files, see the section on decommissioning machines at the end of this chapter.)

Stale data is only part of the problem. You also have to consider the apps installed on the computer. Are there any programs that shouldn't be publicly accessible (e.g., OPAC client software)? What about apparently innocent apps that might have been configured with private logins or personal information, like an address book app or Skype client set up with librarians' personal phone numbers? Again, when it comes to removing apps, Delete doesn't necessarily do what you think it's doing. Modern software often installs itself at multiple locations: the app package itself (represented by the icon you click to launch the program), one or more preference files that may be stored in your user account, support files that could be in your account or perhaps kept at the system level for multiple users, and more. If you delete the app package, you might very well leave all those hidden files behind—and those are often where the app stores your personal preferences and data.

Finally, there's the issue of the machine's system settings, particularly those related to networking. Chapter 3 details the items that you want to consider here, such as configurations for VPNs, DNS servers, and firewalls. Don't overlook your basic Internet connection, either. If at all possible, your public computers should be completely isolated from your staff machines: configure them to use a different network or a DMZ on your router.

The bottom line is this: don't press an old machine into service as a public computer without giving it a thorough cleaning and safety check. If you're working with a used computer, the best approach is to do a complete wipe and reinstall the operating system from scratch (see the end of this chapter for more information).

TEXTBOX 4.1

HOW TO COMPLETELY DELETE APPS

On Macs in particular, people have become accustomed to dragging apps around. Whether in an application or programs directory, on the desktop, or in some other folder, software generally works wherever you decide to put it. Thus it's natural to assume that if you drag an app to the trash or recycle bin and then empty the trash, the app will simply cease to be. That often doesn't do the trick, though. Here are a few options for *completely* deleting apps, their data, and their preferences and configuration files.

- Some apps come with their own uninstaller tools. Since these are custom-fitted to their parent apps, they *should* remove all the additional files that were installed or created by the app. If there is an uninstaller, it will generally appear in the same folder as the original app and have a similar name (hopefully containing the word "uninstaller"). If not, it might be included on the CD or downloaded software package from which you got the app. Launch it as you would any other app and follow its instructions to complete the removal.
- If you're on a PC, then there's an official Windows way to delete apps. (There is no real equivalent to this on a Mac.) Navigate to Control Panel > Programs and Features. You should see a list of installed apps. Select the one you want to remove and click Uninstall. Note that the Windows uninstall tool has not always been completely thorough in its removal of related files. You might be better off trying the following approach:
- For both PCs and Macs, there are dedicated third-party apps that specialize in app uninstallation (often combined with a general-purpose "housekeeping" app that keeps your file system cleaned up and running smoothly). For Windows machines, you can try IObit Uninstaller (www.iobit.com/en/advanceduninstaller.php); for a Mac, CleanMyMac (http://macpaw.com/cleanmymac) is a good choice.

Keeping Data Private among Users (Provisioning)

When it comes to public computers, the biggest privacy threat to users is themselves. If you don't do anything to clean up a user's session after he or she finishes with a machine, then it's all too easy for someone else to sit down at the same computer and find some overlooked personal remnant: a PDF of a job application sitting on the desktop, perhaps, or a logged-in Facebook session. That won't do! It's important to ensure that a session on a public machine is completely erased each and every time it's finished and before the next patron comes along. This means having some way of restoring the computer to its starting point: removing any files or apps the user might have left behind and resetting all app and system settings to their original configuration (this starting point or default state is often referred to as an *image* of the system).

The easiest way to do this is to use dedicated software made for resetting (imaging) computers and administering them remotely. Examples of these systems include Deep Freeze (www.faronics.com/products/deep-freeze), Clean Slate (www.fortresgrand.com/products/cls/cls.htm; Windows only), and Ghost Solution Suite (www.symantec.com/products/threat-protection/endpoint-management/ghost-solutions-suite). This software can be quite sophisticated, giving you very fine-grained control over how your computers are managed: what users are allowed to do or what parts of the file system they're allowed to access; what to keep and what to discard when reverting to a saved system image; when to trigger a restore (e.g., a reboot of the machine, scheduled times, or a certain length of idle time); how system software should be updated; and much more. If you're dealing with a public computing setup of any complexity, you'll probably save yourself a lot of time and trouble by investing in one of these packages and learning to use it effectively. Unfortunately, imaging software can also be fairly expensive.

Another approach is to take advantage of the special "guest" user mode offered in Windows and macOS. Guest mode is discussed in the following section.

But if for some reason you don't want to use guest mode and you're on a limited budget, it's possible to create a basic re-imaging environment using a homebrew approach by combining a few different tools to get the job done. However, it's difficult to do system re-imaging quickly using this approach, so consider carefully how much user inconvenience and how many potential privacy concerns you're willing to accept in the process. It's unrealistic to try to do a complete system restore on your own between user sessions during a busy day in the library, so a more realistic schedule would be to do re-imaging in the evening or during the night once the library is closed. That would leave your users potentially vulnerable to anything unpleasant someone installed on a machine within the same day. You could mitigate that danger by restricting the public's access to the system as much as possible (e.g., only allowing users to save files to certain folders, such as the desktop) and then periodically removing any contents left behind. Here are some ideas you can use to piece together your own system cleanup solution:

- Windows' built-in backup and restore system. This uses what Microsoft calls *system images*: snapshots of your PC's data and configuration that can serve as a basis for backing up and restoring your system to a particular state. Find it under Control Panel > System and Maintenance > Backup and Restore.
- The nearest equivalent to Windows Backup and Restore on the Mac is Time Machine, Apple's system-wide backup solution. It's possible to do a full system restore using a previously saved Time Machine backup, but it's not necessarily the most reliable way of re-imaging an entire machine.

- There are plenty of third-party backup apps that can create full-copy, bootable, restorable images of your disks. Popular options for the Mac include Carbon Copy Cloner (https://bombich.com) and SuperDuper! (www.shirt-pocket.com/SuperDuper). On the Windows side, try Acronis True Image (www.acronis.com/en-us/personal/computer-backup), which is also available for Mac.
- Create a new user account for your library patrons (see the following sections for more information). This will help to ensure a separation between their activities and use by staff or administrators. It also gives you more control over what a guest user is able to do.
- Use your computer's built-in tools to limit user access. Both Windows and macOS provide parental controls that let you set permissions for a user's computing (see below). You can also restrict access to specific folders or directories on an individual basis.
- Restrict user access to all folders except one, designated as a public storage area. Any file that users temporarily save to a public machine goes into the public storage folder. This will (1) make it less likely users will lose track of documents they leave on the computer, and (2) give you a focused target for scheduled cleanup tasks.
- Schedule regular cleanups of your public folder or folders. This can be done using a variety of tools (see below).

Setting Up User Accounts

Limiting your users' access to a public computer begins with logging them in to an appropriate account. It's best to create a fresh account just for your public users.

When you create a new account (Windows: Control Panel > User Accounts and Family Safety *or* Accounts > Family & Other Users in Windows 10; Mac: System Preferences > Users & Groups), both Windows and macOS give you the choice of making it an administrative or standard account. It should go without saying that your public account should be a standard account only; endowing it with administrative rights over the machine would defeat the whole purpose! When you've successfully created your new user account, you can work on restricting its access to the bare minimum someone would need on your public machines.

Actually, though, it turns out that both Microsoft and Apple have anticipated your needs. In addition to regular user account creation, both operating systems provide for a special guest account. (Or rather, Windows *used* to provide a guest account. This feature has inexplicably been removed in Windows 10, with no true functional equivalent, so this trick can't be used there.) This account type is specifically made for transient visitors who should have the ability to use a computer without affecting its configuration. Guest users can't install software or pry into system settings or other user accounts. Guest accounts also don't have passwords, although they must be activated before anyone can use them to log in. In Windows, this can be done within User Accounts and Family Safety by choosing "Add or remove user accounts" in Windows 7 or "Change account type" in Windows 8, then clicking on the guest account. On a Mac, go to System Preferences > Users & Groups, select Guest User in the sidebar, and check the box that says "Allow guests to log in to this computer."

Although the guest accounts in Windows and macOS are similar, each has its own quirks that you should be aware of. The most important difference is that user data is *retained* from session to session within the guest account in Windows, whereas all user data is *deleted* when a user logs out of Guest User on a Mac (see figure 4.1). The guest account on Macs also has a couple of special modes.

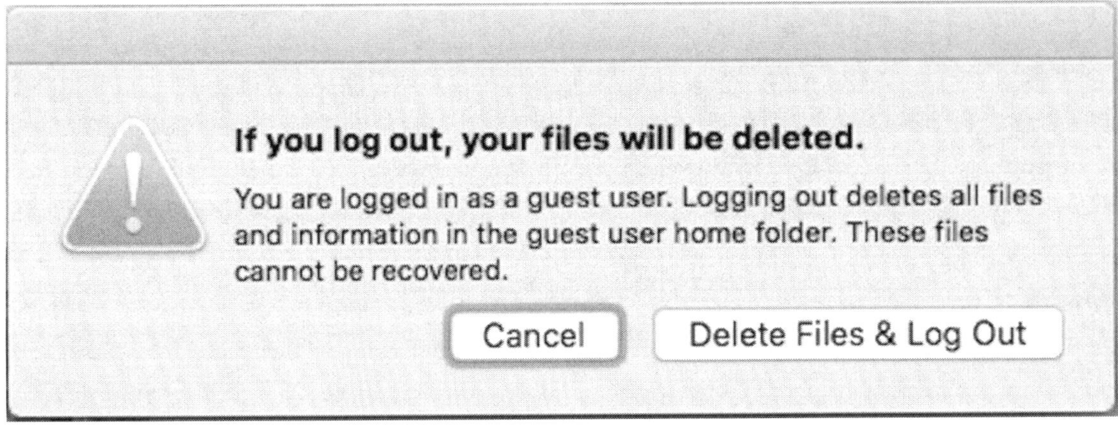

Figure 4.1. Warning message seen when logging out of the Guest account on a Mac. Screenshot from Apple macOS.

One mode concerns FileVault, Apple's whole-disk encryption technology that can be turned on and off under System Preferences > Security & Privacy. While using FileVault is usually a no-brainer—it offers excellent security with almost no effect on user experience—it does have a very pronounced effect on the behavior of the guest account: if FileVault is turned on, then guest users can *only* use Safari. In fact, if you log in to the guest account while logged into another account, the entire system will reboot into a special secured mode. If FileVault is not enabled on the disk, then guests can access most other apps on the computer by default.

The other special mode on the Mac is activated by a somewhat confusing second checkbox that appears right below the "Allow guests" checkbox used to activate the guest account. The second option, "Enable parental controls," makes the guest account behave like a managed account—one where the boundaries placed on the user are defined by the Parental Controls section of System Preferences (see the following section). This means that the behavior of the guest account is not entirely predictable unless you know whether it's being managed or not.

For many use cases, guest mode is the perfect solution to session cleanup, especially on a Mac. Since any changes made to the guest account are cleared after logout, you only have to ask your users to log out when they're done. And since you know that they won't all heed that request, you can set your computers to log out automatically once they've been idle for a specified period (this setting can be adjusted under System Preferences > Security & Privacy > Advanced...). You won't be able to use FileVault unless you want your computer to serve as a Safari-only kiosk; but as long as the machine in question is serving only as a public computer and not being used to store other types of data, that shouldn't be a problem.

Using Parental Controls

Both Microsoft and Apple provide parental controls that can be used to limit the access and actions of a particular user account. Their implementations are a little different—particularly since the appearance of Windows 10, which makes significant changes to Microsoft's parental settings. Windows 10 assumes that an account that is being limited is a child's account set up as part of the Microsoft Family system. Although user accounts can be added to a "family" from a PC (Settings > Accounts > Family & Other Users), parental controls themselves are accessed via the Microsoft Family website (https://account.

microsoft.com/family). The restrictions are synced to Microsoft's cloud services and to any device the child user logs into. This has the advantage of making account restriction a set-once, use-often operation. (Apple's solution has no comparable syncing.) Once an account is set up, you can set limits on web content (whether by blacklisting or whitelisting specific sites or by blocking mature content) and block downloading or accessing apps based on content rating. The ability to block access to arbitrary apps on an individual basis appears to have disappeared, though.

Apple doesn't have a special child user account type (except for its Family Sharing system, which lets you designate members of a family as children for purposes of approving media downloads). Parental controls can be applied to any non-administrator user account by going to System Preferences > Users & Groups, choosing a user account in the list, and checking the "Enable parental controls" checkbox. An account that is under parental control will be labeled "Managed" instead of "Standard." The parental control settings can be accessed by clicking "Open Parental Controls..." on the user account view or by going directly to its panel in System Preferences. From here, you can restrict access to specific apps, specific websites or website content types, and a few particular data types (location services, contacts, calendars, reminders, Twitter, Facebook, and diagnostics).

Scheduling Periodic Cleanups

If you're not using a guest account or carefully managed user account, it may be a good idea to periodically clean up publicly accessible folders on your machines. As with many things, there are several ways to go about this.

- Windows provides a Task Scheduler app (Control Panel > System and Security > Administrative Tools > Task Scheduler) that you can use to set up a regularly recurring custom action. In this case, you would create a new Scheduler entry that ran a batch script containing a simple directive to delete the files in your folder: del /f /q 'C:\Users\Local\path\to\your\directory*.*
- Apple's tools for automating tasks aren't quite so straightforward, but you have several choices. One method is to use Automator, the often-overlooked built-in app that can create automated workflows for any number of different purposes. In Automator, you build a workflow by dragging individual actions into a workflow box where the actions are chained together and executed sequentially. See the how-to sections below for details on creating an Automator workflow for folder cleanup.
- Another Mac technique employs the extremely useful Hazel app (www.noodlesoft.com). Hazel bears a certain resemblance to Automator (see figure 4.2), except that it lets you automatically execute one or more actions in response to specified conditions in a particular folder. For example, you could create a Hazel rule that would watch for PDFs dropped into the Documents folder, tag them with keywords, and upload them to a server. Or, in this case, you can make a rule that will move documents in a folder into the Trash after a given time and then empty the trash. See the how-to sections below for the procedure.

It's also possible to create low-level scripts to handle these cleanup tasks from the command line. The details of how to implement this approach are a little too complex for this book, but it's good to know that they're available if you have the technical know-how. The most venerable method is to create a cron job to run a cleanup script on

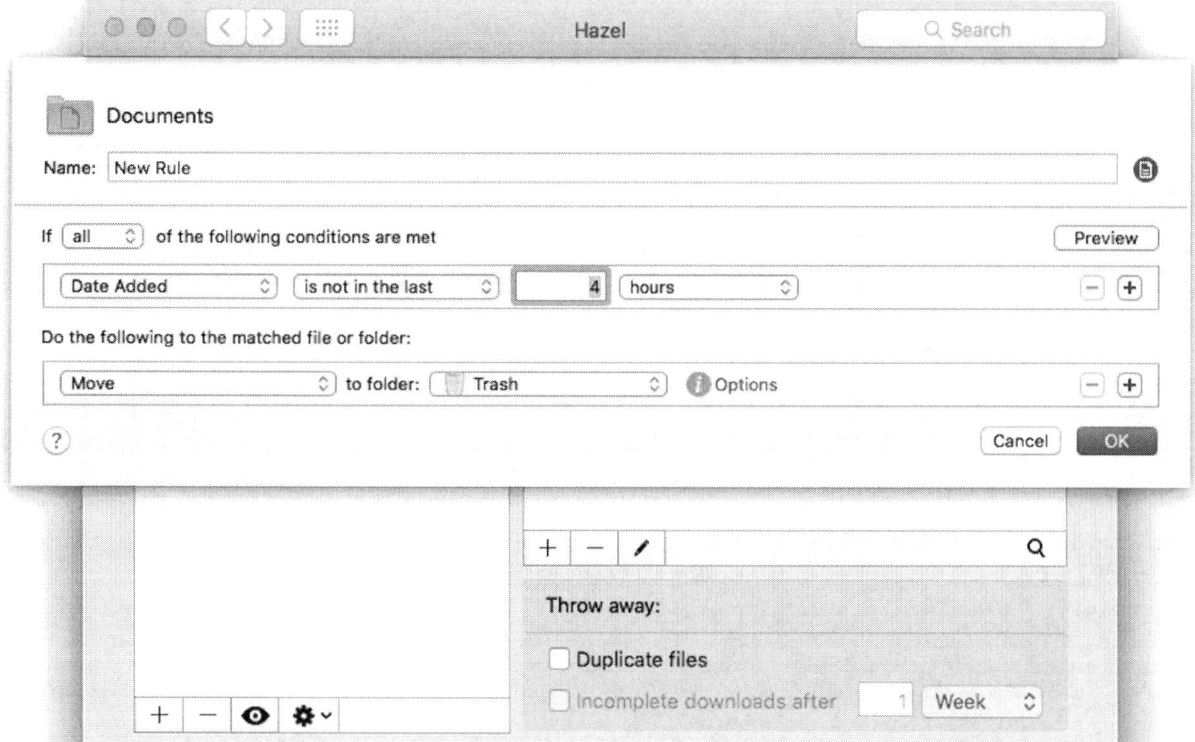

Figure 4.2. Creating a new Hazel rule to empty old files from the Documents folder. Screenshot from Noodlesoft's Hazel app.

a regular schedule (cron is a relatively ancient scheduling tool for Unix/Linux systems). This is basically the same approach as using Windows' Task Scheduler. You can still use cron on modern Macs, but it's been mostly supplanted by Apple's Launchd system (https://developer.apple.com/library/mac/documentation/MacOSX/Conceptual/BPSystemStartup/Chapters/ScheduledJobs.html), which offers better flexibility.

How to Create an Automator Workflow for Folder Cleanup (Mac Only)

To create an Automator task to empty a folder, do the following:

1. Launch Automator, choose New Document, and then select Calendar Alarm as the type for the new task.
2. Under actions, search for "Get Specified Finder Items" and drag the result into the workflow box.
3. Do the same for "Get Folder Contents."
4. Do the same for "Move Finder Items to Trash."
5. In the workflow box, look at the first step (which should be "Get Specified Finder Items"). Click the "Add..." button, then select the folder or folders that you want to empty (e.g., Documents, Downloads, or Desktop, three common locations for saved files).
6. Your workflow should be complete! Try it out. Click the "Run" button in the upper right corner of the window. Any documents in the specified folders should be immediately moved to the Trash.

7. Note that this workflow doesn't *empty* the Trash, so the documents are still hanging around. If you want to have the trash empty automatically at the end of the workflow, you can add one more step. Search for the "Run AppleScript" action and drag it to the end of your workflow. In the text box within the workflow step, enter the following three lines:

```
tell application "Finder"
empty the trash
end tell
```

8. After your workflow is complete (see figure 4.3 for an example) and working to your satisfaction, it's time to schedule it. Save the workflow and give it a name. The Calendar app should appear. Why? Since you specified that your workflow was a Calendar Alarm, it's added to your calendar as soon as it's saved. If you look at the list of calendars, you should notice that there's even a new Automator calendar that's been added to the list (under "On My Mac"). All Automator workflows that you save as calendar alarms are added to this calendar. When you hit save, a new event is scheduled for the current date and time. This event can be changed like any other calendar event to occur or reoccur on specific dates at specific times. You probably want this workflow to run more than once, so be sure to click "repeat" in the event detail box and put it on a regular schedule.

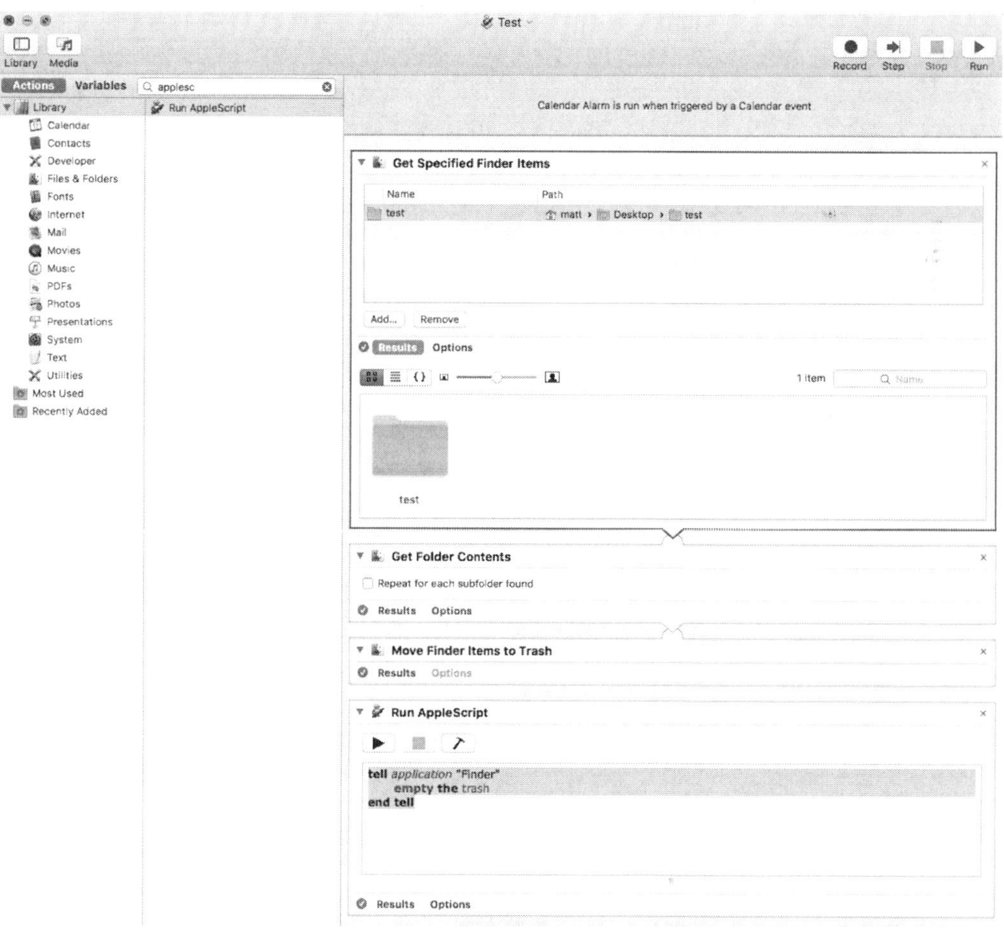

Figure 4.3. Building an Automator workflow to clean up a public computer's folders. Screenshot from Apple Automator app.

That's all! Once you've scheduled your folder cleanup workflow, it should execute on its own whenever it's supposed to.

You can improve your cleanup routine a bit more by reusing that last step in the workflow, the AppleScript that empties the Trash. Right now, the Trash is emptied on a regular schedule—but what if somebody logs out of the public user account and someone else logs in before the scheduled time rolls around? It would be great if you could just have the Trash emptied every time a user logs in—and you can:

1. Launch Automator again and create a new workflow, this time giving it the "Application" type.
2. This workflow will only have one step, and it's exactly the same as the last step in the previous workflow. Find "Run AppleScript," add it to the workflow, and enter the script into the text box.
3. Click "Run" to make sure the workflow is working as you expect it to. Then save the workflow. This time you'll save it to a specific location, just like a normal file.
4. You now have an "Empty Trash" app that can be run like any other app by double-clicking it.
5. In order to run it automatically when a user logs in, first log in to your public user account. Go to System Preferences > Users & Groups. Make sure that the current user (your public user account) is selected, then click the "Login Items" tab. This gives you a list of all the apps that are launched when that user logs in. Click the plus sign below the list to add a new item, locate your new workflow, and add it to the list. It should run the next time you log in as that user.

How to Create a Hazel Rule for Folder Cleanup (Mac Only)

Once you've installed Hazel, you work with it via a custom pane in System Preferences (System Preferences > Hazel). To approximate the Automator workflow detailed above, follow these steps:

1. Make sure that you're in the Folders tab.
2. Select or add the folder or your choice in the list on the left of the pane. In the Rules box on the right, click the plus sign to create a new rule. Give it a good name.
3. In the "if" statement ("if all/any/none of the following conditions are met"), make sure "all" or "any" is selected. Then set the rule to the following: "Date Added" "is not in the last" "4" "hours" (or whatever time period you want).
4. In the "then" statement ("Do the following to the matched file or folder"), set the rule to the following: "Move" "to folder" "Trash"). Click the OK button to finish the rule.
5. To add the second part of the workflow—automatic emptying of the Trash—go to the second tab in the Hazel pane ("Trash").
6. Make sure that the first checkbox is checked ("Delete files sitting in the trash...") and set it to whatever timeframe you want—e.g., have it delete files that have been in the trash for more than one hour.

That should be all you need to get Hazel to take care of your folder and trash cleanup!

Malware

Viruses, Trojans, and Worms

Everybody knows about computer viruses and malware. Even before the Internet was created, hackers were writing software that could spread and reproduce across a network. Most of these early attempts were more in the vein of exploration and discovery of what computers could do and not harmful intent, but more malicious individuals quickly realized the potential of self-replicating code and launched a never-ending campaign to compromise computers and steal private data on a worldwide scale. The umbrella term "virus" can be broken down into numerous subcategories. "Trojans," named for the Trojan horse, are viruses that disguise themselves as normal files. "Worms" are viruses that can propagate themselves across a network, whereas ordinary viruses require human intervention to spread—such as passing an infected flash drive from one computer to another.

Probably one of the most common ways of "catching" a virus is to click on an attachment in an email message. Things aren't always what they seem, and any number of malicious programs can be disguised as innocent images, text documents, or sound files. This is a particularly bad problem for Windows users for various reasons (including the ability to embed executable macros or scripts in the popular Office document formats). Although the email vector for viruses has become less effective over time as users have become more savvy and email clients and providers have strengthened their defenses, malware authors simply shifted their attention to web-based delivery mechanisms and social engineering attacks. The universality of the web and its reliance on many long-in-the-tooth technologies built and maintained (if maintained at all) by diverse sources makes it a particularly effective platform for infection. To take just one example, Adobe's Flash technology can be found practically everywhere on the web, driving audio and video playback, interactive ads, and snazzy screen effects. Yet it's infamous for its long history of serious vulnerabilities that, in some cases, allow third parties to take complete control of a computer running a compromised Flash app. Fortunately, Flash is making a slow exit from the web after a protracted campaign by security-conscious companies and individuals (most notably Apple, who drove the first nail into Flash's coffin by banning it from iPhones and iPads); even Adobe has started encouraging developers to switch to HTML5 and other open standards (Adobe, 2015).

For a long time, Macs were mostly immune to the plague of malware (whether due to "security by obscurity" or inherently better actual security), but that has started to change. Attackers today, drawn by Apple's exponential surge in popularity over the past decade, are dedicating more resources toward cracking Apple's defenses. Reports of genuine, self-propagating malware on Apple systems "in the wild" are still few and far between, but the potential exists.

Malware, once it infects a machine, can have a variety of deleterious effects. If you're lucky, you'll just get someone's idea of a joke: an obnoxious message that pops up randomly on your screen, perhaps. If you're not so lucky, then files or even entire drives can be deleted; confidential information can be stolen and sent to a remote machine; your every action can be spied on; or your computer can be added to a "botnet," a collection of compromised computers that can be remotely controlled and used together for malicious purposes (such as carrying out a denial-of-service attack against a website to force it offline).

If you've followed the advice for keeping data private among users that was outlined in earlier sections of this chapter, then you're off to a good start for keeping malware away from your users. There are three basic dangers of malware infection: infection of the initial computer, infection of other computers on your network, and infection of your users' personal media or devices. If you're diligent about isolating your guest computers from the rest of your network, then you can greatly reduce the risk of spreading infection to other computers in the library system (except, perhaps, for other public computers on the same guest network). And if you're diligent about cleaning up a user session and restoring the computer to its previous state after each use, then malware won't be able to effect any long-term damage to that particular machine either. That just leaves the possibility of infecting user media.

If your user sessions are isolated and wiped clean each time, then any malware that finds its way onto a user's flash drive is most likely self-inflicted, invited in by something that that particular user did during his or her session at the computer. You should still do your best to reduce the risk, though. First of all, use a router- or DNS-level filter to block known malware from entering your network (as described in chapter 3). Then consider whether you should install antivirus software at the computer level as well.

The conventional wisdom for many years was that antivirus software was absolutely necessary on PCs and most likely unnecessary on Macs. That distinction has thawed somewhat; Windows has become a more secure operating system, while Macs have become a more tempting target for malware authors. However, it's still not a bad rule of thumb. If you're fielding PCs, it's probably a good idea to have at least basic antivirus software in place and operational. The good news is that Windows 10 includes a fairly good malware checker known as Windows Defender (Settings > Update & Security > Windows Defender). Make sure this is turned on. There are several other well-known antivirus packages for Windows, and some of them are able to detect more forms of malware, but Windows Defender offers a good balance of protection and performance.

You can purchase antivirus software for the Mac, but many people would argue that it's still unnecessary. Plenty of users have run Macs for years without any malware attacks, and you won't see much in the way of genuine malware infection of Macs reported in the news. (Most security incidents that you do hear about are the result of social engineering—tricking people into revealing their login credentials—rather than technological flaws.) MacOS does not have an explicit user interface for malware protection akin to Windows Defender, but it keeps a careful eye on potential problems with files and apps that you receive via built-in programs like Mail, Safari, and Messages. If you try to open a file that contains known malware, the operating system will refuse to comply; you'll only be able to move it to the Trash. Thus, in today's computing environment, antivirus software for Macs can probably still be skipped—but that could change in the future.

Ransomware

Ransomware is a particularly nasty form of malware that deserves special consideration. In a ransomware attack, a criminal gains access to a computer through some form of malware infection and uses the malware to securely encrypt the files on the victim's machine. The victim is then sent a ransom demand requiring payment in exchange for the keys to decrypt his or her files. Naturally, there is no guarantee that the decryption keys will actually be delivered once the ransom is paid.

Ransomware has been growing in popularity as a malware approach. Public awareness of the technique has also been growing, thanks to a number of high-profile incidents. Early in 2016, ransomware made headlines when the first functional attack was made against Macs, using a compromised version of a popular torrenting app, Transmission, to deliver the malware (Xiao and Chen, 2016). And in one of the most despicable manifestations of ransomware, a survey found that more than half of responding hospitals had been victims of ransomware attempts during the previous year (Sullivan, 2016).

You definitely don't want to be in a position where you have to choose between paying ransom money to extortionists or losing crucial data and files. That's just one more reason to ensure that your public computers are "disposable"—i.e., not storing any mission-critical data, not connected to any important internal systems, and cleaned up and re-imaged on a regular basis. Beyond that, there is no specific, anti-ransomware protection you can implement. (However, on more mission-critical computers, be sure to keep regular, redundant backups of your important data—preferably non-networked backups.) Just make sure that you're using appropriate anti-malware measures—and your common sense. If something looks suspicious, don't click on it!

Keyloggers

A keylogger, or keystroke logger, is a piece of software or hardware that sits quietly on your computer and records every keystroke that a user makes. From this data, whoever installed the keylogger can read the content of email or instant messages sent by a user, pick up login credentials, and view web visits and searches. Keyloggers are not strictly a form of malware; they are advertised and sold in legitimate markets for a variety of "legitimate" snooping purposes, such as parents wanting to monitor their children's Internet use, spouses looking for signs of infidelity, and employers wanting to make sure their workers stay on task. However, for obvious reasons, they pose a security nightmare. Keyloggers are often installed as part of a malware package once a machine's defenses are compromised.

Since keyloggers are designed to go unnoticed and act passively most of the time, it can be difficult to detect when one is running on a machine. Clearing user data and re-imaging on a regular basis should give you some peace of mind, though.

One wrinkle to keyloggers is that they can be implemented as a hardware device instead of as a piece of malware. Since your security attentiveness is primarily attuned to detecting software-based concerns, a hardware logger might be overlooked (and, obviously, remain unaffected by the usual software countermeasures). A hardware logger might be a very small device placed in-line between a keyboard cable and the PC it's attached to. It simply intercepts the keystrokes sent from the keyboard, saves them to internal storage, and waits for its deployer to come back to retrieve it and analyze the data.

Keeping Up to Date with Security Fixes

By now, you've learned a number of ways to configure and maintain your public computers in order to minimize the risk of malware infection or accidental disclosure of users' private data. But everything you do might still be in vain if you're running an operating system that is inherently compromised.

Any programmer will tell you that the simplest programs can hide a multitude of unanticipated bugs or weaknesses. (PHP, one of the most popular programming languages used to build websites, is notorious for enabling developers to write insecure code very easily.) And operating systems are huge, complex pieces of software, often written over the course of decades by thousands of different people. It's no surprise that security holes are discovered in operating systems on a fairly regular basis. Legitimate security researchers and hackers (the "white hats" mentioned earlier), as well as opportunistic criminals and agents of chaos (the "black hats"), devote a lot of time and effort to trying to discover new security problems in Windows, macOS, and other systems. White hats do so for the sake of improving system security and will usually report their discoveries to the software makers, giving them a chance to patch the flaws before a black hat discovers the same security hole and exploits it. Some software makers—and even some ill-intentioned black hat groups—offer bounties to anyone who can successfully defeat security on an operating system.

All this is to say that (1) you should always assume that the operating system you're using has undiscovered security bugs, potentially serious ones; (2) the makers of that operating system want to fix those bugs and release an updated version as soon as possible; and (3) you should do your very best to keep up with those updates so that you don't fall victim to an old vulnerability that was patched long ago. (That would add embarrassment to whatever damage was done to your system!)

For various understandable reasons, some people are reluctant to update to a new major release of an operating system. Perhaps the new version won't run on their older hardware, or they're just used to doing things the same way and don't want all their software to change, or they've heard bad things about the new version (Windows Vista being one notorious example). As a result, there's a sizable number of computers on the Internet that are still running long-obsolete operating systems. One market share survey group estimates that Windows XP, an operating system that was first released in 2001 and that hasn't been officially supported for years, still represents 10 percent of global usage (Net Applications.com, 2016)! If you're still using XP for games or music or other non-networked uses, that's fine. But venturing out onto the Internet with such a setup means that you could be vulnerable to any number of security exploits that may have been discovered after Microsoft stopped bothering to release new patches for it.

Most people aren't running systems that far out of date. But you also have to consider the issue of point releases—the incremental updates, often security-focused, published in between major releases of the operating system. (For example, Mac OS X El Capitan was officially released as OS X 10.11. At the time this chapter was written, the most recent version of El Capitan was numbered 10.11.6, meaning that Apple had issued six incremental updates to fix a variety of issues.) Since these are the updates that tend to nag you with alert messages at inconvenient moments—like in the middle of a PowerPoint presentation to a group of colleagues—it's easy to fall into the habit of automatically dismissing them or ignoring them completely. But this is also a mistake. If you want to be truly careful about security, you generally have to make sure that your computers are kept up to date with the latest operating system incremental releases. (Major releases are a bit different. It's usually okay to wait a year or two before upgrading to a new version of your operating system if you have a good reason to do so. Just don't wait ten years!) One caveat to this principle is that it's often a good idea to wait a short time, perhaps a day or two, before installing a new update. Even though they ought to be tested thoroughly before being released, occasionally an update to Windows or macOS causes significant problems for some users. When a new release is issued, wait, take a look at what early adopters are saying about its effects, and then decide whether or not to go ahead with the update.

Windows 10 handles updates from within Settings > Update & Security > Windows Update. Here you can check for new updates and set a schedule for update-related system restarts (e.g., restrict updates to only restart your computer during the night, when it's not in use). However, there isn't a straightforward way to *prevent* Windows from updating itself. Probably for the reasons discussed above, Microsoft wants to ensure that everyone receives security updates—whether they want them or not. This can be annoying or, occasionally, deleterious. Fortunately, there is a way to defeat this behavior if you need to, as outlined on the How-To Geek website (www.howtogeek.com/224471/how-to-prevent-windows-10-from-automatically-downloading-updates). Just be sure to manually download them as appropriate.

Apple gives you more control over the update process. Operating system updates on a Mac are now handled through the Mac App Store. If there are updates available (for apps or the operating system), a badge will appear in the Apple (leftmost) menu in the system menu bar, next to the "App Store..." menu item. Within the App Store app, you can view the Updates tab to see what updates are available and choose whether to install them or not.

Details of update behavior can be changed within System Preferences > App Store. You can select whether to check for updates automatically, download them automatically, and/or install them automatically.

Remember that if you're using imaging software like Deep Freeze on your machines, you can use it to configure update behavior as well. Consult the manual for details.

Operating System–Specific Security Features

Both Macs and PCs have unique operating system features that are designed to enhance security and protect privacy. Apple in particular has emerged as one of the most prominent defenders of personal privacy in the tech world and makes an earnest effort to protect the privacy of its users in each device it creates. Some of the operating system features have already been described, but this section gives you a summary of some of the more important ones.

On the Mac

Gatekeeper and code signing: Over the past few years, Apple has been making a concerted effort to make software—apps—safer to download and install. In OS X 10.11 (El Capitan), you can choose whether to allow apps to run based on their origin: from the Mac App Store only, from the Mac App Store plus "identified developers" (those developers who are registered with Apple and "sign" their apps with a known code), or from anywhere. Apple calls this system Gatekeeper. The newest version of the Mac operating system, macOS Sierra, drops the "from anywhere" option entirely. In either case, if you try to open an app that doesn't match your Gatekeeper setting, the system will give you an error message and refuse to comply. You can still force it to open, however, by going to the Security > General pane of System Preferences and clicking "Open Anyway." The purpose of Gatekeeper is to guard against malicious code or apps that might harm your system. Every app in the Mac App Store has a digital signature: a cryptographic key that identifies the developer responsible for it (registered developers can also use their key to sign apps not in the App Store). If some malicious code does sneak its way into a code-signed app, Apple can revoke the cryptographic signature, making it impossible for users to run the app.

Sandboxing: This is another change to the way apps are handled at a code level. It used to be that apps on a Mac (or a PC, for that matter) could do pretty much anything they wanted to in the system: install files in protected directories, modify settings, access a camera or other connected hardware, delete other apps. Today, however, apps must be sandboxed: by default, they can only modify files and data within their own confined area of memory or storage; permission to do other things to the system has to be explicitly granted for each point of access the app needs. This limits the damage that a piece of malware can do to your Mac.

Quarantine of suspicious files: Mail, Messages, and other Apple apps that tend to receive a lot of files from external sources are monitored by the operating system. Files that show evidence of malware are quarantined and cannot be opened by the user.

FileVault: FileVault is a secure form of whole-disk encryption that can be activated for individual drives. A FileVault-encrypted drive is very difficult to break into without the correct password or passphrase. This makes it ideal for laptops, rendering their contents useless if stolen, but it's also a good idea to turn it on for desktop machines. FileVault encrypts and decrypts files on the fly as a user interacts with them; the process is transparent to the user, and the performance penalty it incurs is unnoticeable.

Security & Privacy settings: Within the Security & Privacy pane of System Preferences, the Privacy tab contains a set of controls for monitoring and choosing access to various types of sensitive information on an app-by-app basis. You can see a list of all the apps on your system that have requested permission to use your location, contacts, calendars, reminders, social network data, and more. Within the list for each data type, you can use checkboxes to allow or deny each app that permission (see figure 4.4).

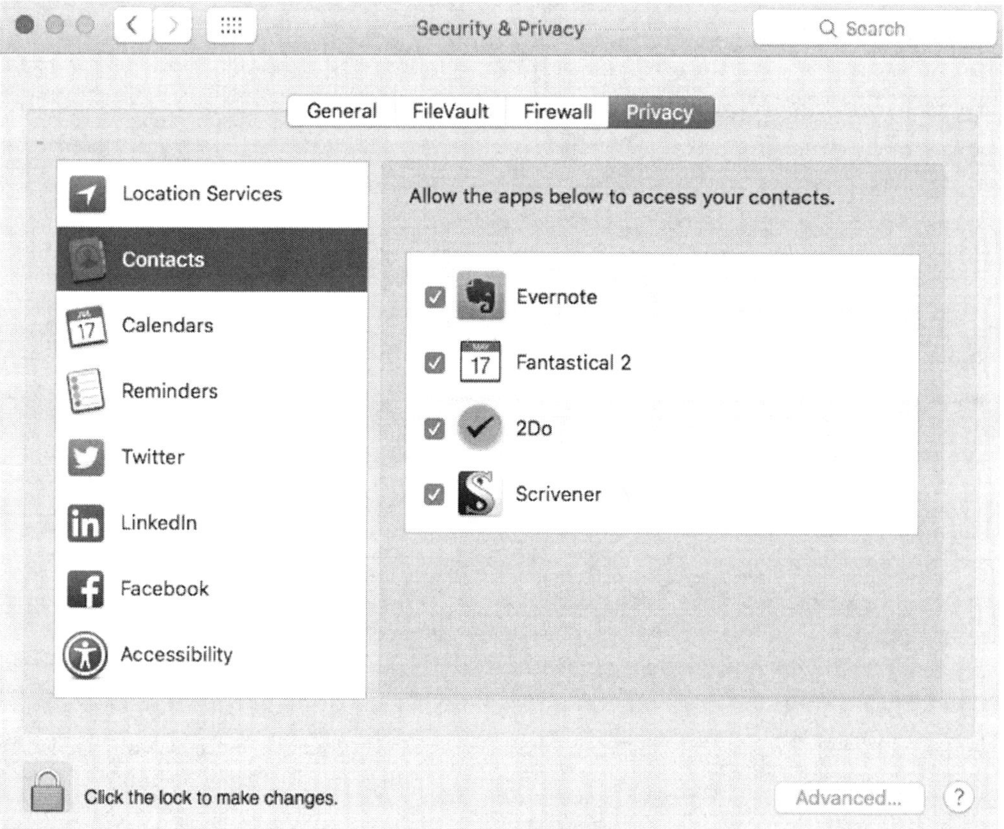

Figure 4.4. Some of the privacy settings in OS X/macOS. Screenshot from Apple macOS.

Deletion of guest account data: If you are using the guest account to log in to a Mac, you can add files and tweak settings to your heart's content, secure in the knowledge that it will all be erased as soon as you log out.

Local data storage: Google has earned a reputation for providing highly accurate and useful contextual information to its users in a variety of situations. Web search results are often exactly what you need them to be, and Google Photos can be spookily accurate at recognizing faces, objects, and places in your picture collection. But this convenience comes at a cost to your privacy: if you opt in to these services, your personal data is uploaded to Google's servers and analyzed. Apple has emerged with its own set of contextual services that is based on a very different philosophy, sacrificing some of Google's magical abilities for the sake of privacy. The latest version of the Mac operating system, macOS Sierra (as well as the latest iDevice operating system, iOS 10), includes a new version of the Photos app that provides better facial recognition and identification of objects and scenes in an image, much like Google Photos. But unlike Google Photos, the Photos app works on your local data only, analyzing your images right on your computer without uploading them to Apple's servers. (iCloud photo backups are a different story.) Likewise, on iPhones and iPads—and now on the Mac, Siri relies on good vocal recognition and contextual awareness to provide useful answers to queries. Its performance could probably be improved by sending reports of user queries to Apple to study and use as baseline data for optimization—but that isn't done. Siri queries are kept locally on your device in order to preserve your privacy.

On a (Windows 10) PC (see Microsoft, 2016)

Device Guard: This is Microsoft's answer to Apple's Gatekeeper, a system that controls which apps are allowed to run on Windows based on origin and code-signing.

Windows Hello and Microsoft Passport: Microsoft is making an effort to reduce the need for passwords, which are often weak and vulnerable to attack (see chapter 5 for more about passwords). Windows Hello lets users log in to a device using either a fingerprint scanner or facial scanner. Microsoft Passport is a single-sign-on system that uses two-factor authentication (e.g., requiring a PIN sent to your phone as well as your login attempt at the computer itself) to identify users.

BitLocker: Similar to FileVault on the Mac, BitLocker provides disk encryption that protects data from theft in the event of a stolen or lost computer.

Anti-malware features: Microsoft's attempt to prevent malicious code from running on a machine using a variety of low-level system features that guard against man-in-the-middle attacks, prevent tampering during system startup, and add sandboxing to prevent web-based malware downloads.

Decommissioning Public Computers

There comes a day when you decide that your public computers have served long enough. It's time to let them go and acquire new equipment. (Your budget may not approve of regular computer upgrades, but your users surely will!) Once you've taken those computers out of circulation, though, you're left with a potential privacy issue if the machines are going to be reused. If you've been careful about maintaining them with good security practices while they were in use, then you probably don't have too much to worry about.

But if you've been diligent up till now, why skimp on the final step? Ensure that nobody will be able to retrieve overlooked, forgotten data from your decommissioned computers.

Preparing for Reuse

If your machines are destined for reuse—whether sold, given away, or passed to a re-use center (and probably sold)—then you'll have to ensure that they remain usable but clean of private data. The best way to do so is to do a complete reinstall of the operating system. (You could also completely erase the computer's hard drive or drives without reinstalling the operating system, but then its next owner would have to do the work for you.)

Windows 10 provides a built-in method for doing a clean install of the operating system. Just go to Settings > Update & Security > Recovery and choose "Get started" (under Reset this PC). Then select the "Remove everything" option and follow the instructions to reset the system. However, by default, the in-house Windows reinstaller will not do a secure erase of your drives before resetting the system. It may delete any user files it finds, but that doesn't guarantee the files couldn't later be retrieved (provided that they haven't been overwritten by new files). For true peace of mind, you'll have to do the job yourself:

1. Make sure that you have a way to reinstall Windows 10 once your drive is clean: an install CD or flash drive.
2. You'll also need software to do the erasing. Recall that simply deleting a file isn't enough to guarantee that it can't be recovered. A secure erasure involves writing random data over the space in the file system that you are trying to clear (at least once, but multiple times for better security). DBAN and Blancco (www.dban.org) are one such set of tools for erasing hard drives (HDDs) and solid-state drives (SSDs) respectively.
3. Follow the instructions for the erasure tool to wipe your drive then let the Windows installer guide you through the reinstallation process. Simple—but time-consuming, especially if you have a large drive to erase.

On the Mac, an installer package is usually included in a hidden area of your primary hard drive or SSD, so you don't have to worry about keeping a separate installer CD or flash drive. To securely reinstall macOS, do the following:

1. Reboot the Mac while holding down the Option, Command, and R keys simultaneously. This will start the computer in recovery mode. You should see the OS X Utilities menu.
2. Select Disk Utility.
3. Select the disk that you want to erase in the sidebar.
4. Choose a disk format—usually "OS X Extended (Journaled, Encrypted)."
5. Give the disk a name.
6. Click Security Options. This is where the "secure" gets added to the "secure reinstall" procedure. You can determine how many times the data on the disk will be overwritten. For most purposes, three overwrites should be more than enough for your peace of mind. Just be aware that the overwriting process can be *very* slow for disks of any appreciable size. For a terabyte hard drive and a setting of three overwrites, the system can easily take multiple days of continuous work to complete the erasure.

7. Click Erase to start the process.
8. When the erasure is finished, quit Disk Utility. You should be back at the OS X Utilities menu.
9. Choose Reinstall OS X (or Reinstall macOS), then follow the instructions to finish the reinstallation process.

Preparing for Recycling

If you know that your computers are destined for the trash heap (or, preferably, the recycling bin), then you don't have to worry about reinstalling the operating system. You do, however, still want to make sure that the data on your hard drives, SSDs, or other physical media can't be recovered.

- If you pull the drives out of the machines to keep for reuse, erase the data using the method outlined in the previous section (but don't bother with the reinstallation steps).
- If the drives aren't worth keeping or reusing, then the best security-minded fate for them is to shred them. Waving a magnet near a disk doesn't do the trick these days! There are industrial media shredders available, although you probably don't want to bother purchasing one unless you're going to be shredding a *lot* of drives. Instead, look for a shredding or data security business that will do the job for you. Sometimes communities will also have local "shredding days," when anyone can bring in media to be destroyed and recycled.
- If you have CDs or DVDs to destroy, you can probably just toss them in with your hard drives if you're going to be shredding other items. Otherwise, some standard business shredders also have the teeth to chew apart an optical disk.
- If you're going to be throwing out the computer anyway and you're in the mood for an experiment, consider destroying its insides with a "USB Killer" flash drive. Invented by a hacker who goes by the handle Dark Purple, this custom-made thumb drive, when inserted into a computer's USB port, will fry the victim machine's circuitry in less than two seconds (Goodin, 2015). This *might* destroy the hard drive as well, or it might not—but shouldn't someone try to find out?

Key Points

Taking the time to secure your public computers correctly can prevent a lot of problems down the road. Crucial steps include starting with a clean computer environment, isolating the public machines' network from the network used by staff or other critical systems, and locking down what users are able to do on the machines. In addition, remember to consider the following points.

- Deleting files or apps on a computer doesn't guarantee that they are truly gone. Apps leave behind support files and data in different locations, and any deleted file may well be recoverable using special tools or techniques.
- User accounts on public computers should be limited in what they can do. Use the operating system's built-in tools to create a limited account and use parental controls to lock down specific apps or media content.

- Periodically clean up user sessions on public computers: delete personal data and reset the machine to a pure state between each session.
- Malware comes in many forms. Besides relatively ancient viruses, worms, and trojans, which can infect physical media or networks, ransomware is becoming a popular technique for extorting money from businesses and organizations.
- Keep your public machines' operating system up to date with security patches and new security features.
- Both Apple and Microsoft are paying attention to the importance of system security these days by including a variety of operating system–specific security features to protect their users and their users' computers.
- When a public machine is due to be replaced, you should take care to ensure that any remaining data on its drives is unrecoverable, either by securely erasing the drives or by shredding or otherwise destroying them.

In this chapter, you've read about techniques for protecting user privacy on public computers at the system level. Next, we'll discuss security issues concerning the primary use of most public computers: web browsing.

References

Adobe Corporate Communications. 2015. "Flash, HTML5, and Open Web Standards." Adobe.com. November 30. http://blogs.adobe.com/conversations/2015/11/flash-html5-and-open-web-standards.html.

Goodin, Dan. 2015. "'USB Killer' Flash Drive Can Fry Your Computer's Innards in Seconds." Ars Technica. October 14. http://arstechnica.com/security/2015/10/usb-killer-flash-drive-can-fry-your-computers-innards-in-seconds.

Microsoft. 2016. "Windows 10 Security Overview." Microsoft.com. August 21. https://technet.microsoft.com/itpro/windows/keep-secure/windows-10-security-guide.

Net Applications.com. 2016. "Desktop Operating System Market Share." August 5. www.netmarketshare.com/operating-system-market-share.aspx?qprid=10&qpcustomd=0&qptimeframe=Y.

Sullivan, Tom. 2016. "More Than Half of Hospitals Hit With Ransomware in Last 12 Months." Healthcare IT News. April 7. www.healthcareitnews.com/news/more-half-hospitals-hit-ransomware-last-12-months.

Xiao, Claud, and Jin Chen. 2016. "New OS X Ransomware KeRanger Infected Transmission BitTorrent Client Installer." Palo Alto Networks. March 6. http://researchcenter.paloaltonetworks.com/2016/03/new-os-x-ransomware-keranger-infected-transmission-bittorrent-client-installer.

CHAPTER 5

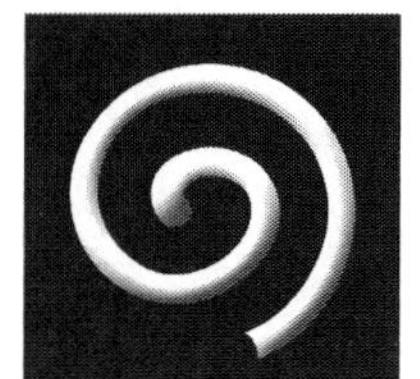

Web Browsers and Websites

IN THIS CHAPTER

- ▷ Understanding the contents of a webpage and the SSL certificate system
- ▷ Learning about browser plugins: Java applets, Adobe Flash, Microsoft Silverlight, and more
- ▷ Avoiding advertising and tracking scripts
- ▷ Using strong passwords and passphrases
- ▷ Implementing more private web analytics
- ▷ Adjusting browser security and privacy settings
- ▷ Securing websites from attack

Threat Assessment

ALTHOUGH DEDICATED APPS ARE USED HEAVILY for popular online activities, especially for social media like Facebook and Snapchat, most people still spend a disproportionate amount of computer time browsing the web. Unfortunately, the web is full of dangers for users, ranging from weak passwords to plugins to tracking scripts. Here's what's at stake:

- Using plugins like Adobe Flash and Java applets can open up your system to severe vulnerabilities if you don't take care to keep them up to date with the latest security patches.
- Not paying attention to security features like certificates on sites running SSL/HTTPS means you can be tricked into visiting a fake copy of a legitimate site that will steal your login credentials for the authentic site it's mimicking.

- Using weak passwords on a site can not only lead to a breach of your account on that particular site, it can cause you trouble in your accounts for other sites as well if you have the tendency to reuse passwords.
- Incautious use of JavaScript and cookies can lead to you being virtually followed around the web by advertisers and tracking scripts monitoring your every move.

This chapter will instruct you in ways to strengthen your browser security and use of passwords for web browsing. You'll also learn about the implications of using web analytics and basic techniques for securing your own websites against attack.

Anatomy of a Webpage

Before delving into the privacy issues surrounding web browsers and websites, it's important to understand how a webpage is put together. This section offers a brief overview of webpage anatomy; if you're already familiar with the basics, feel free to skip it.

A webpage, as seen in a web browser, is the result of a negotiated transaction between a client app (usually a web browser such as Safari, Chrome, Firefox, Opera, or even Internet Explorer) and a web server. The server can be on the same computer that's running the client, but it's more commonly located on a remote machine. A user requests a certain webpage through the browser, either by typing an explicit URL into the address bar or by clicking a link on another page. The browser sends that request to the remote web server that, at its heart, is just a routine for figuring out which file is being requested and sending a copy of it back to the requestor.

If the request is successful, the browser receives an HTML file. An HTML file is nothing more than a text file that contains markup tags—for example, <p>, <h1>, <a>, <ul>, <script>, and all the rest—as well as plain text. The browser uses the HTML tags it finds in the file it receives to figure out how the page is structured and how it should be displayed on your screen.

Unless the page is very basic indeed, it will also contain references to other files that it needs (or at least wants) to download from the server in order to properly display the complete page: CSS files for formatting information; images; script files such as JavaScript for adding functionality beyond what HTML can offer; videos; and even mini-apps in the form of Java applets or Flash code. After unpacking the basic page, the client will request these additional page elements from the server and assemble them into the complete webpage that a user sees in his or her browser. On more sophisticated pages, the exact files that are requested and downloaded may depend on what sort of device the browser is running on: a site may serve up an HTML5-native video file to a smartphone or tablet, for example, but deliver a Flash streaming video to a laptop.

These resource requests and deliveries are executed using HTTP (Hypertext Transfer Protocol), which defines how these client-server transactions are to take place. HTTP defines a set of "verbs" that are used to communicate intent and behavior. For a typical web browsing session, the most commonly used verbs are GET and POST, used respectively to request a resource and to submit a set of data (e.g., a web form submission). In response to a request, a server returns a status code that tells the client whether the request succeeded or not. You're probably familiar with a few such codes: 200 means that everything's okay, while 404 tells you that the server couldn't find what you asked for. There are dozens of others as well.

By default, requests and resources sent using HTTP are sent as unencrypted clear text, meaning that they can be read by anyone who intercepts the transmission. This can be demonstrated by using a Telnet client (see chapter 3 for more information about Telnet), which is also a clear-text, unencrypted tool for connecting to remote machines. First, find a terminal program (such as Apple's aptly-named Terminal) and type the following at the command prompt:

```
>telnet www.isup.me 80
```

That should be enough to launch your very first manual HTTP session. If there are no errors, you should see a response that includes "Connected to www.isup.me." You've just connected to a website by hand, and it's patiently waiting for you to send it a verb to respond to. Oblige it with the following:

```
GET /loc.gov HTTP/1.1
host: bizbiz
<hit enter a second time after the previous line>
```

The IsUp site takes another site URL as its sole URL parameter, checking the specified site's operational status, so this particular request is a little confusing at first glance. But if all goes well, you should see a short burst of HTML—actually the page content for the URL you requested. At the top of the output there should be a status code as acknowledgment: "HTTP/1.1 200 OK." And that's all there is to it! You've sent a simple (unencrypted) request to a remote web server and received unencrypted HTML text in response. You could, if you wished, recreate the full web browser experience by meticulously reading through the HTML, picking out any URLs specified for JavaScript files, CSS, etc., and using the same Telnet method to download those as well—but you've got the point.

SSL and Certificates

If the web were connected solely by unencrypted HTTP requests, much of our use of the web would be ill-advised. We certainly wouldn't want to enter our credit card details in a web form, for example; in fact, it would be a bad idea to submit any personal information at all. Encryption is necessary to keep the modern web working. (It would be nicer to say "keep the modern web *safe*," but safety is a relative measure in this domain. Nothing about networked communication is 100 percent safe.)

As you learned in chapter 3, key-based encryption is a method of enabling secure communication between two machines, typically by creating two keys for each machine or user: a private key, known only to its owner, and a public key, which is shared with anyone who needs to encrypt messages for the private key holder. This system is the basis of SSL, the Secure Sockets Layer (or Transport Layer Security, the successor to SSL that often goes by the same initials). SSL is the primary means of encrypting web communication and securing transactions between your web browser and, say, Amazon or Google. It's SSL that changes the risky "http" at the beginning of a URL to the reassuring "https" that lets you know you're connecting to a security-conscious server. All major web browsers provide some visual indication that you're using HTTPS/SSL in your browsing session, typically by adding a small padlock icon to the location or URL field at the top of the window. Clicking this icon usually brings up specifics about the connection security. Doing so in Chrome, for example, invokes a window that tells you, "Your connection to this site is private" and gives you a link to more details. Clicking the padlock icon in Safari produces a window that immediately starts out with more technical jargon, talking about the digital certificate that's being used.

A digital certificate is what SSL uses to solve the problem of trust. Recall from chapter 3 that it's entirely possible to disrupt the network communication between a client machine and a server and to trick the client machine into thinking that it's talking to a trusted server, when in fact a malicious hacker may have successfully redirected it to a server under his or her own control. If that happens, key-based encryption doesn't do anything to protect you; your carefully encrypted private data is being fed directly to the very type of person you were trying to avoid! In order to mitigate this possibility, SSL uses digital certificates, issued by a certificate authority, that assert that the certificate holder is indeed who they claim to be. Obviously, the value of such a certificate depends entirely on the trustworthiness of its issuer. Certificate authorities (CAs) come in all sizes, and some are more trustworthy—or at least their certificates are far more ubiquitous on the web—than others. CAs typically charge for a certificate then try to verify the owner's identity before providing it.

When a client browser begins an SSL transaction with a server, it first requests the server's certificate then checks with the CA that issued it to confirm that the certificate, and ergo the server itself, is valid. The basic principle is very much like Shibboleth authentication, which relies on a trusted third party to verify the identity of individuals.

In most cases, you can hope that the certificates offered by large, well-known corporations and entities are legitimate, but it may behoove you to take a second look at a certificate if you're conducting a confidential transaction with a site that's particularly small, unfamiliar, or in some way dubious. Trust of the CA is important because simply having a certificate is no proof of authenticity at all. In fact, it's trivial to create a certificate for yourself—a self-signed certificate—with a few commands entered into your computer's terminal. On the other hand, there's nothing wrong with self-signed certificates per se: within a large business, for instance, a self-signed certificate might be perfectly fine to verify connections on a corporate intranet. But seeing a self-signed certificate when you're connecting to a public website out in the wild somewhere should be a warning flag. That's a signal that you should stop and look closely before sending the site any valuable information. Fortunately, major web browsers will warn you if a site's certificate is self-signed.

Despite the ubiquity of SSL-encrypted communication and the certificate system, SSL is not invulnerable to attack. (Are you sensing a pattern here?) Clever hackers have developed a number of ways to game the system or simply to brute-force data out of the encrypted messages. For example: even a certificate issued by a prominent CA may prove to be worthless if the verification methods the CA uses to verify the identity of the certificate requestor are weak. In 2016, a vulnerability was found in the email verification procedure of StartSSL, one of the world's largest CAs, that would let an attacker obtain a certificate for a site he did not own (SecurityWeek News, 2016). Most of the time, though, the certificate system and SSL seem to function without major security issues.

Browser Plugins

The technology trio that defines basic web content is HTML, CSS, and JavaScript. As JavaScript in particular has matured, developers and users have seen impressive increases in the ability of webpages to serve up interactive content, animations and media, and "desktop-app-like" user experiences. The steady development of HTML5, designed with the demands of the modern web in mind, promises to extend the capability of native web content even further. But users, developers, and content providers alike have always wanted to do more than the native technologies or the browser makers themselves allowed. Thus web browsers started to enable the addition of plugins—specialized, non-native code bundles that can be added to a browser to provide specific functionality. (Plugins shouldn't be confused with *extensions*, which provide specific functionality using the *native* tools of HTML, CSS, and JavaScript.)

All major web browsers today provide some form of plugin support, although the extent of that support varies. As much as possible, though, you should avoid using plugins! Why? Because when you add a plugin to a browser, you are adding another vulnerability to your system—another crack in your defenses that a malicious hacker may be able to exploit. A plugin is a piece of third-party code, often proprietary and closed-source, designed to make a browser do something it wasn't intended to do—a hack, really. Anything that can be described in that way should make you nervous. Fortunately, HTML5 and advanced JavaScript are gradually obviating the need to load a lot of proprietary plugins into your browser. Certain types of activity or interaction are now possible using native, open HTML5 that previously required the use of a plugin. For example, making use of the hardware a browser client was running on was impossible in earlier versions of HTML and JavaScript; to record audio or video, a user would have to resort to a Java applet or Flash plugin. Now it can be done with a few lines of JavaScript.

A few of the major plugin types still in common use are discussed here.

Java Applets

Not to be confused with JavaScript, just plain Java is a much more powerful, desktop-level programming language. Until now, it has provided a way to create native Java apps that run as "applets" in a web browser. Java applets can provide surprising amounts of functionality in a browser window: databases, remote terminal access, games, access to a user's camera or microphone, and much more. It's not surprising that applets became pretty popular on the web—but it's also unsurprising that giving developers that much power has led to some pretty serious security vulnerabilities.

Applets can be completely invisible to the user, so they can be undetectable once they have permission to run in a particular browser. In theory, there are supposed to be multiple levels of protection set up to ensure that applets can't do anything a user doesn't want them to do. Like web servers, applets use a signed-certificate system to confirm their identity; they also operate as sandboxed apps, prevented from accessing software or hardware features that they're not supposed to use. Web browsers have also become increasingly cautious about allowing applets to run. Typically, a user has to click on a button or link to launch an applet and then confirm its permission to operate—and that's assuming that it can run at all. Apple, for instance, has stopped including Java in its laptops and desktops at all, meaning that applets are, by default, off the table completely on

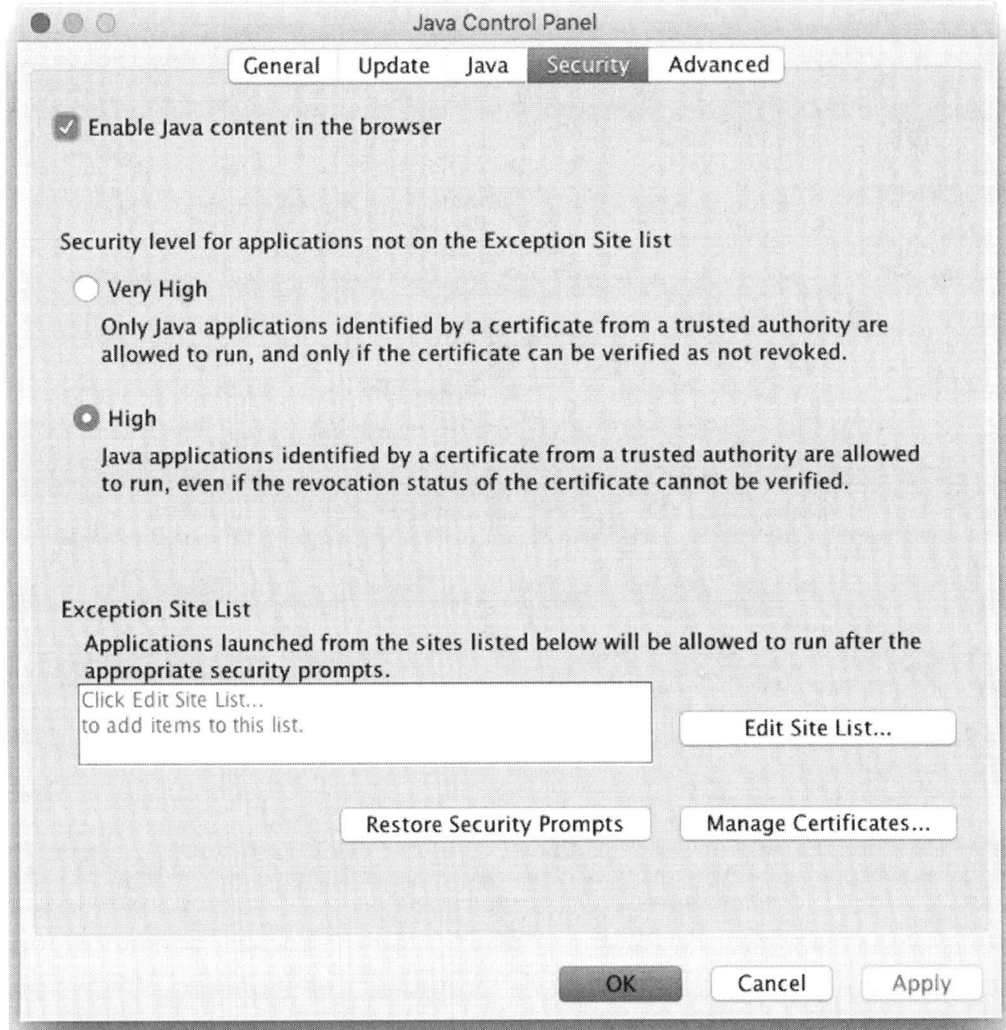

Figure 5.1. The Java Control Panel on the Mac. Screenshot from Apple macOS.

Macs (and they've never been permitted on iOS devices). A user can still install a version of Java, but even then the Java Control Panel (see figure 5.1) includes an intimidating set of security controls for applets. Oracle, which controls Java, sensing which way the wind was blowing, finally threw up its hands and declared applets dead; the next version of the Java Development Kit will do away with them for good (Camarda, 2016).

Applets have been burdened with security issues and concerns since their inception. McGraw and Felten's *Securing Java* (1999) gives a good early overview of the many ways in which applets could be abused or mishandled (you can read the relevant chapter online at www.securingjava.com/chapter-five). Unfortunately, the next fifteen or so years of applet history didn't clear their name: as recently as 2016, Oracle was still issuing vulnerability alerts for applets with the dire possibility that "successful exploits can impact the availability, integrity, and confidentiality of the user's system" (Oracle, 2016).

Adobe Flash

Without a doubt, Adobe's Flash technology is the most infamous of plugins when it comes to privacy and security. Nevertheless, it has become a far more popular way of implementing certain types of web functionality, particularly animation and visual effects ("flash," in other words) and media recording and playback. Part of this success is due to ease of implementation: the technical knowledge needed to write a Flash applet is not necessarily as involved as that needed to write extensive Java code. Another factor is the low overhead needed to load and start Flash objects on a page. Java applets are at a disadvantage in a speed contest since a browser must start up a Java "virtual machine" on the page before the applet itself can be launched; this often incurs a noticeable delay, potentially of tens of seconds for complex applets. Thus, until very recently, Flash reigned as the king of interactivity on the web. (For some reason, restaurants in particular were fond of building Flash-heavy websites and online menus—leading to a crisis among foodies when the Flash-free iPhone became popular!) Even if you didn't actively use Flash yourself, it was impossible to avoid: the vast majority of banner ads and other attention-grabbing advertisements on the web was Flash-based.

Unfortunately, Flash's codebase is, and always has been, rife with serious vulnerabilities. A brief history of Adobe-issued security updates for Flash can be viewed online (https://helpx.adobe.com/security/products/flash-player.html), and at the time this chapter was written, there were nearly 250 entries on the page (other lists peg the number much higher). In 2015, Flash Player had the dubious honor of being the most-used technology seen in so-called exploit kits, or commercialized malware. Eight of the top ten vulnerabilities found in such kits were Flash-related (Recorded Future, 2015). Even Adobe's numerous attempts to patch these vulnerabilities, as evidenced by their 250 security updates, arguably contributes to the problem: users who are repeatedly asked to update Flash on their computers may contract "alert box fatigue" and start automatically hitting the Cancel button each time a new alert appears.

Many of Flash's vulnerabilities are extremely serious, potentially leading to data breaches or complete system takeover on a target computer. Worse, many of these problems are so-called zero-day exploits—discovered in the wild and exploited by malicious hackers before Adobe is aware of them and has an opportunity to fix them.

Like Java, Flash applets are slowly being done away with on the web—a change long overdue, in many developers' opinion! HTML5 is providing viable, native-web solutions to the problems that required Flash or Java for so long. As noted, the first nail was driven into Flash's coffin by Apple when the company declined to include Flash on its newly announced iPhone. In an article published on Apple's website, CEO Steve Jobs wrote, "Symantec recently highlighted Flash for having one of the worst security records in 2009. We also know firsthand that Flash is the number one reason Macs crash . . . We don't want to reduce the reliability and security of our iPhones, iPods, and iPads by adding Flash" (Jobs, 2010). The meteoric rise of the iPhone and iPad guaranteed the slow demise of Flash, but other technology companies gradually followed Apple's lead as well. Chrome and Mozilla, like Safari, now block Flash by default, requiring users to jump through a couple of hoops before letting them use Flash applets. An April Fool's joke published in 2011 was titled "Adobe Quits Flash, Goes Full HTML5" (Chone, 2011), but now that absurdity doesn't seem so far-fetched: at the end of 2015, Adobe announced that, while not quitting Flash entirely, it was now promoting HTML5 development as the way forward (Adobe, 2015)!

Microsoft Silverlight

Microsoft's Silverlight plugin, while not as well known as Flash, enjoyed steady, stealthy growth in adoption—not for its own sake, but because both Amazon Video and Netflix adopted it for their increasingly ubiquitous streaming video services. That growth appears to be coming to an end, though. As with other plugin technologies, browser makers and content providers are turning away from proprietary systems and adopting the more open HTML5 standards. As early as 2013, Netflix was already announcing a switch away from Silverlight (Park and Watson, 2013). Google announced the impending demise of Silverlight in its Chrome browser the following year (Schuh, 2014).

Like other types of plugins, Silverlight is prone to numerous security vulnerabilities. The CVE Details website, which maintains a database of vulnerabilities for different technologies, lists twenty-eight known security issues for Silverlight (www.cvedetails.com/vulnerability-list.php?vendorid=26&productid=19887) compared to several hundred for the various versions of Java and nearly one thousand (!) for Flash Player. It only takes one good, exploited vulnerability to cause massive damage, though. As recently as 2016, reports were surfacing that Silverlight security holes were being actively used in online attacks and exploit kits (Goodin, 2016).

Wrap-Up

Java, Flash, and Silverlight are by no means the only third-party browser plugin technologies that exist, but they are covered here by way of example. The takeaway message is that although it's tempting to use plugins to make your web browser do more for you, they constitute a serious privacy hazard if they're not handled carefully. Fortunately, browser writers are making it harder to misuse plugins. Safari, Chrome, Opera, and even Internet Explorer will all soon disable most plugins by default, forcing the user to take very deliberate steps to enable Java, Flash, Silverlight, and similar technologies. Over the next few years, the need to use those sorts of plugins will continue to decrease as native web technologies like HTML5 and JavaScript gain additional functionality.

The best privacy-conscious choice, then, is to live without plugins. Use the latest versions of your browser or browsers of choice, and remove or disable any plugins that aren't blocked by default. If you must use a plugin, limit it to a case-by-case basis. MacOS Sierra, for example, will display a dialog box when it detects a plugin on a webpage you're visiting, letting you choose whether to allow the plugin to play once or every time you visit the page. If you really need that content, then choose "Use Once"; even though it's inconvenient to take that extra step each time you visit that page, it forces you to repeatedly review your security choices.

If you choose to leave plugins enabled, it's crucial that you keep up to date with new versions, especially if they're security patches. As soon as a plugin vulnerability becomes common knowledge, two things happen: the development team responsible for it begins working on a fix and publishes a new version of the plugin for you to install, and malicious hackers start scanning the Internet to find computers that are still running the older, vulnerable version. If you don't update when a patch becomes available, you're a sitting duck; there's a decent chance that you *will* fall victim to an attack through that outdated plugin. Each plugin has its own mechanism for alerting you to updates: Silverlight's notifications tend to manifest as in-browser alert boxes, while Flash has an unpleasant habit of launching its own updater app on your system. Don't fall into the habit of automatically dismissing and ignoring these alerts! Take the time to update your plugins for the sake of your own privacy and that of your users.

Scripts, Ads, and Trackers

The above section alluded to the fact that the need for third-party plugins is being obviated in part by the growing capability of JavaScript. JavaScript, which once was used primarily for making page elements and photos look different when you hovered your mouse over them, has matured into a technology that can manipulate virtually any aspect of a webpage, even to the point of mimicking or recreating full-blown, native desktop apps. Crucially, they can also communicate with the rest of the Internet, receiving data from remote servers—or sending it out to them. That's where privacy and security become an issue.

You can see the ubiquity of JavaScript on the web very easily by inspecting the HTML source of any webpage. (Every browser has a different way of getting to this view. In Safari, for example, you first have to activate the hidden Develop menu through Safari preferences, then choose Show Web Inspector from the menu.) JavaScript scripts hang out inside <script> tags on the page (not every script in a <script> tag is JavaScript, but most of them are). Occasionally you may see actual JavaScript code just sitting there on the page, but a more common approach—particularly for more complicated code—is to reference an external script file. This pulls in the JavaScript on the fly, as the HTML page is assembled, from an outside source via a tag that looks something like this:

```
<script src="../scripts/SneakyPrivacyHole.js" type="text/
javascript">
```

It's rare to find a website of any complexity these days that doesn't rely at least partially on JavaScript scripts, and many sites may invoke dozens of different scripts to do their work.

Of course, some common-sense rules apply when judging the nature of a script. If you're visiting an innocuous website, you can probably assume that the scripts running on its pages are at least *intended* to be innocuous as well; likewise, visiting shadier sites invites trouble in the form of malicious scripts that can start running as soon as a page starts to load. You could always disable JavaScript altogether in your browser for the greatest peace of mind. Unfortunately, because JavaScript plays such an important role on the web, disabling it will probably break, or at least cripple, your web-browsing experience; on some sites, you might not see anything but a blank page. No JavaScript, no content.

Assuming then that JavaScript is almost a necessity at this point, what steps can be taken to minimize the risk of privacy violations? The best approach is to try to regulate the type of scripts that will run in your browser. And the best way to do this is to make use of a "content blocker."

Content blockers, as the name suggests, control the types of content that can be executed in a web browser. They are usually implemented as browser "extensions," which are akin to plugins, adding nonstandard functionality to a browser, but doing so using the native languages of the web. Blockers have been around for a while, but they have gained popularity over the past few years due to a couple of factors: the growth in script-based advertising and tracking, and Apple's enabling of content blockers for Safari on iPhones and iPads in iOS 9 in 2015.

It turns out that one of the things JavaScript scripts are particularly useful for is tracking browser activity. Such tracking is crucial to a lot of modern web advertising and marketing systems. By including invisible scripts on a website, all sorts of information can be gleaned about you: the type of browser and computer you're using, the pages you're looking at, the search queries you're entering, and more. Furthermore, the tracking doesn't end when you leave one site and go to another; large advertisers have scripts embedded everywhere, and your actions on one site can haunt you on others. If you've ever searched for a product on Amazon and seen ads for that very thing appear on sites you visited days afterward, you're familiar with this effect. While this behavior may sometimes be a convenience if you happen to want directed advertising custom-tailored to your preferences and interests, it can otherwise seem rather creepy and invasive. And when it comes to privacy, online tracking is a huge threat. The metadata collected about your online behavior might not include your name, phone number, and address, but it might be enough to uniquely identify you nonetheless. Privacy is not the only concern with tracking, however. Tracking scripts pose a performance issue as well: running additional, superfluous scripts on a page can sometimes significantly slow down the site's response time. They can also greatly increase the overall amount of data that needs to be downloaded to construct a page in a browser—and that can be a problem for mobile devices on strict bandwidth budgets.

Thus the primary reason for the recent surge of interest in content blockers is their ability to selectively stop JavaScript scripts from running on a page. By intercepting requests for remote scripts before they can be loaded and comparing their origins and filenames to databases of known advertising and tracking scripts, a blocker can filter out the "bad" JavaScript and let the "good" through. One of the best browser extensions for this job is Ghostery (https://ghostery.com), which claims more than fifty million installations and a database of more than two thousand tracking scripts. After being configured to block the types of scripts you don't want to encounter, Ghostery pops up a little overlay each time you visit a website, indicating the number of scripts running—or blocked—on that page and their type (the emphasis is on advertising and tracking, but Ghostery also detects social widgets like share buttons for social media, beacons, and analytics systems like Google Analytics). The numbers can be truly staggering in some cases. A few examples: Cornell University Library's home page (https://library.cornell.edu) shows a grand total of one script running on the page (for Piwik Analytics). The *New York Times* home page (http://nytimes.com) includes fifteen. The *Daily Record* (www.dailyrecord.co.uk) hosts thirty-one. And so on.

How to Block Tracking Scripts with Ghostery

To start using Ghostery, follow these steps:

1. Ghostery's browser extension is available for the big five desktop/laptop browsers (Chrome, Firefox, Safari, Opera, and IE) as well as for Android and iOS. Go to the download page at www.ghostery.com/try-us/download-browser-extension and select your browser of choice. This example will use the Safari browser.
2. Download and install your browser extension. The installation procedure varies from browser to browser; in the case of Safari, the download comes in the form of a Ghostery.safariextz file and can simply be clicked to open the Safari preferences and give you two options for installation: install the file you just downloaded ("from the developer") or install an equivalent file from the Safari Extensions Gallery, which is a sort of mini app store for Safari extensions. In this case, choosing the Extensions Gallery version is actually the preferable option because it enables

Safari to automatically update the Ghostery extension when new versions are released. Click "Install From Gallery."

3. Once Ghostery has been installed, you'll see it listed in the Extensions pane of Safari's preferences (under the Safari menu). Safari will also add a small Ghostery button to the browser toolbar, near the search/URL box, and automatically open a couple of new browser tabs with information about Ghostery. Find and open the Ghostery Configuration Walkthrough tab.
4. The content in this tab walks you through four pages of setup for the extension:
   a. The first page (after an introductory page) asks if you want to opt in to sending anonymous data about the trackers you encounter back to Ghostery to help them improve their filtering. It's up to you to decide whether you want to or not—no pressure.
   b. The second page asks if you want to see a list of trackers overlaid on each page that you browse to (the Alert Bubble). This is entirely optional; you can access the same information from the Ghostery button in the toolbar. The overlay can also become quite distracting, so it's probably better to leave that box unchecked unless you're very curious about the scripts you're encountering during your browsing.
   c. The third page is the essential one. Here you're presented with a list of all the trackers Ghostery can potentially block, grouped into five sets: Advertising, Analytics, Beacons, Privacy, and Widgets. This is where you decide which trackers—or sets of trackers—you want to block in your browser. You can disable an entire category of script by checking the box next to the set name (e.g., Advertising) or drill down and disable selected scripts within a category. Clicking on the title of any script reveals additional information about it (see figure 5.2); for example, a related website, any industry affiliations, and sometimes a company's own description of what the script is for (typically couched in vague, marketing language).
   d. Click the Next button, and you're all done! Ghostery is operational.
5. Try it out: Browse to any website you want. If there are any ad or tracking scripts on the page, the Ghostery button in the toolbar will display a little red badge with the number it found. Click the button for information about the scripts in question. (The first time you do this, Ghostery will take you through a brief tutorial to understand the information box's content.) From here you can see a summary of all the scripts on the page. For each script, you can temporarily enable or disable it for your current browsing session on that site or permanently enable or disable it globally; you can also pause Ghostery's script blocking or whitelist the site you're on.

Peace and Advertising

Marco Arment is a well-known programmer in the Apple world. He was instrumental in the development of Tumblr, created the Instapaper tool for online reading, and now maintains a popular podcast app called Overcast. But when iOS 9 was rolled out allowing the addition of content blockers on mobile Safari for the first time, Arment also released an ad blocker app that he called, simply, Peace. The app was sure to sell well simply on the basis of Arment's reputation, but it also boasted a unique feature: for its database of advertising and tracking scripts, it used Ghostery's comprehensive and well-maintained

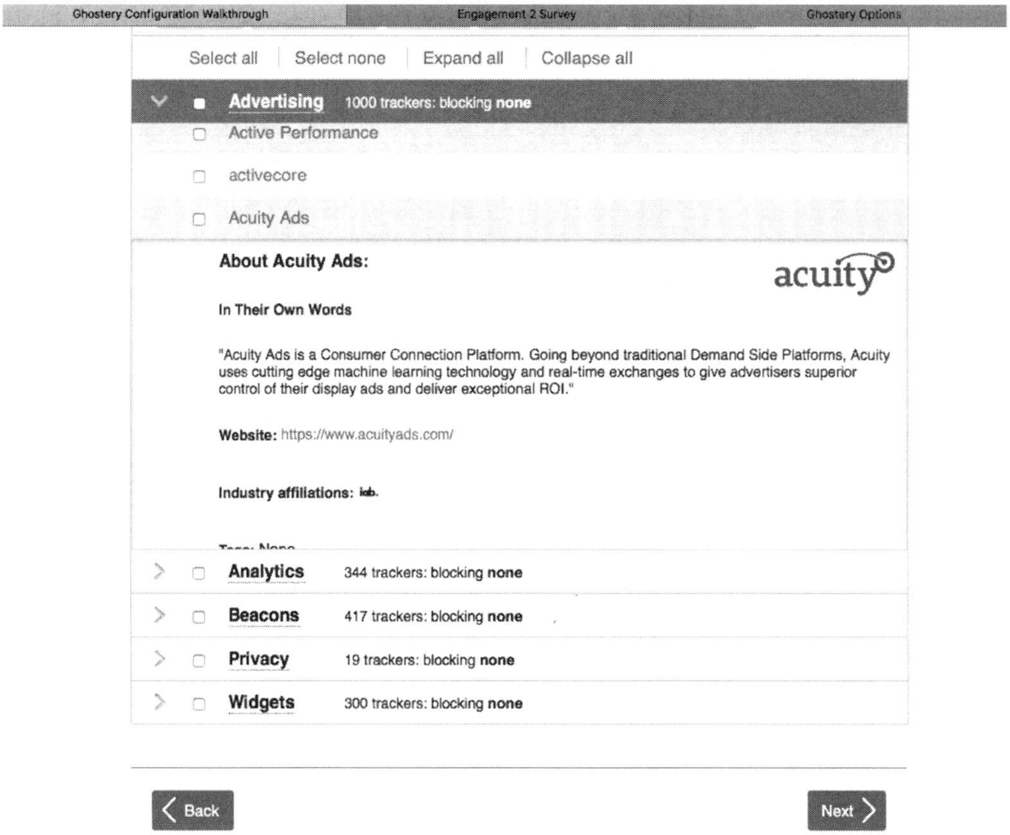

Figure 5.2. Inspecting an advertising script in Ghostery. Screenshot from Ghostery browser plugin.

collection. Peace appeared in the iTunes Store on the same day that iOS 9 was released, offered for $2.99. In a blog entry announcing the app, Arment explained why he'd created it in this way: "Ad and tracker abuse is much worse on mobile: ads are much larger and harder to dismiss, trackers are harder to detect, their JavaScript slows down page-loads and burns battery power, and their bloat wastes tons of cellular data. And ads are increasingly used as vectors for malware, exploits, and fraud" (Arment, 2015a).

And yet, just three days later, Peace was gone. Arment removed it from the App Store and told his customers how they could request a refund through Apple. In a follow-up blog post, he explained that it just "didn't feel good" that his new app was as successful as it was for its brief lifetime (Arment, 2015b). His conflicted feelings stemmed from his concern that ad blockers like his blocked ads for the good guys as well as the bad: innocuous websites that depended on ad revenue to keep their publications or businesses going. Ultimately, he decided that the revenue from his app wasn't worth the price of an uneasy conscience.

The blink-and-miss-it story of Peace was a dramatic moment in the otherwise quiet but ongoing debate about the morality of using ad blockers—and, especially, about using them indiscriminately. Given the intrusive nature of many advertising and tracking scripts, along with their impact on browser performance and data use, it's no wonder that people are starting to use content blockers more and more to neutralize them. And while few people would argue that online advertising and tracking is out of control, there's less agreement about how much of it is truly *bad*. While you may not appreciate having your every move tracked as you browse your way across the web, some advertising—often commingled with tracking scripts—is a necessary evil that keeps many a website afloat. If everyone were to start blocking all online ads (admittedly an unlikely scenario), then what would become of the sites that depend on ad revenue for funding?

Meanwhile, some sites have started to fight back against ad blockers, blocking their own content from being viewed if they detect a blocker in action. A typical example is City A.M. (http: cityam.com), which blurs out most of the content of an article and advises the reader to "disable any ad blockers . . . [and] reload the page to see the rest of this content." For now, it's up to each individual user to decide if and how to use ad blockers while browsing the web.

Passwords

Strong passwords are a crucial element in any defense against malicious hackers and criminals. Unfortunately, many computer users are still clueless about good password practices—and about what constitutes a good password. Analyses of common passwords (usually conducted on lists of passwords revealed in website database breaches) repeatedly show that the most popular passcodes in use today are words or phrases that were barely excusable in the much less computer-literate 1980s: "password," "123456," "qwerty," "abc123," etc. One problem with these passwords should be immediately obvious: the fact that they're the most popular means that they're easy to think of and thus easy to guess. But the trouble only starts there.

These days, hackers don't have to guess at a trivial password. Instead, they can employ *brute-force attacks*: essentially, running a script that repeatedly tries different password combinations until the right one is found. Thanks to the raw processing power of modern computers, millions of combinations can be tried in a second, covering the entire alphanumeric space in a feasible amount of time. An eight-character password consisting of only digits and upper- and lowercase letters could be any one of 218 trillion combinations ([26 + 26 + 10]^8). That's actually not too bad; a brute-force attack on a truly random, eight-character alphanumeric password might take on the order of six thousand hours to find a match (estimates in this section were made using the Brute Force Attack Estimator tool offered by Mandylion Research Labs, www.mandylionlabs.com/PRCCalc/BruteForceCalc.htm). That's probably not worth the effort for a casual hacker unless you're a particularly tempting target. But that's for a single computer. If someone has a lot more resources at his or her disposal—a botnet, say, consisting of one hundred machines—then that time drops down to sixty hours. To make matters worse, most simple passwords *aren't* random. A common practice is to use ordinary words as at least part of a password: "henry2006," for example. Knowing this, hackers don't start with a naive brute-force attack. Instead, they use a "dictionary attack," which is just what it sounds like: they load their password-cracking script with the contents of a dictionary, which is fairly likely to produce a working password in far less time than a brute-force approach that starts with "AAAAAAAA" and works through the whole space to "99999999."

One caveat to keep in mind with these rather bleak numbers is that they are theoretical estimates. On the web, most savvy sites that employ user logins and passwords take steps to prevent brute-force attacks against their user accounts. A site may limit the number of unsuccessful attempts a user can make to log in, or it might limit the frequency of attempted logins. Either approach will very effectively discourage a brute-force attack. But when considering passwords in other contexts, that might not be the case. An encrypted hard drive, for example, typically doesn't have that sort of limit for someone trying to access it. It doesn't matter if your drive is encrypted with the very latest, most sophisticated encryption algorithms available; if you connect to it by typing "password" into a text field, you're practically giving your data away to anyone who is able to gain physical access to the drive.

And it seems that 218 trillion combinations just isn't good enough these days. That's why many password systems today require you to get a little more creative, including non-alphanumeric characters in your passwords. Simply adding an exclamation point to the end of your eight-character password boosts the number of possible combinations to seven *quadrillion*, costing a malicious hacker two thousand hours on his one-hundred-machine botnet to discover your secrets. But clearly, merely increasing the length of your password will improve the situation. If you used 12 alphanumeric characters (uppercase letters, lowercase, and digits), you would get 3 sextillion combinations—which would require 938 million hours to crack.

Now, you could just throw caution to the winds, start using random twenty-character passwords, and call it a day. There's a problem with that approach, though: you have to be able to enter those passwords to log in, perhaps frequently. Remembering passwords is one of the biggest weaknesses of the password system—it's the reason people use easy-to-guess passwords in the first place. (And some people still write down their passwords on a scrap of paper near the computer. Please don't do that.) Many users have turned to password manager apps to do the remembering for them; and most browsers have started to provide built-in password managers as well. A password manager can autofill your credentials when you come to a login page, or you can just use it as a secure list that you can consult to find the right password for the page and copy or enter it yourself. Of course, you need to have some way of securing the password manager itself, which is usually done using a master password. And thus you have the same problem to deal with as before, just at a different level.

These days, many security experts are advocating the adoption of "passphrases" instead of passwords. A passphrase consists of two or more words, sometimes with spaces just as in a regular sentence. Typically, the words themselves are ordinary. The advantage of a passphrase is that it can be easy to remember, much easier to type in than a random string of letters and numbers, and yet it can still remain relatively out of the reach of most hackers. Why? Simply put, length is the most important factor in password and passphrase security. Since the number of combinations for any password length is multiplicative, the size of the potential search space grows exponentially with each additional character. Using the word "password" alone makes the problem trivial for an attacker: it could be determined in less than a second, even if it weren't the very first password a smart hacker would try. On the other hand, using the passphrase "password aardvark lacks determinate wings" catapults the number of potential combinations into the octillions, a search space that could occupy a hundred thousand machines for several trillion hours to cover.

To summarize a few best practices for using passwords and passphrases:

- Never use common, easy-to-guess words as passwords. If you don't want to use a passphrase, make sure that your password is long and random and uses a variety of special characters.
- Never write down your passwords in such a way that other people could use them.

- Never send a password through email. Email is insecure and difficult to remove from servers once it's been sent. In general, it's best to avoid sending passwords through the Internet at all.
- Use a passphrase instead of a password. Thirty to forty characters is a good length to aim for.
- Keep your passwords unique—don't use the same one across multiple sites.
- Use a password manager so that you don't have to remember passwords yourself. Secure it with a good, long passphrase that you won't forget (because you can't very well store your password for accessing the password manager within the password manager itself).

Web Analytics

One potential privacy problem on websites comes into play when considering the impact of web analytics. Web analytics systems carry an inherent tension between obtaining data and respecting users' privacy. The more data and metadata a web analytics tool can collect about a visit—and visitor—to a website, the more useful it may be to the site's creators and developers; but clearly, collecting more data is potentially more harmful to a user's privacy and anonymity.

Older analytics tools, such as the venerable Analog—https://en.wikipedia.org/wiki/Analog_(program)—analyzed web data by processing web server logs. Many newer tools, however, rely on tracking code inserted into a webpage—commonly JavaScript, although not exclusively. The most popular of these is Google Analytics (https://analytics.google.com). When you sign up for a Google Analytics account, you're given a snippet of JavaScript to place in the HTML source of your webpages. Each page that the script appears on will be tracked in the Google Analytics (GA) system, and each visit to each of those pages will be analyzed, quantified, and logged. The popularity of GA lies partly in its ease of implementation, but mostly in the quantity and variety of data it reports to you about visits to your site: browser and computer details, geographic location of visitors, demographics, sessions and engagement information, and so forth. And best of all, you don't have to track or store any of that information yourself; it's all neatly compiled and maintained on Google's servers for you—oh, wait.

For many users, the tradeoff is worth it: a wealth of accumulated web analytics data, offered for free, easily collected, in exchange for giving up control of that data. Many people consider Google trustworthy. On the other hand, once your Analytics data lands on Google's servers, you have no idea what might happen to it. Google says that it anonymizes the data it collects, but even anonymized data can be used to identify individuals. When you use a third-party cloud service like Google, the privacy policy that represents your library (see chapter 2) is no longer comprehensive—you are subject to Google's data policies as well, including any guidelines they may have about usage, retention, and access by third parties.

Due to these concerns, privacy-conscious users of analytics have started to embrace an alternative. Piwik (https://piwik.org) is an open-source analytics package that emphasizes personal control over data (their home page prominently advertises "100% data ownership" and "User privacy protection"). In setup and behavior, it is comparable to Google Analytics: you insert bits of tracking JavaScript code on your website, and the analytics app collects data and reports it back to you in a variety of useful visualizations. However,

Piwik offers a plugin system stocked by third-party developers; if you're not satisfied with the preconfigured reports, you may be able to find a plugin that will add the information that you need. Furthermore, you can host Piwik yourself. Though there is a cloud-hosted Piwik solution you can subscribe to, there's no need if you have the resources to host a simple LAMP (Linux-Apache-MySQL-PHP) application on your own server. That way, the data you log about your users' activities online need never leave your hands!

Security-Conscious Browsing and Searching

Developers have started to build security and privacy tools directly into web browsers. The five major browsers all offer a private browsing mode (aka "incognito mode"). When you're in private browsing mode, all the usual things that a browser does to remember your activity are shut off: sites you visit don't appear in your browser history, data you type into web forms isn't retained to be offered later as autofill values, and cookies aren't added or used. However, private mode is not *completely* private. Research has shown that it is possible to retrieve information about a private browsing session using a variety of techniques to analyze hidden caches and operating system data on the host computer (Satvat et al., 2014). Furthermore, you should remember that private browsing mode only operates on your own computer. Regardless of whether you're in private mode or not, your IP address and information about your browser will still be visible to the web servers you visit.

Most browsers also provide a growing list of security and privacy options that affect the behavior of your browser whether you're in private browsing mode or not. The exact choices and implementations vary, so Safari's preferences will be used here as an example (see figure 5.3). The main principle to remember is that you should only select the options that you really need; as with other aspects of security, fewer holes in your defenses means lower risk of a successful attack.

In Safari, relevant options are found under two panes in the Preferences window: Security and Privacy. In the latest version of Safari, they include the following.

Warn when visiting a fraudulent website. When you enter a URL or click a link while this feature is selected, Safari checks the target site against a database of sites known to spread malware or phishing attempts. Instead of taking you directly to the site, Safari will display a dire warning message to deter you from visiting it. You can still opt to go to the site despite the warnings, but Safari doesn't make it easy for you to do so.

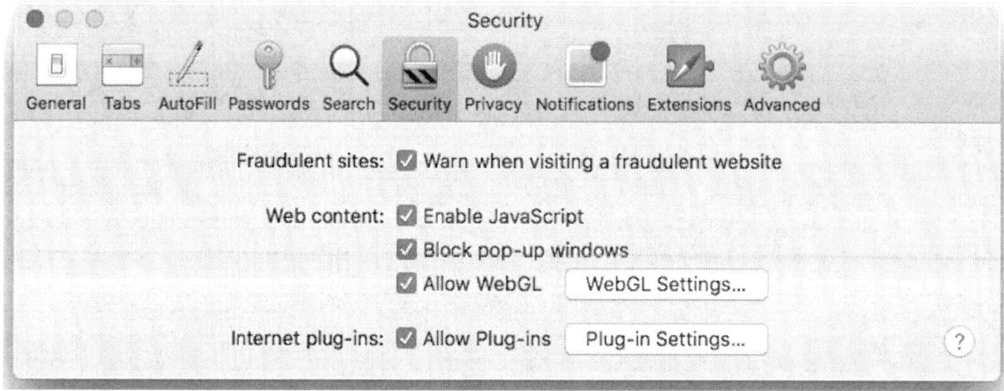

Figure 5.3. Safari's security settings. Screenshot from Apple Safari.

Enable JavaScript. Disabling JavaScript in your browser certainly lowers the risk of encountering malicious scripts and odious trackers, but it will also significantly limit your experience of the web. Many modern websites rely heavily on JavaScript for basic functionality.

Block pop-up windows. While some pop-up windows are legitimate, many are used to aggressively thrust ads or phishing attempts in your face. It's best to leave them blocked by default, only disabling this option as needed for specific sites.

Allow WebGL. WebGL is a JavaScript graphics library used to natively display 2D and 3D graphics on a page. Although it creates a potential vulnerability for your computer, the seriousness of the threat is a matter of debate. It's probably okay to leave this one selected.

Allow plugins. This is an important one. Recall that plugins allow non-native code to run in your browser. While plugins have their uses, they pose a significant security risk. Fortunately, Safari provides a fairly granular set of permissions for plugins. Click the Plug-in Settings button and you'll be taken to a secondary pane that lists all the installed plugins. For each plugin, you can choose to let it run or not run on each individual webpage you have open (and any you have previously permitted to use the plugin). You can also disable plugins completely from this page. Safari warns you if it considers a plugin's security measures to be insufficient. Unfortunately, this view doesn't tell you what a plugin does; if you're not sure, you'll have to find information about it somewhere else.

Manage cookies and website data. Cookies, fairly ubiquitous on the web, are chunks of data and settings stored in your browser by the websites you visit. A site can store almost anything it wants to in a cookie, including login information, site preferences, and browsing history. As in the case of JavaScript, disabling cookies entirely will make your browsing experience somewhat rougher since sites will have no way of "remembering" you when you visit them more than once. Safari lets you choose whether to always block cookies (undesirable), never block cookies (bad for privacy), or allow them only from the current site or sites you visit. You can also access a secondary pane here that shows you the cookies saved in your browser and allows you to selectively remove them. In general, accepting cookies only from sites you visit is a good practice. Allowing all cookies opens the door for advertisers and trackers to store unwanted data on your machine and to use it to track your browsing activity across multiple websites.

Manage location services. Sites you visit are able to query your computer to reveal its location, which can be useful for presenting users with local results—a list of nearby restaurants, for instance. But the privacy implications of revealing your location are obvious. Safari is especially restrictive with this setting: there's no way to always allow sites to read your location; instead, you can choose between automatic denial or forcing each site to ask permission to get your location.

Ask websites not to track me. This is a fairly new feature on the web, known as "Do Not Track." The intent is to let users decline to have tracking scripts and cookies monitor their web browsing. There's really no downside to turning this option on. But this is a weak privacy feature at best because it relies on the goodwill of sites to respect your preference. There's nothing to stop a website from ignoring this setting and placing a tracking cookie in your browser anyway.

Manage Apple Pay. Safari has a unique feature relating to the Apple Pay system: if a website wants to accept Apple Pay as a way for customers to buy products online, Safari works in conjunction with your Mac to see whether you have a nearby Apple Watch or iPhone. (A Watch or iPhone is needed to authenticate your identity before using Apple Pay.) Since this has potential privacy implications, it's included in the settings here.

Securing Websites

Before leaving this chapter, it's important to consider security and privacy from the other side of the browser window. If you're a website owner, what should you be doing to ensure that your site can't be used as an attack vector for a malicious hacker? This is by no means a trivial question, and the stakes are high: if hit by a successful attack, a vulnerable website running on a server can compromise the security of the entire server it's running on—or worse yet, be repurposed to deliver malware to your unsuspecting visitors.

As mentioned in the last section, web browsers have started to block access to sites thought to be compromised by malware. This is often done at a higher level too. If you have a central IT unit that controls network access at your institution, it may very well be running its own malware checks on sites users try to access and blocking them if it suspects there's anything wrong. Search engines do this too. Google, for example, maintains an active database of sites believed to contain malware and blacklists them, preventing users from accessing them. You really, really do not want your website to end up on this list! The best way to ensure that that doesn't happen is to do your best to protect your site from attack.

Protecting your network and computers at a systems level has already been addressed in earlier chapters, and of course those items still apply. At the *website* level, though, one of the most important things you can do is to keep any code you're running safe and up to date. Popular CMSes (Content Management Systems) like WordPress carry a significant risk associated with them. The sheer number of sites running them, combined with the plethora of third-party plugins that can be added to base sites, make them a tempting target for malicious hackers. WordPress, for example, is regularly updated with important patches to close security holes discovered in the wild. But the very simplicity of installing WordPress makes it trivial to launch one or more WordPress blogs and quickly forget about them. Letting a WordPress site languish unmaintained in an obscure corner of your server is a prime way of getting your entire server compromised. Criminals actively scan the web for older, unpatched instances of WordPress running where they can exploit known—and already fixed in newer versions!—security holes to break into your systems. Don't let this happen to you! Make sure that you keep *all* of your CMS-based sites updated with the latest security fixes. Another best practice is to aggressively cull any old blogs or sites running on your servers that are no longer being actively used. It's too easy to forget about them and let them fall behind in the upgrade cycle.

A second thing to do for all your sites—whether using a third-party CMS or your own code—is to run a security audit. There are a number of open-source apps that will analyze your site and identify any significant security vulnerabilities in the code. You can even run checks using online tools, no download required. One such tool is Scan My Server (https://scanmyserver.com). While other tools may let you scan any URL you enter, Scan My Server requires you to verify that you control the site in question by placing a small badge on your webpage. Running a scan will produce a report of any malware or site vulnerabilities the scanning tool discovers.

Key Points

The web and web browsing are integral parts of the modern Internet, and as such they are targets of many types of privacy attack. However, you can mitigate a substantial amount of risk while using the web by remembering some simple points and behaviors, including the following.

- The native languages of the web are HTML, CSS, and JavaScript. Web browsers interact with web servers via HTTP requests.
- Secure HTTP, or HTTPS, uses cryptography and a system of trusted certificates to encrypt data being transmitted between servers and browser clients.
- Plugins extend the functionality of a web browser by allowing non-native code (e.g., Java) to run. However, this comes at the cost of significant security risks.
- JavaScript is heavily used on the web for adding content and functionality to webpages, but it is also commonly used to track the activities of visitors. Content blockers can be used to prevent advertising and tracking scripts from reaching you, but this may adversely affect legitimate scripts and sites as well.
- Many people still use weak, easy-to-break passwords. You should only use strong (long) passwords or passphrases, and you should keep them unique.
- Web analytics systems can be a privacy risk if your server activity data is uploaded to a third party. Piwik is an alternative that lets you keep your data secure.
- Web browsers include many security and privacy safeguards. Take the time to learn how they are configured in your browser preferences.
- Web servers that run outdated CMSes, such as older versions of WordPress, are highly vulnerable to attack. Always keep your sites updated with the latest available security fixes.

This chapter examined the privacy threats that impact web browsers as a general category but with a more specific focus on desktop and laptop browsers. In the next chapter, we'll move on to consider a platform that has overtaken desktops and laptops in popularity: mobile devices.

References

Adobe Corporate Communications. 2015. "Flash, HTML5, and Open Web Standards." November 30. http://blogs.adobe.com/conversations/2015/11/flash-html5-and-open-web-standards.html.

Arment, Marco. 2015a. "Introducing Peace, My Privacy-Focused iOS 9 Ad Blocker." September 15. https://marco.org/2015/09/16/peace-content-blocker.

———. 2015b. "Just Doesn't Feel Good." September 18. https://marco.org/2015/09/18/just-doesnt-feel-good.

Camarda, Bill. 2016. "Goodbye and Good Riddance: Oracle Finally Ditches Java Browser Plug-In." Naked Security by Sophos. February 2. https://nakedsecurity.sophos.com/2016/02/02/goodbye-and-good-riddance-oracle-finally-ditches-java-browser-plug-in.

Chone, Jeremy. 2011. "Adobe Quits Flash, Goes Full HTML5." *Bits & Buzz*. April 1. www.bitsandbuzz.com/article/adobe-quits-flash-goes-full-html5.

Goodin, Dan. 2016. "Malicious Websites Exploit Silverlight Bug That Can Pwn Macs and Windows." Ars Technica. February 25. http://arstechnica.com/security/2016/02/malicious-websites-exploit-silverlight-bug-that-can-pwn-macs-and-windows.

Jobs, Steve. 2010. "Thoughts on Flash." Apple. April. www.apple.com/hotnews/thoughts-on-flash.

Oracle Corporation. 2016. "Oracle Security Alert for CVE-2016-0636." Oracle.com. March 23. www.oracle.com/technetwork/topics/security/alert-cve-2016-0636-2949497.html.

Park, Anthony, and Mark Watson. 2013. "HTML5 Video at Netflix." *Netflix Tech Blog*. April 15. http://techblog.netflix.com/2013/04/html5-video-at-netflix.html.

Recorded Future. 2015. "Gone in a Flash: Top 10 Vulnerabilities Used by Exploit Kits." *Recorded Future Blog*. November 9. www.recordedfuture.com/top-vulnerabilities-2015.

Satvat, Kiavash, Matthew Forshaw, Feng Hao, and Ehsan Toreini. 2014. "On the Privacy of Private Browsing—A Forensic Approach," *Journal of Information Security and Applications* 19 (1): 88–100. doi:10.1016/j.jisa.2014.02.002.

Schuh, Justin. 2014. "The Final Countdown for NPAPI." *Chromium Blog*. November 24. http://blog.chromium.org/2014/11/the-final-countdown-for-npapi.html.

SecurityWeek News. 2016. "StartSSL Flaw Allowed Attackers to Obtain SSL Cert for Any Domain." *SecurityWeek*. March 22. www.securityweek.com/startssl-flaw-allowed-attackers-obtain-ssl-cert-any-domain.

CHAPTER 6

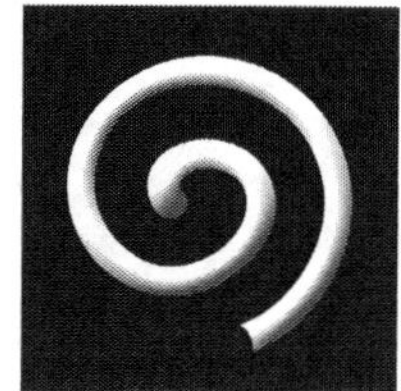

Mobile Devices

IN THIS CHAPTER

- ▷ Securing mobile devices with a strong passphrase
- ▷ Understanding the threat of operating system backdoors
- ▷ Tracking mobile devices by cellular or wi-fi signals
- ▷ Learning about man-in-the-middle attacks on cell phones
- ▷ Restricting app and operating system access to location data and other private information
- ▷ Protecting yourself against Bluetooth attacks
- ▷ Keeping your devices up to date with security improvements
- ▷ Jailbreaking your mobile devices (or why you shouldn't)
- ▷ Summarizing good mobile device security practices

Threat Assessment

MOBILE DEVICES HAVE PROLIFERATED throughout the library world, just as they've taken over large swathes of the rest of society. They appear primarily as the personal tablets and smartphones used by library staff and library patrons; however, some libraries also loan out mobile devices (primarily iPads and other tablets) to users. Many of the privacy strategies described in this chapter are more applicable to personal devices than to library-loaned devices (like public computers, the latter should be cleared of data and re-provisioned after each loan). However, part of a well-rounded library privacy protection strategy entails educating your users about how they can limit their own vulnerability. This chapter will help you to do that.

In this day and age, a smartphone or tablet can be a fairly comprehensive representation of your digital self. With built-in cameras, links to cloud services, and ever-increasing on-board storage space, a single device can hold a surprising amount of very personal, very private information about you or the library you're working for. Yet they're so easy to lose or misplace or have stolen from you. If that should happen, you want to be able to groan about the cost of replacing the device without having to mourn over the exposure of your private data. While modern operating systems on mobile devices do a great job of trying to erect sturdy barriers around such data, it's up to you to make sure that the gate is secured with a strong passphrase that won't be easily decrypted.

Mobile devices, especially smartphones, are also multifaceted communication devices. They can talk to the world using wireless networking, cellular networks, Bluetooth, and occasionally less-conventional technologies. Every communication with the outside world, though, is—not to be paranoid—an opportunity for third-party snooping or worse. Each communication protocol used is vulnerable to different forms of attack, both active and passive. At best, such attacks may merely intercept some of the data stream flowing from your device to the outside world or vice versa. At worst, they can use your signal as a vector to infect or compromise the device itself, potentially accessing everything on it.

While device makers (particularly Apple) are continually improving security features in their operating systems and device hardware, those improvements won't do you much good if they don't get into your devices. Devices that run older versions of an operating system that haven't been patched with the latest security fixes are vulnerable to attackers who exploit those known weaknesses and know how to detect devices that haven't been upgraded. Staying up to date with operating system releases is crucial to a good personal or library security strategy. Android users face an additional challenge in this area due to the complexity and fragmentation of the Android device market, which in some case hinders them from updating to the latest and greatest operating system versions. This chapter will inspect each of these three problems: locking devices, securing communications, and maintaining an up-to-date security environment.

Device Access

Locking Devices and Passcodes

Smartphones and tablets contain a wealth of personal, private data. Keeping one with you at all times is like carrying around your address book, photo album, family movies, diary, medical records, and trip planner, all rolled into one—and in a much smaller, easier-to-lose-or-steal package. And just as you wouldn't leave your diary or your credit cards lying around in public where anyone could pick them up, you shouldn't leave your mobile devices unprotected.

Android and iOS devices have always had the ability to be locked with a passcode, but many people never bother to enter one. It's an inconvenience, after all, to have to enter a code every time you want to check your text messages or take a picture. Over time, this burden has been reduced—most significantly by the advent of fingerprint scanners, which can obviate the need to enter your passcode under most circumstances. In fact, Apple's newer fingerprint scanner (found in the iPhone 6s/6s+ and newer models) was so fast that users complained about the speed; they didn't have enough time to look at the information on the lock screen before their phones established their identity and brought them to the main dashboard! (In iOS 10, Apple redesigned the unlocking process to account for this problem.) Manufacturers too have tried to encourage users to adopt passcodes. When you set up a new iOS device, for example, one of the steps is to create a new passcode. You can skip it, but you have to make a little more effort to *not* use a passcode than you would otherwise.

Adding a passcode to your mobile devices should be a no-brainer if you are concerned with privacy. The default for a long time was to use a four-digit code akin to a PIN. Recall the discussion of passwords from the previous chapter, though. A four-digit, purely numeric passcode only affords you ten thousand potential combinations. That's well within the reach of a brute-force attack, although device makers do their best to reduce the risk. Apple, for instance, intentionally structures the unlocking process in such a way that each unlock attempt must be performed on the device itself (i.e., not through remote access) and takes eighty milliseconds to complete, while subsequent attempts are delayed by increasing time periods when an incorrect code has been entered (Apple, 2017). Both iOS and Android also support an optional failsafe mechanism: if you so choose, you can instruct your device to erase all its data and reset to factory default mode after ten failed passcode attempts. If you don't use that option, then it's not difficult to imagine a brute-force device being constructed to physically enter different codes and plow through the ten-thousand-combination space. That's why Apple now encourages you to use, at a minimum, a six-digit combination instead. A six-number code expands the search space to a million combinations. Android uses similar methods to block brute-force attacks. In fact, both iOS and Android support—and encourage—the use of arbitrary-length, alphanumeric passcodes (or passphrases) instead of short, numeric codes. Simply adding letters to a six-digit code will increase the size of the search space exponentially and the time required to search it to years or decades.

A long, random, alphanumeric code is even more of a nuisance to type in on a phone or tablet keyboard than it is on a laptop, so the fingerprint scanner is a tempting alternative. (Even with the scanner enabled, though, you still need to remember your code; it has to be entered under special circumstances, such as after a device has been restarted or when you're trying to disable security features in the device settings.) Apple in particular has gone to great lengths to protect your fingerprint data, even creating a separate physical location in its chips (the "Secure Enclave") to guard it against misappropriation. However, it's impossible to protect your fingerprints *outside* a device. You leave fingerprints everywhere; in fact, if you look closely at the fingerprint scanner on your phone, you may very well see a nice, clear fingerprint sitting right there. That's a bit like leaving the combination to a safe written on a piece of paper taped to its door! Long a favorite plot point in spy movies, it turns out that it is actually possible to create a false "finger" with a lifted print that can trick a scanner into unlocking a device (Brandom, 2016). Of course, under the wrong circumstances, you could also be physically forced to place your thumb on a scanner to unlock your device.

In the end then, simple numeric passcodes are only sufficient to deter casual, opportunistic snooping or theft. Fingerprint scanners are convenient alternatives to entering a code, and they may encourage the use of more complex codes, but ironically, they introduce their own vulnerabilities into the system. If you are determined to protect your devices from intrusion by more sophisticated criminals or government agencies, your best bet is to disable the fingerprint scanner and manually enter a complex (alphanumeric) passphrase that follows the guidelines described in chapter 5.

Backdoors

You may have five different deadbolts on the front door of your house, but they won't do you a bit of good if you leave the backdoor unlocked. The same holds true for your mobile devices. Unfortunately, there's one important difference: you probably won't be able to tell whether your phone's backdoor is open or not.

A *software* backdoor is a hidden, deliberately created vulnerability in an app, operating system, or other piece of software that bypasses the normal system entry and any associated security features. Anyone who has the key to the backdoor can use it to access your mobile devices without knowing your passcode or fingerprint. Generally speaking, backdoors at the app level are installed by developers, or hackers who gain access to the app code, to be used for illegitimate purposes. This is a larger problem in the Android world than it is for iOS; Apple's greater control over iOS and iDevice hardware means that they are able to enforce restrictions on how apps are installed. For the most part, iOS apps can only be installed on an iPhone, iPad, or iPod by downloading them from Apple's own iTunes App Store. Every app in the store is carefully screened for suspicious or malicious code, so the risks of unauthorized backdoors is kept to a minimum. On Android, however, it is possible to install apps from sources other than the official app stores—and even those official sources, such as Google Play, have accidentally let malware slip through the app vetting process on multiple occasions.

If apps are properly sandboxed—only allowed to operate within strictly defined limits on the type of data or set of documents they can access—then an app backdoor can only compromise your privacy up to a certain point. On the other hand, a backdoor in the operating system itself is a much more serious matter; it potentially opens up your entire device and all its data for inspection. Because of the way that operating systems are written and protected, it's fairly unlikely that a third party would be able to insert a backdoor into operating system code without its authors realizing it. The likeliest way for an system backdoor to be added, then, is for the operating system company itself to insert one, either for its own purposes or at the request of a third party. Today, that third party is most probably going to be a government agency. Agencies like the FBI have become increasingly vocal about their desire (stated as a need) to be able to defeat mobile device security and cryptography for criminal investigations or for anything relating to the "terrorism" keyword.

Since backdoors tend to be kept secret (both in order to protect them from being illicitly exploited and because they tend to be very unpopular with the public), you could very easily own a backdoor-enabled device and never know it. Your only real protection against backdoors in mainstream phones is to keep up with security news and try to catch any new revelations that are disclosed. As an alternative, you could consider a device like the Blackphone (www.silentcircle.com), which advertises itself as "private by design." The Blackphone runs Silent OS, a version of Android modified with additional security features and privacy protections.

Law Enforcement vs. Encryption

Digital security and cryptography is a cat-and-mouse game between the "good guys" and the "bad guys." In this day and age, modern computers have enabled both strong, mathematically complex encryption techniques that can be used to lock away information for centuries and supercomputing techniques that have the potential to defeat any encryption that is not sufficiently strong. Recognizing this situation, law enforcement and government agencies like the FBI and the NSA in the United States have become increasingly vociferous about their need to be able to bypass device security and access information. Tech companies and many technical users of mobile devices have resisted this call, arguing that weakening encryption or requiring backdoors into devices is harmful for everyone.

The dramatic climax to this debate, at least for now, came in the spring of 2016 when the FBI requested that Apple help them access the iPhone of Syed Rizwan Farook, one of the two perpetrators of the San Bernardino terrorist attack in December 2015. The FBI approached Apple to ask that they create a customized version of the iOS operating system that would bypass its normal security measures. The modified operating system would be installed onto Farook's phone and enable the FBI to review its contents. Apple, which for years had been advertising its commitment to customer privacy, rejected the FBI's request. In an open letter posted to the company website, CEO Tim Cook explained the conflict in this way:

> The U.S. government has asked us for something we simply do not have, and something we consider too dangerous to create. They have asked us to build a backdoor to the iPhone.
>
> Specifically, the FBI wants us to make a new version of the iPhone operating system, circumventing several important security features, and install it on an iPhone recovered during the investigation. In the wrong hands, this software—which does not exist today—would have the potential to unlock any iPhone in someone's physical possession.
>
> The FBI may use different words to describe this tool, but make no mistake: Building a version of iOS that bypasses security in this way would undeniably create a backdoor. And while the government may argue that its use would be limited to this case, there is no way to guarantee such control. (Cook, 2016)

Despite increasing pressure from the government, both legally and in attempts to sway public opinion, Apple stood firm in its refusal to cooperate. Dozens of tech and security companies filed amicus briefs in court when the Department of Justice sought a court order to force Apple to comply. Finally, only a day before the hearing was scheduled to begin, the government backed down, claiming that they had found another way of accessing the phone.

This odd drama is significant for privacy protection in a number of ways. First, it confirms Apple's commitment to protecting the privacy of its customers. The evidence is strong that the iDevice teams are working hard to make Apple's iPhones and iPads truly secure, immune to outside attacks, and accessible only by their owners. Second, the conflict demonstrates that the U.S. government is willing to pressure tech companies to go to extraordinary lengths to compromise privacy protection. Finally, although the showdown was ultimately cancelled, many security observers are concerned that this was an attempt to set a precedent that could be leveraged into more widespread compromises in the future. There are concerns that the government blinked first because it saw that public opinion was against it but that it will most likely try something similar again in the future.

Communication and Device Tracking

Tracking Device Movement

Cellular Connections

It's important to realize that mobile devices are inherently trackable. Seamless cellular connectivity depends on a device's ability to discover nearby cell towers and connect to them as needed. If your phone is powered up and not in airplane mode, it is probably doing something Internet-related in the background: syncing data with cloud services, communicating with messaging systems or email servers, etc. When you're using a cell service provider for these tasks (i.e., you're not connected to a wi-fi network), each communication leaves a record in the cell tower you're currently using. Even if your phone isn't actively connecting to the cell system to complete a task for one or more of your apps, the phone itself is continually checking for the presence of new cell towers and switching to use the one that affords the best connection to the service. Each of these connections and "probes" leaves a record in a cell tower that identifies you via your phone number or subscriber ID. And since the towers are in known, fixed locations, these records also reveal where you are or where you've been. With very little effort, a fairly accurate history of your movements could be constructed by analyzing cell tower records.

A connection to a single cell tower only reveals your general location; the precision of the measurement depends on, among other factors, how widely spaced the towers in the area are. However, if you are within range of several towers simultaneously, your phone's precise location can be determined through triangulation of the different signals. Furthermore, modern phones are legally required to have an emergency feature that also returns a precise reading of your location so that emergency responders can find you if necessary (Blaze, 2013).

In the United States, at least, all of this data can be requisitioned by law enforcement agencies, either after the fact or in real time. Such agencies can even compel cellular providers to use the emergency location feature to find someone (Blaze, 2013). And while cell tower records are *supposed* to be used only for legitimate, legal investigations of specific individuals, you should assume, as always, that this data is available to any interested parties that have the technical ability to access it through nefarious means.

Wi-Fi Connections

Your response to the above might be to reach for the Airplane Mode toggle on your phone to disable your cellular connection and to rely solely on wireless networks for connectivity. Unfortunately, this won't do you much good. It's just as straightforward to track mobile devices (and laptops, for that matter) using wi-fi as it is to track those on cell networks. This is because your devices discover new wi-fi networks in much the same way as they learn about new cell towers. As you move through an area, your device—a smartphone, say—is constantly on the lookout for new networks that you might be coming in range of. It does so by sending out queries on wi-fi frequencies that can be answered by a wi-fi signal provider. This is how the phone gives you a list of available networks that you can join; a similar message is sent to a specific network in order to actually join it.

One of the chunks of data broadcast in these messages is your phone's MAC address (Sweeney, 2014). The MAC (media access control) address is a unique identifier associated with the hardware in your device. Any device that you have that connects to a larger network—your phone, your iPad, your laptop—has a MAC address different from any other MAC address in the world. (Thus it's even more specific than your IP address, which is assigned at the network level and can be dynamically changed or recycled.) Just as you leave a record of your movements in cell towers when connected to a cellular network, wi-fi networks can identify and track you by recording your MAC address. Government agencies like the NSA in the United States and the Communications Security Establishment in Canada (Khandelwal, 2014), as well as retailers (Sweeney, 2014), have been shown to be using this technique to monitor people's movements.

Now, although a device's MAC address is permanently associated with its hardware, it's only revealed to the outside world through software. This means it can be changed or spoofed. Such alteration is increasingly being done systematically at the operating system level. Apple (which has repeatedly demonstrated that it's the large tech company most concerned with protecting user privacy) started the trend in 2014 with iOS 8 for iDevices: in iOS 8 and subsequent OS releases, MAC addresses are randomized when they're used to signal and connect to wi-fi networks, rendering them useless for tracking purposes. Similar techniques have since been added to Android (version 6.0 and above) and Windows 10. (Depending on your device and operating system, randomization may be turned on by default or may have to be manually set in the system preferences.) Address randomization is not yet as common on the laptop and desktop front, but there the increased flexibility of operating systems affords you more options for temporarily changing your MAC address. It can be done by using the command line in most cases, or you can download an app or tool (e.g., SpoofMAC, https://github.com/feross/SpoofMAC) that will do the work for you.

There are a couple of caveats to consider when spoofing or randomizing your MAC address. One is that doing so all the time can cause you problems; networks and servers use MAC addresses to identify specific devices for legitimate purposes, not just for tracking, and deliberately frustrating those purposes might interfere with your work on those systems. The second issue is a related one. Since MAC address identification is often needed to ensure that a wi-fi connection is routing information to and from the correct devices, randomizing your address *within* a connection can be problematic; thus, randomization is more commonly used when a device is discovering new networks, and a fixed address is used once a connection is made. That means that there is still the potential for you to be identified and tracked while you're connected to a specific network.

Man-in-the-Middle Attacks

The preceding section considered the potential privacy violations inherent in connecting to a cellular network. However, it only addressed issues related to an *official* network. It's possible that you may not be connecting to what you think you are.

Recall from chapter 3 that network communications are vulnerable to man-in-the-middle attacks in which an eavesdropper inserts a device, real or virtual, between your device and the server or router with which you're attempting to communicate. By tricking your device into thinking that his or her device is the legitimate one, the eavesdropper can intercept messages being sent back and forth and potentially read their contents.

Since the process of connecting to a specific cell tower in a network is conceptually very similar to channeling your Internet communications through a router or server, you may be able to guess that cellular communication is vulnerable to the same sort of interception. An IMSI (International Mobile Subscriber Identity) catcher (popularly known as a StingRay) is a device intended primarily for military or law enforcement use that enables man-in-the-middle attacks on cell networks. It does so by spoofing the signals and responses generated by legitimate cell phone towers while, critically, providing a higher-power signal than the ones used by the existing towers. Since a cell phone maintains its call or data quality by connecting to the strongest available cell signal, it will usually preferentially choose a StingRay if one is operating in the area. Once this happens, the StingRay can either passively collect data about the devices connected to it—making it possible to identify individual subscribers and their locations—or actively eavesdrop on the voice or data messages being passed through it.

Since their debut, StingRays have grown steadily more popular with law enforcement groups and government surveillance agencies. Unfortunately, they are sometimes employed indiscriminately, and their use is very controversial.

Like many man-in-the-middle attacks, it's difficult to know if you've been hit by a StingRay or not. Fortunately, the physical structure of the cell tower networks makes a clever solution possible. With a suitable app, such as the Android IMSI-Catcher Detector (https://github.com/CellularPrivacy/Android-IMSI-Catcher-Detector), your device can compare the characteristics of the cell tower it's supposedly connected to with the open-source databases of known cell towers in your area. If the ID sent back by your connection doesn't match a known tower, there's a good chance that someone's interfering with your signal. The Android IMSI-Catcher Detector uses this and other techniques to ascertain a threat level for your current connection, ranging from green ("no threats detected") to black ("Someone is trying to remotely manipulate your handset, YOU are the TARGET!"). Sadly, there doesn't appear to be an equivalent app available for Apple devices.

Location Services

Find My Device

Of course, your smartphone has a dedicated location sensor in the form of a GPS receiver (as do some, but not all, tablets). Your mobile devices can use GPS data to determine location even if their wi-fi and cellular connections are turned off. This ability is a great thing to have when you're trying to find your way or have your pictures geotagged as you take them. But you should be conservative about allowing apps to access and use your location data. Always follow the basic security rule of minimum access: only grant permission to an app to use personal data if it's necessary, and then only allow it to access the subset of data that it truly needs.

One system-wide application of location data is to maintain an awareness of where all your devices are at any given time. This requires coordination of a device's location data with a cloud-based service that can keep track of the device's position. On Apple devices such as iPhones and iPads, this functionality is branded Find My iPhone. In the Android world, it's called Android Device Manager. Both services work in roughly the same way. If you elect to activate Find My iPhone (which, despite the name, also applies to iPods, iPads, and Macs) or Android Device Manager, you'll be able to locate your device in real time on a map either on a webpage or in an app. You'll also have other options: post a message to the device—something that an honest person might see and act upon if the device is found; lock the device so that it can't be used; cause your device to emit a loud beeping or ringing sound to help you locate it; or, as a last resort, wipe all your data off the device. If you've instituted a mobile device lending program in your library or librarians and staff are using devices for work, you probably want to make sure that you have the appropriate service activated for your device type. At the very least, you want to be able to locate a public iPad if it somehow fails to return to the circulation desk. And if there's work-related data on a missing device, the remote lock and remote wipe options provide a comforting safety net to keep that data from being accessed. To set up and use Find My iPhone on an Apple device:

1. Open the Settings app and tap into iCloud > Find My iPhone (or Find My iPad—the name changes with device type).
2. Tap the Find My iPhone (or iPad) switch to the On position. Note that you will have to enter an Apple ID password to turn it off again (which should be done if, for example, you are selling or giving away the device).
3. Tap the Send Last Location switch to the On position. If the device's battery is failing, this will tell it to use its dying breath to log one last location data point before it goes out completely.

4. To locate devices using the web, visit iCloud.com and sign in with your Apple ID. Select the Find iPhone app. This should display a map with the location of any devices that are associated with your ID and that have Find My iPhone activated. Click on one of the green dots to see the device name and how long ago its position was last reported. Click the "i" icon in the information box to play a sound, lock the device, or erase it.
5. Alternatively, launch the Find iPhone app on your iPhone, iPad, or iPod. The display map, info box, and remote controls work the same way as they do on iCloud.com.

To set up and use Android Device Manager:

1. Go to Settings > Permissions > Security > Device Administrators.
2. Tap the checkbox next to Android Device Manager. Tap the Activate button on the permissions page that appears.
3. To locate devices using the web, visit www.google.com/android/devicemanager and sign in with your Google ID. You should then see a map with all of your registered devices and their last known locations. There will also be options to ring, lock, or erase each device.
4. Alternatively, launch the Android Device Manager app (you may have to install it from the app store first) and follow the instructions to view the map.

Apps Using Location Services

One of the best uses of apps on a smart mobile device is to provide contextually relevant information to a user. Location is a key piece of context in many cases: geotagging photos, Facebook posts, or FourSquare check-ins; providing local recommendations for restaurants, hotels, and tourist attractions; and determining which Pokémon can be caught at any given time, for example. In order to provide this magic, you must grant each app that you're using permission to access your location data. On an Apple device, this is done when you first launch the app after installing it—or sometimes a bit later, the first time the app wants to use location information. A system message will pop up over the app, explaining that the app would like to access location services and giving you the option to allow or deny the request. If you allow it, then the app may use your location data indefinitely while the app is running in the foreground. If it wants to use data all the time, even when it's in the background, you may see another system message later asking if that's okay.

It's very easy to lose track of all these requests and allowances. When you're trying to do something on your smartphone, it's annoying to have a dialog box interrupt you to ask a question, and it's tempting to tap "OK" just to make it go away. While this is something that you really shouldn't do (in the same sense that you shouldn't click "I agree" on a software license without reading the legalese first), we all do it from time to time. Fortunately, mobile devices give you a straightforward way to go back later and check to see what you've agreed to. On an iOS device:

1. Open the Settings app, then tap into Privacy > Location Services.
2. At the top of the Location Services view, there is a global on/off switch to disable Location Services entirely. If you disable services, then the operating system itself, as well as third-party apps, will be unable to determine your position accurately. This could impact your use of the phone in many ways. If you're not worried about

legitimate use of your location, leave the global switch turned on and continue. Otherwise, switch it off and you're done!

3. The next option on the page, Share My Location, is a sub-page that can be used to enable location sharing in Messages and the Find My Friends app (similar to Find My iPhone, but for people). Unless you have a reason to use this, leave it turned off.
4. The rest of the Location Services view consists of a list of all the apps that have ever requested permission to use your location data. The main page shows the currently set permission for each app. By tapping on an app's entry, you can change the permission. There are three possible permissions that can be set: "Never," "Always," and "While Using." For a given app, you may or may not have a choice of "Always" versus "While Using": some apps use one or the other, but not both. A small arrowhead symbol may appear next to an app's permission setting. As the legend at the bottom of the view explains, a purple arrowhead means that the app has used your location data recently, while a gray one indicates use within the past twenty-four hours. Figure 6.1 shows what this view looks like.

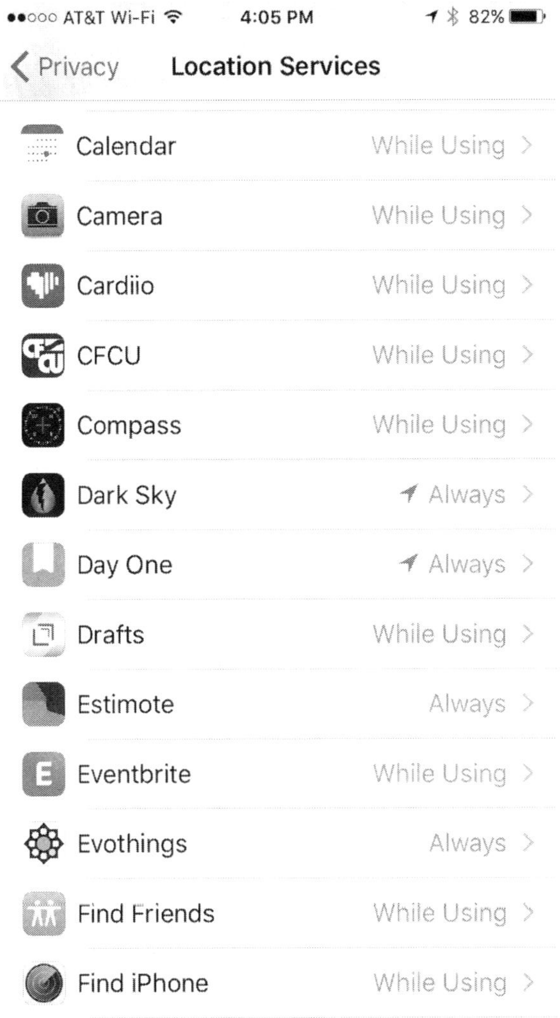

Figure 6.1. A partial list of apps using Location Services in iOS. Screenshot from Apple macOS.

a. The "Never" permission indicates that the app does *not* have the ability to read or use your location. Location-related features of the app will not work until you switch to one of the other permissions.
b. The "While Using" permission means that the app can use your location data only while you are actively using the app—i.e., it's in the foreground, visible on the screen. This is the pro-privacy option; it follows the principle of minimum necessary access.
c. The "Always" permission means, simply, that the app can use your location any time it wants to, even if it's only running in the background. Apps can continue to update themselves even if they're not being actively used. You should be conservative about granting "Always" permission to apps, but you have to balance privacy against convenience.

5. At the very bottom of the list of apps is a link for System Services, which lists in a sub-page the various uses that location data has for the operating system itself. There are approximately twenty such services, including everything from Cell Network Search to Routing & Traffic. Unlike third-party apps, system services can only be switched on or off.
6. At the bottom of the System Services page is an option to display an arrowhead symbol in the status bar (the very top of the screen, where the network information, time, and battery status are normally shown) whenever a system service uses your location data. If you want a visual indicator, switch this option on.

On an Android device:

1. Open the Settings app, then tap into Location (or Privacy and Safety > Location).
2. At the top of the Location view, there is a global on/off switch to disable location services entirely. If you disable services, then the operating system itself, as well as third-party apps, will be unable to determine your position accurately. This could impact your use of the phone in many ways. If you're not worried about legitimate use of your location, leave the global switch turned on and continue. Otherwise, switch it off and you're done!
3. The next pane in the view lets you choose a mode. The choices are "high accuracy," "battery saving," and "device only." The first and third options use the GPS receiver for location determination, while "battery saving" only uses wi-fi and Bluetooth to approximate a location. For purposes of privacy protection, there's not much benefit to using an approximate location over a precise location, so pick the setting that you prefer.
4. Below the Mode setting, Android lists "Recent location requests" with an entry for each app or service that has recently accessed your location data. To change the permission, tap on the app name, then Permissions, then switch Location (or Your Location) on or off. (On some Android devices, this process is reversed: from Location, you must first tap App Permissions, then Location, to get a list of apps accessing your location data.)

Location History

Buried deep within both the Android and iOS settings pages is an obscure feature with extremely important privacy implications: location history. By default, both systems keep a record of places you visit. This information is used in various ways, but mostly in the pursuit of creating intelligent assistants to provide you with useful contextual information. For example, iOS uses this data to predict where you might be going at a particular time of day. If you stop at a coffee shop every morning on your way to work, your iPhone will notice the pattern and provide you with an estimated travel time and current traffic conditions as soon as you get into your car. Understandably, though, having your phone or tablet record this amount of detail about your movements makes some people nervous. Here's how to turn it off in iOS:

1. Open the Settings app, then tap into Privacy > Location Services > System Services > Frequent Locations.
2. Use the main switch at the top of the view to disable Frequent Locations.
3. If necessary, use the Clear History... button at the bottom of the view to remove any locations the device has already recorded.

And on an Android device:

1. Open the Settings app, then tap into Location (or Privacy and Safety > Location).
2. Below Recent Location Requests, find the Location Services section and tap into Google Location Reporting.
3. Tap Location History. Use the switch at the top of the view to disable the service.
4. If necessary, tap the Delete Location History button at the bottom of the view to remove any locations the device has already recorded.

Apps Accessing Device Hardware

Although location data gets a lot of attention in modern privacy debates, it is by no means the only type of personal information that your apps may be using. Software in modern smartphones and tablets has access both to device hardware (which includes cameras, microphones, motion sensors, and GPS receivers) and personal databases such as your photos, contacts, calendars, notes, and health data. The same basic rules apply for giving apps permission to use this data that should guide you when granting access to location data: pay attention when an app asks you for a new permission, grant only the minimum access needed to use the app, and occasionally go back and check to see what permissions are in effect.

Android and iOS handle app permissions in similar ways, although Android provides a second path to the data. Although you can review permissions by category in both operating systems—i.e., view a list of apps that have permission to use the camera, or the apps that can read your contacts database, etc.—only Android lets you choose an app and see all the permissions associated with it (by going to Apps > [app name] > Permissions in the Settings app). For the common method, the following steps will help you review permissions. In iOS:

1. Open the Settings app and navigate to Privacy. Below Location Services, which was described in the previous section, you should see a list of other data types: Contacts, Calendars, Reminders, etc. (see figure 6.2).
2. Tap a data type. You should be taken to a subview for that data (e.g., Calendars).
3. In the Calendars view (or whatever data type you chose), you should see a list of apps that have, or had, permission to use the data. (The list may be empty if there are no apps using that data type.)

4. Tap the switch for an app on or off to adjust its access. Even if an app does not currently have permission to use the data, it will remain in the list until it is uninstalled.

With an Android:

1. Open the settings app and navigate to Apps.
2. Tap the configuration icon in the upper right corner of the screen and select App Permissions. You should see a list of data types and the number of apps that have permission to use each one.
3. Tap a data type. You should be taken to a subview for that data (e.g., Calendar).
4. In the Calendar view (or whatever data type you chose), you should see a list of apps that have, or had, permission to use the data. (The list may be empty if there are no apps using that data type.)
5. Tap the switch for an app on or off to adjust its access. Even if an app does not currently have permission to use the data, it will remain in the list until it is uninstalled.

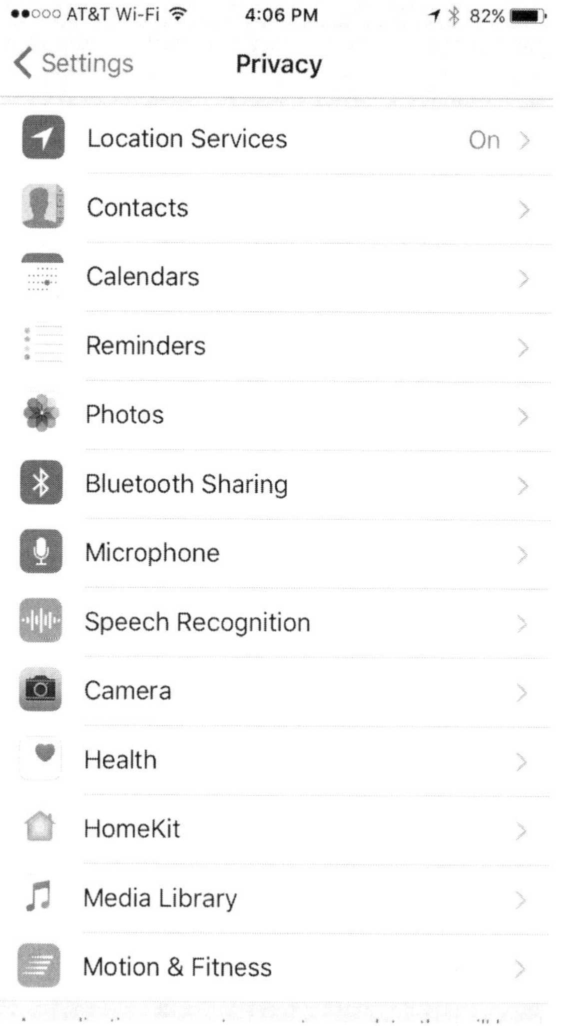

Figure 6.2. The iOS Settings app's Privacy view, listing data types. Screenshot from Apple iOS.

Eavesdropping on Bluetooth

So now you've ensured that you only connect to encrypted wi-fi networks, you've familiarized yourself with the threat of man-in-the-middle attacks (whether on wi-fi or cellular), you've slimmed down your app permissions for private data, and you've deleted your location history. You're good to go, right? Well, not quite. There's one more type of connection on mobile devices that people tend to forget about: Bluetooth.

Like cellular and wi-fi communication, Bluetooth is a wireless radio-communication protocol; it is specifically intended to operate at low power for very localized communication and networking between devices. First developed in the late 1990s, Bluetooth has become increasingly popular as a way of pairing mobile devices with one another and with a bevy of peripherals—everything from cars to headphones. More recent versions of the protocol also support the use of "beacons," Bluetooth signal generators that can provide proximity-based information and advertising when used in conjunction with an app that is aware of them. Although it's notoriously finicky and a nuisance to try to use with multiple devices or peripherals at the same time, Bluetooth has become ubiquitous. Most computers, smartphones, and tablets now come with Bluetooth built in by default. And many people walk around with their mobile devices' Bluetooth transmitters activated all the time.

This is a privacy problem because Bluetooth, like any other wireless communication system, is vulnerable to hacking and disruption. The problem is compounded because there is a relatively complex matrix of different versions of the protocol and connection types within a given version, each with its own security holes and weaknesses. Delving into each of these is beyond the scope of this book—and unhelpful because in most consumer systems you won't find an easy way of telling which version of the protocol is in use. But the general concern is this: just as you can easily procure a packet sniffer to eavesdrop on data transmissions in a network (see chapter 3), it's trivial to find apps that will monitor the Bluetooth connections of everyone within range. Since Bluetooth transmitters send out a unique identifier when trying to discover other Bluetooth devices in their vicinity, monitoring these broadcasts can identify unique users and help to track their movements. In a more active attack, someone with a malicious Bluetooth system could potentially force your device to pair with his, giving him access to your phone or tablet and the personal data stored there.

For the time being, there is only one way to ensure that your Bluetooth connection isn't hijacked for illicit purposes: turn it off when you're not using it. It only takes a second to enable or disable it, and most people don't have a good reason to leave it transmitting and receiving all the time. When you're done listening to music through your Bluetooth earbuds or you're leaving your car after using hands-free Bluetooth calling, just pause and turn off your Bluetooth receiver on your phone. Your peace of mind is worth the minor inconvenience.

Keeping Up to Date with Security Fixes

It's important to understand how to secure the privacy features of your mobile devices and how to manually adjust related settings as needed. In the end, though, the primary line of defense against attacks on your mobile devices is the operating system itself. While it's the flashy new features that usually grab people's attention when a new system update rolls out, there's typically a whole slew of new security- and privacy-related features or fixes that accompany even minor updates.

Every new version of a piece of software contains new bugs, especially software as large and complex as an operating system. However, it's reasonable to assume that, all other things being equal, the value of the security *fixes* in a new operating system update probably outweighs the threat of potential new vulnerabilities. Thus it can be considered a best practice to update your operating systems with new versions promptly for the sake of your continued security. Even if the presence of a particular vulnerability on an older operating system version was kept secret while the vendor worked to fix it, its existence will most likely be announced in the new operating system's release notes (the document that relates all the significant changes made in the newly released version). Malicious hackers pay attention to things like release notes because learning about previously unknown vulnerabilities will help them to target systems that haven't yet updated to the operating system version that fixes the issues. On the other hand, updating your operating system as soon as possible is often undesirable for other reasons, as noted earlier. One might be feature compatibility; if you have to work with other devices that may not be as quick to install an update, updating unilaterally may cause relationships with those other devices to break. For example, a document or database format may change between versions, rendering documents created on the newer device unusable on older devices. Another issue is unanticipated problems with the new operating system version or the installation process itself. Many pro users advocate waiting at least a day before installing an update, or preferably a week or two, just to make sure that an undetected bug doesn't wipe out all your data when you update.

As usual, there's a tension between security and usability or convenience. Some compromises are necessary. Fortunately, not all operating updates are equally significant, so you can adopt different strategies for dealing with each type. Many large software projects, including the major mobile device operating systems, use a three-point numbering system for software versions. For example, as of now, the newest version of iOS that has been released is 10.1.1. There is no absolute definition of what each of the three numbers mean, but in general, they signify major, minor, and revision releases. In this case, 10.1.1 shows that iOS 10 is the major version (and the blanket term that Apple uses for this year's operating system release); there's been one minor update since the initial iOS 10 release; and there is now one additional revision to iOS 10.1. (In macOS, the versioning is a little different; the major release number, OS X as it used to be called, remained fixed for many years so that Apple could use it as an established brand. Yearly updates to the operating system were reflected in the "minor" number.) Changing the first number in a sequence often indicates a complete rewrite to the software. A minor update usually signifies that new features have been added. Revision number updates generally only include bug fixes—and security fixes. This fact suggests an approach to handling operating system updates. Fortunately, revision number updates (e.g., 10.1.1, 10.1.2, 10.1.3) are the updates that have both the smallest impact on overall use of the software and backward compatibility *and* the greatest potential impact on security and privacy protection. Therefore, you can usually apply a revision update as quickly as possible (or after a wait of a day or two if you want to be cautious) without worrying about features changing or compatibility with other devices breaking. Major and minor updates are less urgent from a security standpoint. Although they will usually include new or improved security features, any important security *fixes* will be back-ported to a revision update for earlier versions of the software—or for a while, at least (backward compatibility isn't guaranteed forever). For example: the last version of iOS 9 to be released is currently 9.3.5. If Apple were to discover a new vulnerability common to iOS 9 and iOS 10, they would work to fix it as soon as possible and release iOS 10.1.2 with that security update, but they would also release iOS 9.3.6 to fix it for users who can't or won't upgrade to iOS 10.

The iOS environment makes a better example for these points because of its relative simplicity. All iOS devices are made by Apple in a relatively small number of configurations, and it's easy to keep track of the different hardware models and software versions. Not so in the Android world. Android users face an additional challenge in keeping their devices updated with security patches because of the fragmentation of the Android market. There are over a thousand manufacturers of Android devices, and not all of the devices produced are even capable of being updated with new operating system versions for more than a year or two. In 2015, more than 5 percent of devices were running a version of Android more than five years old (Swanner, 2015)! Unlike Apple, which has boasted high adoption rates of new operating system versions when they become available (Reisinger, 2016), the Android world has seen many users lag far behind the leading edge of updates (and security fixes). To the greatest extent possible, then, you should be cautious when choosing an Android device. Be sure that it can be updated with new operating system releases for as long as possible.

Information about new updates can be found in the Settings app in iOS under General > Software Update. In Android, look under About Phone/About Tablet > Software Update (or an equivalent—the actual button name may vary).

Jailbreaking and Its Risks

Jailbreaking, or rooting, is the process of "breaking" certain components of a device's operating system in order to allow greater flexibility in its behavior or abilities. For example, one of the primary purposes of jailbreaking iOS devices is to enable the ability to download and install apps from sources other than the official iTunes Store (a procedure known as "sideloading"). Jailbreaking is another cat-and-mouse game. Although operating system makers typically don't condemn jailbreaking very loudly, they certainly don't encourage it, and new versions of an operating system usually include patches for the exploits that allowed the previous version to be jailbroken.

In general terms, it's not advisable to attempt to jailbreak your phone or tablet unless you know what you're doing. You could end up damaging your phone or even turning it into a useless "brick." Even if you succeed, you may encounter problems with the device's normal operations. Apple publishes a support document that warns of instability, reduced battery life, and disruption of Apple-related services (such as iMessages and iCloud) on jailbroken iPhones (https://support.apple.com/en-us/HT201954).

When it comes to privacy and security, the main concern with jailbreaking is that it opens up the device to malware or other attacks and compromises. By its very nature, jailbreaking involves defeating some of the built-in security features of the operating system—otherwise the device couldn't be jailbroken at all. It's quite possible for a jailbreaking "kit" itself to include malware that gets installed onto the device during the jailbreaking process. Even if it doesn't, subsequent installs of apps—particularly apps sideloaded from an unofficial source—can also introduce malware packages. Depending on how the jailbreak kit has altered the operating system, such malware might be able to operate beyond an app's normal confines and sandbox. All in all, jailbreaking is a bad idea for most people.

Good Security Practices

Here are some good security practices to follow when using mobile devices, either devices in library lending programs or devices used by library staff for work:

- Use a strong passphrase to lock mobile devices. If you are lending devices for public use, you probably won't want to use a passcode. For any work-related devices, especially those that may have access to sensitive data, use a complex passcode (not a four-digit number!). For added security, consider disabling the fingerprint scanner if you have one.
- Pay attention to news items about mobile device security. There may not be too much you can do about the disclosure of a backdoor in your device, but the information may influence your future purchasing decisions.
- Keep your Bluetooth receiver turned off when you're not using it. On a similar note, disable automatic joining of wi-fi networks (this can be done from within the Settings app in iOS or Android). Be careful about joining unfamiliar networks, especially when they are unsecured.
- Be parsimonious when granting permission to apps to use your location or other private information.
- Perform a security audit on your devices once a month or so. Use the information provided in this chapter to review the permissions granted to apps, revoke them where necessary, and ensure that you're maintaining minimal access to personal data.
- Keep up to date with new operating system versions, especially when they contain crucial security updates.
- Don't jailbreak your devices, which can compromise the built-in security protections that the operating system offers you.
- Before you dispose of a device, make sure that you've cleared any private data stored on it, signed out of accounts, cleared your passcode, and, ideally, reset the device to its factory settings.

Key Points

Mobile devices are ubiquitous, but it's possible to use them in relatively secure ways. Here are the main takeaways for this chapter:

- Protecting your mobile devices against physical access is crucial. Always use a strong passphrase to unlock your devices if they contain any information that you wouldn't want to share with the public. A fingerprint scanner can be a convenient alternate method of entry, but it's also a security risk.
- Your device's operating system could potentially include a backdoor that circumvents normal security features. Backdoors are difficult to detect by non-expert users. Governments and law enforcement agencies have begun to lean heavily on tech companies to provide them with backdoors for so-called official use.
- A phone or tablet's communication protocols—including cellular, wi-fi, and Bluetooth—typically expose more identifying information than you realize. This information can be used for tracking the movements of specific users, setting up man-in-the-middle attacks, or introducing malware onto the device.

- Apps often want to use a wide variety of private data to enhance their functionality, but you should be sparing in granting this access. Follow the principle of minimum viable access to place limits on what your apps know about you. Perform an occasional security audit to make sure you know how your data is being used.
- Operating system updates are important for maintaining a secure environment on your mobile devices. Not all operating system updates are equally important for security purposes, though. Counterintuitively, the releases with the most minor change in version number often contain the most time-sensitive and crucial security patches.
- Jailbreaking a mobile device compromises its built-in security features and should be avoided.

This chapter considered the security features of mobile devices at the hardware and operating system levels. The next chapter will dive deeper into the software layer and look at a more familiar aspect of smartphones and tablets: apps themselves.

References

Apple. 2017. "iOS Security." Apple.com. www.apple.com/business/docs/iOS_Security_Guide.pdf.

Blaze, Matt. 2013. "How Law Enforcement Tracks Cellular Phones." *Exhaustive Search*. December 13. www.crypto.com/blog/celltapping.

Brandom, Russell. 2016. "Your Phone's Biggest Vulnerability Is Your Fingerprint." *Verge*. May 2. www.theverge.com/2016/5/2/11540962/iphone-samsung-fingerprint-duplicate-hack-security.

Cook, Tim. 2016. "A Message to Our Customers." Apple. February 16. www.apple.com/customer-letter.

Khandelwal, Swati. 2014. "Spying Agencies Tracking Your Location by Capturing MAC Addresses of Your Devices." *Hacker News*. January 31. http://thehackernews.com/2014/01/spying-agencies-tracking-your-location_31.html.

Reisinger, Don. 2016. "Apple's iOS 10 Adoption Rate Nears 20% in Just Two Days." *Fortune*. September 15. http://fortune.com/2016/09/15/ios-10-adoption-rate.

Swanner, Nate. 2015. "This Is What Android Fragmentation Looks Like in 2015." *Next Web*. August 5. http://thenextweb.com/insider/2015/08/05/this-is-what-android-fragmentation-looks-like-in-2015.

Sweeney, Latanya. 2014. "My Phone at Your Service." *Tech@FTC*. February 12. www.ftc.gov/news-events/blogs/techftc/2014/02/my-phone-your-service.

CHAPTER 7

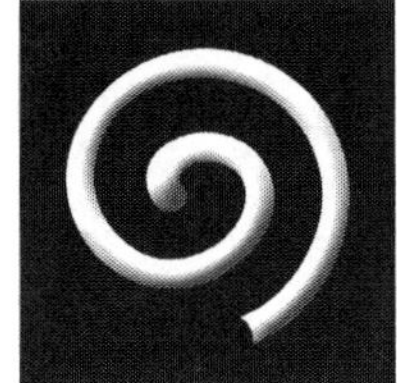

Apps

IN THIS CHAPTER

- ▷ Installing and distributing apps on mobile devices
- ▷ Understanding privacy in the context of social media apps
- ▷ Creating your own library apps
- ▷ Reviewing messaging apps
- ▷ Using private web browsers
- ▷ Applying content blockers to your web browsing
- ▷ Understanding the role of password managers
- ▷ Adding a VPN to your network connections for privacy and security

Threat Assessment

SMARTPHONES AND TABLETS WOULD NOT BE NEARLY as compelling as they are without the proliferation of apps that enable users to extend the functionality of their devices in ways that were unimaginable just a few years ago. Apple's tagline "There's an app for that" was more than just a snappy marketing slogan; it accurately summarized the arrival of an "app lifestyle" for many people.

While the benefits of having so many app-enabled abilities at one's fingertips are myriad and obvious, there is the danger of complacency that comes with familiarity. The convenience of apps, and the ease with which they can be installed and used, encourages users to overlook potential threats to their privacy from apps that have the ability to communicate with the outside world *and* access their personal data. Even a well-intentioned app can leak personal or identifying information in ways that neither the user nor the app developer anticipated.

This chapter considers the privacy concerns of several common categories of apps. If your library is lending mobile devices to users, you may want to consider some of the apps discussed here for inclusion on the device's standard setup so that your users can take advantage of them for private work or communication. Or if you are offering workshops on online privacy and security, you can use the information in this chapter to inform your audience about the pros and cons of using the apps in each category.

App Stores and App Distribution

As discussed in chapter 6, the preferred mechanism for downloading and installing apps on a mobile device is to use the appropriate official app store for your device type—e.g., the iTunes Store for iPhones and iPads, and the Google Play store for Android devices. These stores are supposed to provide a layer of protection against malware; apps that appear in the stores are evaluated and tested for the presence of malicious code, malware, or vulnerabilities—at least, in theory. In practice, results vary. Apple's app store has remained malware-free for the most part, with one glaring exception. In 2015, Apple discovered that hundreds of apps in the iTunes Store, mostly from Chinese developers, were infected with malware. It was inadvertent on the developers' part: the source of the infection proved to be unofficial copies of Xcode, Apple's primary app development tool, that had been modified to insert malware into any app created using the tool (Finkle, 2015). Android has fared less well, with repeated malware breaches of the Google Play store over the past few years. One security researcher puts the number of Google Play malware instances at more than two dozen over a four-year period, with the most recent dozen alone affecting more than five million devices (Yu, 2016). To be fair, the diversity of Android hardware and operating system variants makes it more difficult to anticipate malware exploits on that platform.

Because of the protection afforded by the official app stores, it's strongly recommended that you only install apps found and downloaded there. Sideloading apps onto jailbroken devices or downloading them from third-party sources is usually asking for trouble. In fact, on iOS, you usually *can't* install apps from anywhere but the iTunes Store unless you deliberately break the protections built into the operating system. Newer versions of Android have the same restriction by default, but you can disable it within the system settings. Don't.

Now there's one reasonable exception to the preceding advice that may appeal to you as a library professional. Both Android and iOS permit the distribution of apps through an enterprise deployment system. A business or organization—such as a library—can create their own website or app server where a very specific target group of users can go to download apps (usually apps created by or for the particular organization distributing them). If your library, college, or university affiliate is developing custom apps, this is one way to create a curated list of apps for patrons to find and install without having to search for them in the very large, often confusing app stores.

In keeping with its careful restrictions on the entire iOS platform, Apple makes it just a little bit tricky to use its enterprise program to distribute apps. These are the broad steps necessary to do so. They assume that you are in the process of developing your own apps in-house.

1. Enroll in the Apple Developer Enterprise Program (https://developer.apple.com/programs/enterprise). Enrollment in this program currently costs $299 per year, compared to $99 per year for the normal developer program.

2. Once you are enrolled in the program, you will be able to obtain two crucial items: a digital certificate that you install in Xcode enabling you to sign the apps you create with your organization information, and a provisioning profile that users must install on their devices before they can use your apps.
3. With your certificate installed, follow the usual app development process. You will end by generating a special .ipa file that is suitable for enterprise distribution (but not for iTunes Store submission).
4. Both your app (.ipa) file and your provisioning profile can then be placed on a website for downloading or distributed via email to users.
5. Alternatively, homebuilt apps may be distributed to devices that you have control over (e.g., iPads in an iPad lending program) using Apple's Configurator 2 software tool (available in the Mac App Store).

Details of iOS app development and deployment, including use of Configurator, are outside the scope of this book. For more information, consult *Using iPhones, iPads, and iPods: A Practical Guide for Librarians* (Connolly and Cosgrave, 2015).

On the Android front, the procedure is simpler. All that needs to be done is to enable downloads from sources other than the official app stores, which can be done from within Settings by going to the Security pane, looking for the "unknown sources" setting, then enabling it. Then you can create your apps (they still need to have a code signature, but you can create a "self-signed" certificate and proceed without Google's blessing), host them on a site, and have users download them at will. There is a better way, though. Google now offers what it calls Private Channels within the Google Play store. Businesses and entities can sign up for a private distribution channel within the official Google Play store if they are members of Google's G Suite program (formerly Google Apps) and host their apps there, controlling who has access to download them. Doing so affords businesses the normal malware protection of the official Google Play store while letting them customize the suite of apps that their specific user-group can download.

Hosting your own homegrown apps may make sense if your library has the resources and desire to create or curate multiple apps—perhaps because it's affiliated with a large university that produces a variety of apps in different schools or programs, or because it's a member of a consortium of libraries where sharing app resources can be useful. For many smaller libraries, though, it may require too much effort to maintain. An easier way to suggest apps to your users is to simply link to their entries in the official app stores. Once you have the links you need, you can create a basic webpage with your unique descriptions and advice for using the apps. App store links can be created in a number of ways:

- In iTunes on a laptop or desktop, navigate to the specific page for the app within the App Store (the Apps section of iTunes). Find the Get button below the app icon on the page, then click the small down-arrow button next to Get. Select Copy Link from the list of options, then paste it into your list.
- From an iPhone or iPad, open the App Store app. Find the app you want a link for, then tap the share icon in the upper right corner of the view. Choose Copy Link from the list of actions.
- For a link to an iOS app without using iTunes or the App Store, use Apple's Link Maker page (https://linkmaker.itunes.apple.com). Beneath the search box, click the Media Type link to reveal a drop-down menu. Choose iOS Apps as the media type. Then search for the name of the app. Choose the correct app from the list of

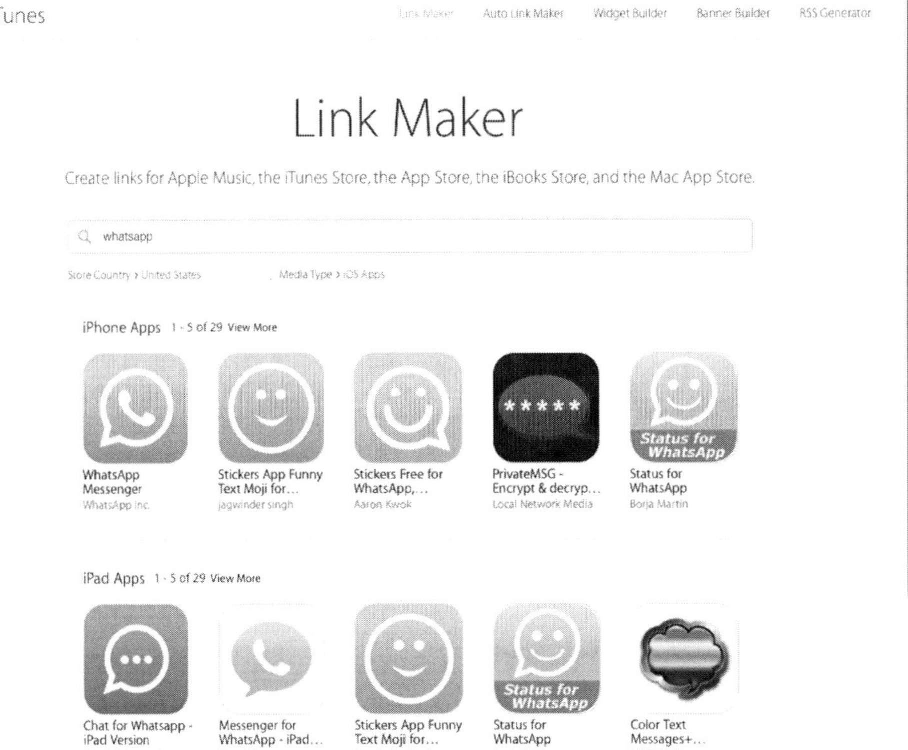

Figure 7.1. Creating an app link to the iTunes Store using Link Maker. Screenshot from Apple website.

search results and click its icon to open its detail page. Scroll down to the bottom of the page and copy the Direct Link URL (e.g., https://itunes.apple.com/us/app/signal-private-messenger/id874139669 for the Signal Private Messenger app). See figure 7.1 for an example.

- For Android apps, the Google Play store can be accessed directly from the web at https://play.google.com/store. Search for the name of the app and click the appropriate icon from the results list. The URL of the app detail page that opens can be copied from the browser's address bar and used as a permanent link to the app (e.g., https://play.google.com/store/apps/details?id=org.thoughtcrime.securesms for the Signal Private Messenger app).

Social Media

People use social media obsessively. For many, checking Facebook or Twitter has become second nature, a fact of life that's inserted into free moments whenever they occur throughout the day. But when use of an app becomes automatic, the user may stop thinking about the potential consequences of what he or she is doing. If you're going to include social media apps on a curated list, or pre-fill iPads or tablets in a lending program with them, then you have to understand when privacy in social media becomes an issue. Of course, you can't stop users from violating their own privacy in the content they post—but you can raise awareness. Consider adding some text to your website about privacy concerns. If you're running a tablet lending program, you may even wish to create a custom background image that appears on the home screen and contains similar information (or a link to your webpage).

Facebook

Facebook is the heavyweight of the social media world. Its immense popularity has propelled it from a novelty used exclusively by students at colleges and universities to a gigantic network that spans the world and is populated by, well, everybody (or so it might seem to Facebook users). Facebook has also extended its membership beyond individual users to include businesses and organizations such as libraries. Unfortunately, that incredible growth in size has been accompanied by a similar growth in complexity: new ways of finding friends, new algorithms for determining what appears in your news feed, the intrusion of advertising, third-party apps within Facebook, location data, likes, interests, settings, and on and on.

Furthermore, Facebook has at best a mixed track record when it comes to protecting user privacy. They face the same conflict of interest that impacts any company that derives a majority of its revenue from advertising (e.g., Google): their continued profitability depends on users opening their personal data to the world so that they can (1) draw more connected users into the social graph and service, but more importantly (2) keep advertisers happy by enabling more targeted, custom ads. Mark Zuckerberg, the company's founder, infamously stated in 2010 that Facebook's system was adjusted to match "current social norms" when it came to privacy—or the lack thereof (Paul, 2010). This approach has led to a number of clashes with privacy advocates over the years, such as Facebook Beacon (2007–2009), which used a tracker script on third-party websites to feed Facebook users' activities and purchases to Facebook advertisers and individuals' news feeds—whether users liked it or not. Such failed experiments have usually been followed by revisions to the service's privacy policy or privacy controls, adding uncertainty to an already complex system. If you haven't looked at your profile's privacy settings in a while, they may not be doing what you thought they were doing. Facebook also makes it difficult for you to make your profile entirely private, and its use of location data is potentially problematic as well. The Electronic Privacy Information Center provides a detailed history of Facebook's relationship with user privacy (https://epic.org/privacy/facebook).

Since most people and businesses aren't going to stop using Facebook anytime soon, they should at least be aware of the sort of data that they might be leaking to the rest of the network (and to the rest of the world, effectively). Facebook maintains a Data Policy page (www.facebook.com/fulldatause_policy) that describes the information about you that they collect and what they do with it. To their credit, they have also placed a Privacy Shortcuts menu in the main Facebook menu bar. It contains useful controls to adjust settings for who can view your posts and who can contact you, with links to other parts of the privacy system. The main privacy controls can be found at https://facebook.com/settings?tab=privacy. Since the controls are liable to change from time to time, it's a good idea to get into the habit of conducting a quick Facebook privacy audit every now and then. Libraries as organizations using Facebook should be equally conscious of the implications involved. Posting photographs of users in the library can be a potential privacy violation (especially with the increasing sophistication of facial recognition software). Even letting people follow, like, comment, or check in on your library's page leaves a trail of personal data that could potentially be used in unanticipated ways.

Flickr

The popularity of Flickr as a photo-sharing platform has waned in recent years thanks to a lack of updates and strong competition from other services like Google Photos. It still offers a free terabyte of photo storage, however, which is a pretty great deal. Some libraries have begun posting parts of their photo collections to Flickr (e.g., www.flickr.com/photos/boston_public_library/collections).

Flickr itself has not been plagued by the controversial sort of privacy issues that Facebook has repeatedly had to deal with, but its parent company, Yahoo, made headlines in late 2016 by announcing that it had suffered a massive data breach in 2014 (Perlroth, 2016)—a breach that went undetected for almost two years. Around the same time, reports surfaced that the company had cooperated with a government request for information by secretly scanning hundreds of millions of its users' email messages (Menn, 2016).

Fortunately, privacy settings within Flickr itself are fairly transparent and understandable. The Yahoo/Flickr privacy policy page (https://policies.yahoo.com/us/en/yahoo/privacy/products/flickr) does a good job of explaining the types of information that the service collects about users and photos, the effect of changing certain privacy settings, and a lengthy note about the use of location data. Most privacy-related settings can be found at www.flickr.com/account/privacy.

There is one significant privacy flaw in Flickr that is shared by many similar photo-storage services: the app-based uploader (or Uploadr, as Flickr prefers to call it). This is a handy tool for ensuring that you have a backup of all the photos you take with your phone; just enable auto-uploading, and every picture will be added to your account on Flickr. (With any such service, you should be sure to check to see what viewing permissions the uploaded photos are given. Flickr is good enough to make them private by default, but other sites may not be so considerate.) The problem with auto-uploading is that it's easy to forget about or overlook. You may not remember that a new picture is being uploaded to the cloud each time you tap the shutter button! While this is less of an issue for library collections, which tend to be a little less personal, it should still be kept in mind.

Instagram

Instagram, the photo-sharing app that popularized square photos and instant filters, is now owned by Facebook. It maintains its own privacy policy, which can be viewed at https://help.instagram.com/155833707900388. There are a couple of sections that might give privacy advocates pause. For one, Instagram's policies explicitly state that your personal information may be shared with advertisers for the purpose of directing targeted ads at you. Another concern is that Instagram can share anonymized and aggregated information about you with a very nonspecific set of "other parties." The problem with anonymized user data is that it can often be analyzed or cross-referenced with other data in such a way that it turns out to not be very anonymous at all. This is one potential concern to consider for library Instagram accounts (e.g., www.instagram.com/nypl) where users can like or comment on photos.

Despite being owned by Facebook, Instagram's reputation for privacy and security is reasonably good. The service stirred up controversy a few years ago when its terms of service changed to allow the possibility of users' photos being shared with advertisers, but there was nothing underhanded about the way it was done or announced. Like any online service, though, Instagram is vulnerable to exploits enabled by hidden bugs. Observing how a company reacts to the discovery and disclosure of such vulnerabilities is an indicator of how serious its commitment to user privacy and data security is. In 2015, a professional security researcher became embroiled in a confrontation with Facebook over his handling of major weaknesses he discovered in Instagram's back-end systems (Fox-Brewster, 2015).

LinkedIn

LinkedIn, a professional social networking site now owned by Microsoft, keeps its privacy policy at www.linkedin.com/legal/privacy-policy. Helpfully, it summarizes each clause of legalese with a side-by-side translation in more understandable English.

Unfortunately, LinkedIn's history with user privacy is flawed at best. The service has faced high-profile lawsuits for spamming users' contacts email via a contact-scraping system and for selling private work-history data to potential employers. However, there is a growing expectation among some employers that you *must* have a LinkedIn profile to be taken seriously as a potential hire, so it might be difficult to quit the service.

Snapchat

Snapchat began as a unique twist on a photo-sharing app with the conceit that photos sent through the service would be ephemeral, viewable for a short time before they were automatically deleted. The app also attempted to prevent viewers from saving the images that appeared on their screens. When chat was added to the system, messages would also disappear after being read. Such a feature set would be very intriguing to users concerned about privacy! Over time, however, the transient nature of Snapchat content (which now includes audio and video as well as still photos and messages) has been reduced. Media and messages now linger longer—indefinitely, in some cases. But that's apparently what users want. With the lingering impression that content *will* disappear, though, users may become confused about how private their Snapchat content truly is.

Of greater concern is the fact that content that is deleted from Snapchat may actually be retained on the local storage of a phone or tablet used to view it. It turns out that deleted Snapchat images are not removed from your device, merely transferred to an obscure, hidden directory (a fact acknowledged in Snapchat's privacy policy, www.snap.com/en-US/privacy/privacy-policy). When you know where to look, the files are easy to locate and transfer from the device using any of the numerous smartphone or tablet file-manager apps that are available for both Android and iOS. In later versions of the Snapchat app, the retained files are encrypted. Snapchat's use of encryption is flawed, however, and so content may still be accessible.

Due to Snapchat's popularity, especially with younger users, some libraries have started to use the service as a way of engaging their patrons. One middle school library in San Antonio, for example, encourages teenagers to post photos of the books they're reading (Alfonso, 2016). Unfortunately, this circumvents one of the long-standing tenets of library privacy: what a patron is reading or studying is a private matter that should be kept confidential.

Tumblr

Tumblr is used as the back end for hundreds of millions of blogs, including library blogs. Like Flickr, it is owned by Yahoo. Although the system allows for private blogs and certain types of private communication, everything is public by default. Tumblr is refreshingly frank about this in its privacy policy (www.tumblr.com/policy/en/privacy): "You should assume that anything you publish is publicly accessible unless you have explicitly selected otherwise." (Like LinkedIn, Tumblr provides plain-English translations of the more technical language in the main clauses of its policy.) It also maintains a webpage (www.tumblr.com/security) with a form for easily reporting any security flaws users may discover on the site.

Tumblr recently attained a rather dubious honor: it was recognized as the victim of the fourth-largest data breach on record when it was discovered that a three-year-old attack had led to the theft of more than sixty-five million user records that were now for sale on the so-called dark web (Vaas, 2016). Libraries using Tumblr—or any other service, really—should practice good password behavior to minimize the risk of similar compromises.

Twitter

Twitter's privacy policy is maintained at https://twitter.com/privacy. While Twitter became the victim of yet another high-profile, massive data dump of private user credentials, it's believed that the information was obtained not through a breach of Twitter's own security but rather was the result of individual users' computers being hacked or infected with malware (McMillan, 2016).

Twitter's greater user privacy concerns center around its reputation as a magnet for abusive messages, harassment (especially of women), and cyberstalking. Although the company has made noises about curbing such behavior, the steps it has taken haven't been enough to satisfy many users and commentators. Also troubling—if understandable from a legal perspective—is the revelation that Twitter provided personal information about a complainant in a Digital Millennium Copyright Act takedown request to the recipient in at least one case, leading to harassment of the complainant (Bort, 2016).

Homegrown Library Apps

The preceding section should have alerted you to the difficulties and risks of trying to create a truly secure app experience. Even the largest tech companies in the business are vulnerable to security breaches (whether through their own system's vulnerabilities or through weaknesses in a partner company that has access to its data) and conflicts of interest between user privacy and advertising revenue. Hopefully, for a library, the latter isn't too much of an issue; by and large, libraries have historically maintained a strong interest in preserving the privacy of their patrons. (Otherwise, why would you be reading this book?) But the technical hurdles in closing all the security holes in a system are an even bigger problem for libraries, many of which do not have the expertise or resources to ensure that app source code is as secure as possible.

If your library wishes to develop its own apps for users, you must give this problem serious thought. It is very easy to write bad, insecure code. (PHP, one of the most popular languages for coding websites and web services, is infamous for enabling coders who know just enough to be dangerous to build websites full of security holes—but really, the same thing can be done with various degrees of ease in all web scripting languages.) The best way of protecting user privacy with a homebuilt library app is to steer clear of private data altogether. Besides the dangers on the technical side of the process, retaining private information about your users also puts you in potential conflict with various national and local privacy laws, which in the United States will vary from state to state. Sorting out the legal implications of your data collection could be complex.

Unless it's absolutely necessary, don't create a way for users to log in to your app (and if you must, then don't try to store their login information within the app). If your app lets your users search the library catalog or databases, then make sure that their search queries aren't retained within the app either. If, however, you need to allow your users to create a profile or store personal information in your app, at the very least (1) give them a way to delete their profile or data permanently and completely, and (2) make sure you give them a way to view your (prominently displayed, clearly worded, and user-friendly) privacy policies.

If your library doesn't have the technical resources to develop a mobile app in-house and do it well, a better alternative might be to hire a third-party app development service to do the work for you. Be sure that you go with a reputable company, though. One of the most popular choices for mobile app development in the library world is Boopsie (www.boopsie.com), which is used by thousands of libraries around the world for this purpose. Boopsie-developed library apps can provide catalog searching, user account management, integration with other services like OverDrive, news and events content, and other widely used functionalities. The service also handles the intricacies of building an app and then deploying it to multiple incompatible app stores (the iTunes Store, the Google Play Store, etc.). If you employ Boopsie or another service, be sure you understand up front what their policies are regarding privacy, data retention, and security. If the answers are satisfactory, then letting someone else develop an app for you is a good way of skirting the technical pitfalls of app development.

Messaging Apps

Another increasingly popular segment of the mobile app market is messaging apps. What began as something of a novelty with limited, text-only SMS (Short Message Service) messages has grown into the preferred method of mobile communication for many users, with elaborate suites of functionality for sharing audio, video, formatted text, emoji, and more. Two services alone, Facebook Messenger and WhatsApp, handle more than sixty billion messages *per day* (Goode, 2016). Given such volume, mobile messaging offers a tempting target to anyone interested in stealing a user's personal data. Messaging apps are less of a concern for libraries as institutions, but library staff should be aware of the risks involved in using them, especially if the messages sent involve library business or patron information. Here is a rundown of some of the most popular messaging apps and the state of their privacy protections.

Facebook Messenger

Facebook's entry in the messaging market offers text messages, video and voice calling, photo and video sharing, group chats, location sharing, and money transfers. It has also recently begun allowing ads into the service. Perhaps because of Facebook's popularity, its Messenger app has been the subject of a lot of attention and misinformation, with false rumors circulating about Facebook unreasonably using Messenger to read your personal data, use your camera and microphone without permission, and even take control of your phone or tablet. While the app does ask for your permission to access various types of personal information on your device, this is hardly unusual. As we discussed earlier, mobile phone and tablet operating systems have well-established (and well-used) procedures for enabling an app to request such permission for any number of legitimate uses. As one obvious example, you can't realistically expect Messenger to help you with a video call without accessing the camera on your phone!

Facebook recently added end-to-end encryption as an option for text messages and photos, billed "Secret Conversations." With end-to-end encryption, you can be reasonably confident that your conversations will remain private to all but the most sophisticated intruders. Unfortunately, this option is not turned on by default in the app, and encryption must be explicitly chosen for every conversation in which you want to use it. On the plus side, Facebook gives you a method of verifying that your conversation is encrypted, and you even have the option of creating "self-destructing" messages that will automatically disappear after a chosen duration.

iMessage

iMessage is Apple's proprietary messaging system, used to exchange text messages, audio, and video among users of Macs, iPhones, and iPads. (Audio and video calls are relegated to FaceTime, a separate app.) Its popularity is undoubtedly due to its close integration with the iPhone (and to a lesser extent, the iPad). While there have been rumors that Apple is planning to bring iMessage to Android devices, it remains Apple-only for now.

As we've seen, Apple has been one of the strongest proponents of user privacy in the tech community. It was the first to add end-to-end encryption to messages sent through its service (and to add it to all conversations by default), and it makes a point of publicly stating that the company couldn't read your iMessages even if it wanted to, which it doesn't. There are a couple of caveats to this, though. One is that like any technology, iMessage encryption is vulnerable to undiscovered bugs and exploits. Some weaknesses in the system have been found in older versions of iOS, although they have already been fixed in newer versions. A bigger problem is the way in which Apple handles backups of your messages to iCloud (an optional feature that you have to enable on your iPhone or iPad). Although your messages are encrypted end-to-end with personal encryption keys, meaning they can only be decrypted by you and your correspondent, your iCloud backups are encrypted with a single key belonging to Apple. This means that Apple *could* theoretically access your messages if, say, they were legally compelled to do so; also, a hacker who managed to defeat Apple's own security and gain access to its encryption key could also snoop through your messages. If you're worried about this possibility, then you might want to turn off the automatic iCloud backups. Apple is reportedly working on a solution to this security hole for the latest versions of its operating systems.

WhatsApp

WhatsApp, now owned by Facebook, offers text, voice and video calls, voice messages, photo and video sharing, and document and file sharing. It gained popularity due to its simplicity, speed, and low barrier to entry—although one of its techniques for lowering that barrier, using your personal contacts data to identify other WhatsApp users via phone numbers, raised some eyebrows among privacy advocates. Newer versions of WhatsApp enable end-to-end encryption for messages *and* calls by default. Like Facebook Messenger, it also provides a way of verifying that encryption is in place for a particular conversation.

Skype

Another venerable messaging system, Microsoft's Skype, owes its popularity to being one of the first easy-to-use ways of making free voice calls across the Internet. In addition to voice calls, Skype enables text messaging, video calls, screen sharing, and—another big winner—calling to phones other than those of other Skype clients. Unfortunately, although Microsoft claims that all of its Skype communications are encrypted, it doesn't use full end-to-end encryption, and there are enough questions about its privacy protection—including an intermediate decryption step in the messaging process that could be used as a point of interception; specially compromised versions of the software used in China and Russia for government spying; and a number of instances of Skype-targeted malware appearing—that it stands as a poor choice for the privacy-conscious user. In fact, Skype earned a special rebuke from Amnesty International as an app "not protecting users' privacy" (alongside Snapchat; Amnesty International, 2016). Skype is often used as a business tool. If your library is conducting any confidential business during online meetings, however, it should consider using one of the more secure messaging apps instead of Skype.

Kik Messenger

Kik has gained widespread adoption as a cool messaging app, especially among teenagers. It does not provide end-to-end encryption for its communications. It does, however, make it easy to sign up for and use the service anonymously: contact details are not verified, and only a user-chosen nickname is used to identify and connect users of the service.

Privacy-Centric Apps

The aforementioned apps are more prominent in terms of their popularity than for their security and privacy features, although some of them (e.g., WhatsApp and iMessage) fare quite well across the board. There is, however, a respectable list of messaging apps that while less popular, have a strong focus on protecting the privacy of their communications. These include Silent Phone (from Silent Circle, maker of the Blackphone), Signal, Wickr, ChatSecure (which uses open-source code for its encryption, increasing transparency), Telegram, Ricochet, and Tor Messenger (in beta). This is the class of messaging apps that libraries should consider providing on public computers or loaned mobile devices.

Web Browsers and Search Engines

When it comes to web browsing on mobile devices, your choices are a little more limited than in the desktop environment. Deep system integration with the system's defaults, such as Mobile Safari on iOS devices, can be a disincentive to look for more secure options. However, if your library is running a mobile-device lending program with an emphasis on privacy, you might consider installing some of the apps listed here for more secure browsing and searching.

Web Browsers

The paradigm of the "standard" web browser doesn't do much to protect your privacy; using one is akin to leaving your fingerprints everywhere you go. Most browsers keep track of your browsing history, cached webpages, search queries, and cookies by default. It's all done in the name of improving your browsing experience, but it's a potential privacy nightmare! (Note that in this context, the concern is the trail you leave behind *on the devices you use*, whether those devices are personal or library-supplied. Of course, your web browsing is also registered elsewhere in server log files and JavaScript trackers, as discussed in chapter 5, but that's a different story.) It's not advisable to try to delete your default web browser, such as Safari, but you can tuck it away in a folder somewhere and feature a secure alternative more prominently. If you do use the default browser, keep in mind that your account settings may mean that your browser bookmarks and history are synced with your other devices (as is the case with Safari and iCloud syncing).

If you browse through one of the app stores for the different mobile platforms, you may find dozens of different apps named or advertised as "private browsers." In most cases, these are merely apps that take the common privacy mode a little more seriously by discarding common types of browsing data—history, caches, queries, cookies—each time you stop using the app. Some of them take things a step further by adding password protection to the app to prevent others from using it. However, there are a few that take private web browsing to the next level.

Onion Browser (and derivatives). The Tor project is a special network designed to preserve anonymity and privacy through a system called "onion routing," which uses multiple layers of encryption and routing to prevent a client from being identified. Although the primary way of using Tor is through a custom desktop web browser, the technology can be accessed from a number of different systems, including messaging apps—and now through mobile device browsers as well. There are a number of different browsers that claim to employ onion routing and connect to Tor. Onion Browser is a representative example. The primary attraction in such browsers is their ability to use Tor, so feature-parity with other browsers may lag in some respects.

Ghostery Browser. The company behind the excellent Ghostery ad-blocker browser extension (see chapter 5) has now developed its own mobile browser that incorporates all of its own script-blocking functionality. Although script blockers can be added to standard mobile browsers as extensions (as you'll see in the next section), Ghostery's browser saves you the trouble of installing them and keeping them up to date.

Firefox Focus (iOS only). Not to be confused with the main Firefox browser, Firefox Focus is another browser that provides built-in blocking of ads and tracking scripts, along with a focus on privacy in the retention of browsing data (or the lack thereof). Focus's largest drawback for some users may be its extreme simplicity—it lacks features like tabs that have become standard-issue across most modern browsers.

Search Engines

Web browsers are usually complemented by search engines, which add a new wrinkle to the battle for privacy. Google's exemplary search-engine results come at a price: your search queries, search history, and as much other personal information as the company can glean about you from your use of its systems are all pooled to customize results for you but also to make larger inferences about result relevance for different groups of users—and to be sold to advertisers who want to target you with custom ads. A small number of privacy-conscious search engines have emerged over the past few years. The best-known one is DuckDuckGo. DuckDuckGo advertises itself prominently on its search page as "The search engine that doesn't track you," and it emphasizes that it keeps no record of your search history and does not sell your personal data to advertisers. Despite this, it often provides search results comparable to those produced by Google or other less-private search engines, and it has enough special features of its own to keep users coming back to it. DuckDuckGo is available as an extension for most major web browsers, and some even offer it as a first-tier alternative for a browser's built-in search box (e.g., Safari and Chrome). One interesting effect of DuckDuckGo's no-tracking policy is that identical search queries made to the service by different users will produce identical sets of search results—in contrast to Google's search engine, which factors its knowledge of who you are into its decisions about what results to show you!

Content Blockers

The concept of using content blockers in conjunction with a web browser to prevent certain elements from loading on a webpage—most commonly JavaScript added for advertising or tracking purposes—was introduced in chapter 5, where the focus was on desktop and laptop browsers. There you read about the short-lived drama surrounding Peace, a content blocker introduced for Mobile Safari when that browser enabled the use of content blockers in iOS 9. On mobile devices, there are two basic ways to get content blocking when browsing: use a custom browser that has blocking built in, such as Ghostery Browser or Firefox Focus; or install extensions that enable blocking for a standard browser, such as Peace.

Installing extensions for content blocking is straightforward. Both iOS and the Android operating system provide a mechanism for browser extensions to filter out certain types of content. Since the user experience on mobile devices is app-driven, however, these extensions are usually packaged within apps. All you have to do to use them is to download and install the app and configure it according to the maker's instructions.

Password Managers

Password managers play an important role in practicing good password safety. Chapter 5 described some of the challenges inherent in creating and maintaining good passwords. Unfortunately, most of the things you *should* do to keep your passwords secure (such as using long, complex passwords or passphrases; not reusing a given password for multiple sites or systems; and not writing passwords down) also discourage people from using good passwords due to their complexity. That's where password managers come into play. A good password manager reduces the friction of password use by doing all the hard work of creating, remembering, and entering them for you. In the library, password managers should be deployed on staff computers and workstations to minimize the risk of sensitive passwords being written down on scraps of paper somewhere. They can also be installed on public computers if the managers can sync data through the cloud (thus allowing a temporary user to sign in to his or her password account during a session). Of course, you should also encourage users to take advantage of password managers for their own computing.

As with most categories of apps these days, you're spoiled for choice with password managers. However, a few venerable names stand out from the crowd. Top among them are LastPass and 1Password, but there are other good ones out there as well. Every typical password manager offers a few core features and then a variety of nice-but-not-necessary functions. Chief among the core features is a secure password vault—the very reason for a password manager's existence. The password vault enables you to create new entries for every login or other authenticated credentials you need to enter to access a website. Browser plugins allow the vault to work with your web browsing directly. When you encounter a login form on a website you've previously created an account for, a click or two into your password manager browser extension will fill in your login information directly (see figure 7.2). If you choose not to use the browser plugins, you can still open the password manager's vault and read or copy your username and password.

The more comprehensive password managers, such as 1Password and LastPass, also provide separate categories for storing software licenses and keys, encrypted notes, credit card numbers, personal profile information, and more. As an example, here is how to enter credentials using 1Password on an iPhone or iPad:

1. Browse to the site in question using Safari and navigate to its login page. Tap into the username field.
2. 1Password is accessed within Safari through the Share sheet, which is a little counterintuitive. Tap the Share icon in the bottom toolbar (a little square with an arrow pointing out of the top). This brings up the Share sheet.
3. In the lower row of the Share sheet (actions), scroll across until you find 1Password. Tap it.
4. On the 1Password pane that appears, you can either enter your master password or, if enabled, use Touch ID and enter your fingerprint.
5. If the site is recognized, your login information should appear first in the list of results. If not, you may have to search for it. When you find the correct site information, tap the site name.
6. The 1Password sheet should close, and your credentials should be autofilled into the form. Depending how it's set up, the form may be automatically submitted as well (or you may have to hit the submit button yourself).

Other password managers and other operating systems will behave similarly.

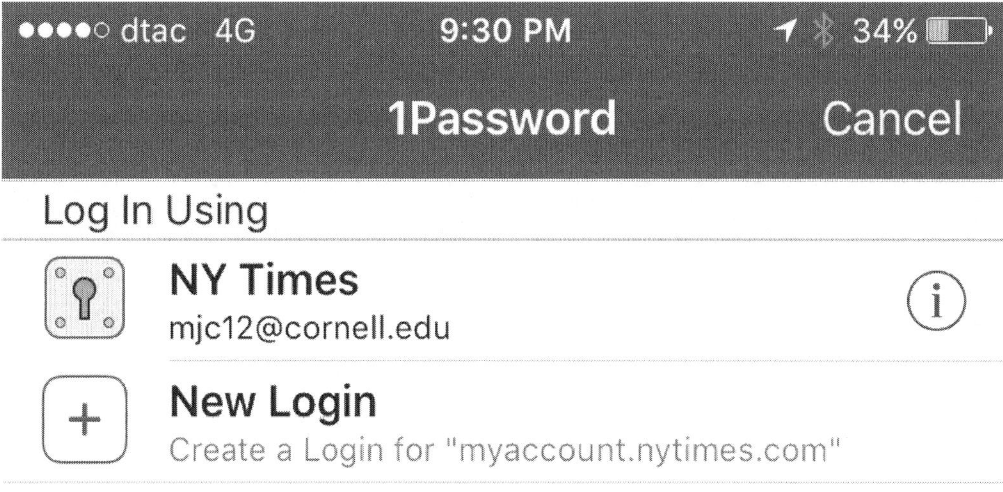

Figure 7.2. Using 1Password to log into a website. Screenshot of AgileBits' 1Password app.

Password managers also encourage good password hygiene. Once you start using a reliable password manager that syncs your vault across all your devices—phones, tablets, desktops, laptops—then you have little excuse not to fill it with reliable passwords. You can stop limiting yourself to short, easily hackable passwords constrained by the need to remember them. A best practice is to use a different password (and, ideally, a different user ID) for each site where you enter credentials. That way, a breach of one website that you use won't reveal your password information for multiple sites. Apps like 1Password also provide password-audit services, identifying potentially vulnerable passwords due to weak password structure, duplication of passwords across sites, or old passwords that should be changed just on principle.

Of course, password managers have one major weakness: they seal your vault using a single master password or passphrase. If you use a weak password for that, or the encryption and security used by the app and its developers aren't strong enough, then there's the potential that you'll lose everything in one fell swoop if your master password is compromised.

Apps like 1Password have the ability to sync your account data across devices (1Password can sync through Dropbox or iCloud). This means that you can provide 1Password on your public devices, whether desktop machines, laptops, or for a mobile lending program. If they want to, users can log in to their own accounts and sync from a network to use their own password vault during their work sessions. Naturally, you should ensure that the credentials they enter are cleared when their session is completed—ideally, by using a provisioning system as we discussed in chapter 4.

VPNs

Virtual private networks (VPNs) are immensely useful for protecting your personal data while using a mobile device, particularly if you have to connect to an insecure network. As we saw in chapter 3, VPNs encrypt your data as your device communicates with other devices or servers, even over an otherwise unencrypted wi-fi network; they also mask your true IP address from outside servers. Thus, if you visit a website while using a VPN client, the site will register a visit from an IP address belonging to the VPN service, not your own IP. Besides protecting your privacy, this behavior has a couple of other uses: it can be used to circumvent government-imposed firewalls or censorship technology in countries like China; and it can be used to make it appear that you are connecting to the Internet from a different country, which is a popular technique for getting around geographic restrictions on streaming media (e.g., watching content from Netflix's European catalog while you're in the United States).

In libraries, VPNs are widely used to provide access to ejournals and ebooks hosted on third-party servers. They are also useful for connecting to library systems remotely—to get some work done while away at a conference, for instance. Providing an easy-to-use VPN client on public machines in the library can also be a useful service for your patrons for the aforementioned activities.

There are many mobile apps that provide VPN functionality. In order to use them, you have to have access to a VPN to begin with. If your library is affiliated with a college, university, or other larger institution, it may very well have access to a VPN that authorized users can connect to. If you don't have an institutional VPN, you're still in luck: there are a number of VPN services that you can subscribe to on a yearly or permanent basis.

Several of them promise that they keep minimal connection logs that could identify you, or indeed no logs at all. Some are also based in territories where subpoenas or government requests for data may prove ineffective.

A popular choice of providers is ExpressVPN (https://expressvpn.com). A subscription to ExpressVPN buys you unlimited bandwidth, strong encryption, a choice of servers located in almost a hundred countries, no logging of user activities, three simultaneous connections, and a thirty-day guarantee. ExpressVPN uses an app to control its behavior, but installation is a little more involved than simply downloading the ExpressVPN app from an app store. Since VPN use involves routing all of your Internet traffic through its server, it must integrate with a mobile device at the system level. This is done by downloading a special configuration file from the ExpressVPN website. It's best to follow the online instructions to make sure you get all the steps correct. Once installed, you can activate or deactivate the VPN at the touch of a button.

Key Points

Although the world of mobile apps is almost infinite in its breadth, this chapter has concentrated on highlighting the privacy and security implications of using certain popular categories of apps—and why your library might want to use some lesser-known categories, such as content blockers and VPNs. Here are the essential points.

- Methods for installing apps include downloading them from an official app store or using an enterprise deployment system to distribute them within a business or university. The safest approach is to use an app store, however.
- Your library might consider creating a curated list of privacy-conscious apps for concerned users to adopt. When lending devices or configuring public workstations, you can pre-install these apps for your patrons.
- Creating and distributing your own library apps can be risky unless you really know what you're doing. Professional alternatives like Boopsie are a better way of creating custom apps without having to worry about the technical side of security.
- Social media apps, although popular, should be approached carefully due to their checkered history of privacy breaches. Make sure that you understand how a service provider handles and protects personal data.
- Messaging apps are starting to take privacy seriously, and many offer strong, end-to-end encryption of user communications and data. Carefully selected, they can be an asset to privacy management.
- Specialized web browsers and search engines can be used to improve the privacy of your web browsing and search sessions. If you're using standard web browsers, content blockers can be added to provide some of the same benefits.
- VPNs are a useful way of protecting a networking session even if the channel itself is insecure. They also mask your IP address and, in some cases, promise not to log your online activities.

Thus far, this book has discussed security and privacy within the environment that you or your library has immediate control over: your network, public computers, web browsers and websites, mobile devices, and apps. In the next chapter, you'll step out of that zone of control and into a much more mysterious area: the cloud.

References

Alfonso, Paige. 2016. "Snapchat in the Library." *American Libraries*. November 1. https://americanlibrariesmagazine.org/2016/11/01/snapchat-in-the-library.

Amnesty International. 2016. "Snapchat, Skype among Apps Not Protecting Users' Privacy." Amnesty International. October 21. www.amnesty.org/en/latest/news/2016/10/snapchat-skype-among-apps-not-protecting-users-privacy.

Bort, Julie. 2016. "Twitter Sent a Woman's Address to the Man Who Was Harassing Her after She Filed a Complaint." *Business Insider*. May 26. www.businessinsider.com/twitter-sent-a-womans-address-to-her-stalker-2016-5.

Connolly, Matthew, and Tony Cosgrave. 2015. *Using iPhones, iPads, and iPods: A Practical Guide for Librarians*. Lanham, MD: Rowman & Littlefield.

Finkle, Jim. 2015. "Apple Cleaning Up iOS App Store after First Major Attack." *Reuters*. September 21. www.reuters.com/article/us-apple-china-malware-idUSKCN0RK0ZB20150921.

Fox-Brewster, Thomas. 2015. "Researcher Finds 'Shocking' Instagram Flaws and Ends Up in a Fight with Facebook." *Forbes*. December 17. www.forbes.com/sites/thomasbrewster/2015/12/17/facebook-instagram-security-research-threats.

Goode, Lauren. 2016. "Messenger and WhatsApp Process 60 Billion Messages a Day, Three Times More Than SMS." *The Verge*. April 12. www.theverge.com/2016/4/12/11415198/facebook-messenger-whatsapp-number-messages-vs-sms-f8-2016.

McMillan, Robert. 2016. "Twitter: Passwords Leaked for Millions of Accounts." *Wall Street Journal*. June 9. www.wsj.com/articles/twitter-millions-of-accounts-at-risk-of-breach-1465510623.

Menn, Joseph. 2016. "Exclusive: Yahoo Secretly Scanned Customer Emails for U.S. Intelligence—Sources." *Reuters*. October 4. www.reuters.com/article/us-yahoo-nsa-exclusive-idUSKCN1241YT.

Paul, Ian. 2010. "Facebook CEO Challenges the Social Norm of Privacy." *PCWorld*. January 11. www.pcworld.com/article/186584/facebook_ceo_challenges_the_social_norm_of_privacy.html.

Perlroth, Nicole. 2016. "Yahoo Says Hackers Stole Data on 500 Million Users in 2014." *New York Times*. September 22. www.nytimes.com/2016/09/23/technology/yahoo-hackers.html.

Vaas, Lisa. 2016. "65 Million Tumblr Passwords Stolen and Up for Sale." *Naked Security*. May 31. https://nakedsecurity.sophos.com/2016/05/31/65-million-tumblr-passwords-stolen-and-up-for-sale.

Yu, Rowland. 2016. "The Secrets of Malware Success on Google Play Store." Presentation, RSA Conference 2016, San Francisco, March 2. www.rsaconference.com/writable/presentations/file_upload/crwd-w13-the-secrets-of-malware-success-on-google-play-store_.ppt.pdf.

CHAPTER 8

The Cloud

IN THIS CHAPTER

- ▷ Evaluating cloud providers for privacy and security
- ▷ Understanding the implications of using cloud services in libraries
- ▷ Encrypting your data in the cloud
- ▷ Classifying legal risks to cloud-stored data
- ▷ Hosting your own cloud storage system
- ▷ Using two-factor authentication
- ▷ Assessing the risks of always-on voice assistants

Threat Assessment

THUS FAR, THE TECHNIQUES FOR PROTECTING PATRON PRIVACY discussed in this book have concerned systems that you (personally or as an organization) have some control over. From the server and network level down to the choice and use of individual apps, you can choose tools and practices that are more or less secure as deemed appropriate for your library's particular circumstances.

When you start to store data in the cloud, that all changes. The term "cloud," such as in "storing your photos in the cloud," is one that, although having grown popular in recent years, actually describes a very basic and well-established concept. Simply put, the remote servers that you interact with on a daily basis when, say, browsing the web can host not only an outside entity's websites and data but also your own personal data. This is really nothing very exotic; any email system that uses IMAP (see chapter 3) to store your messages on a server, not to mention every social media platform, like Facebook, is making use of the cloud. As the technology for servers and networking has improved and the associated costs have been driven down, cloud storage and computing have become ubiquitous. Using a cloud storage solution for important personal data, like your photo collection, is often strongly encouraged as a safe backup solution. Major computing platforms use cloud storage extensively to improve the user experience on their devices. Apple, for example, urges the use of iCloud not only to store your photos, videos, music, and documents in the cloud, but also to seamlessly connect your activities between your iPhone, iPad, and Mac by syncing bookmarks in Safari, passwords, network settings, desktop files, and more. More recent versions of iOS and macOS also support Handoff, a blanket term for a collection of technologies that let you begin work on a document or webpage on one device then pick up another device and continue where you left off—also realized through iCloud.

The downside to storing data in the cloud is that it's outside your control. A good general rule of thumb when publishing content on the web—e.g., updating your Facebook status—is to assume that anything you publish is potentially accessible by the entire world. It's a good way to save yourself from major embarrassment if something leaks out in unexpected ways. Using cloud storage is a little bit different in that many cloud solutions for personal data management promise that your information is safe, private, and secure, and that you can rest easy with the knowledge that it's in good hands. They create an expectation of privacy—arguably an unreasonable expectation, as a seemingly unending string of news items about large-scale data breaches (both new and old but undisclosed) would seem to indicate. Doing without cloud services completely these days is unrealistic and probably unbearably inconvenient. But as with every other aspect of networked computing, you should tread carefully and abide by the same axiom: nothing that you send out across a network can ever be said to be truly 100 percent secure. Cloud storage providers are vulnerable to two major categories of threat: criminals and other malicious hackers who want to steal your data or credentials; and legal subpoenas for personal data from law enforcement or government agencies. You might think that a large, experienced company would be well-equipped to defend itself against the former threat, but sometimes that's not the case. Likewise, you often can't be sure just how much heat a company is willing to take if it's being threatened with legal consequences if it doesn't hand over a user's information or data. This chapter will take you through the process of evaluating cloud providers, encrypting the data you upload to the cloud, hosting your own cloud storage, and skirting the pitfalls of new, cloud-backed hardware.

Evaluating Cloud Providers

Before committing sensitive library or personal data to any cloud service, including the big players, you should take some time to evaluate both the technology and the ideals that they use to protect the privacy of their users. It's crucial for library personnel to weigh these factors before committing any data to them. Both factors are important; a well-intentioned company that uses inexperienced developers to build its tech stack or a technically savvy firm that simply doesn't care about user privacy—such as Uber (Evans, 2016)—are both potentially disastrous if you put your trust in them. It can be difficult to evaluate those key points, however. Technology in particular is usually a black box unless the system is open source. That's why you'll have to spend a bit of time researching a provider. The company's website is a reasonable starting point. A good cloud provider should state clearly that it is using secure communication (SSL/HTTPS transmission) and file encryption to protect user data. You can also hope that it will be transparent about any breaches of its security, notifying users clearly and immediately if their data or credentials have been compromised. Sadly, this is not always the case. So don't end your research with the provider's own materials; hunt around for security advisories or news items about the site. A potentially useful resource for evaluating a site's policies is a website called Terms of Service: Didn't Read (https://tosdr.org), which grades major sites based on the contents of those legal documents that often go unread. Although the TOSDR project seems to have lost some momentum in recent years and scores a somewhat small number of sites, it is a concept worth supporting.

You should also consider the company's data-retention policies. Even on your own personal computer, deleting a file usually does not really erase it from your hard drive or SSD until the actual bits are overwritten with new data (which doesn't happen predictably and perhaps not even frequently). In a cloud-based system, that uncertainty is multiplied; your service provider may be maintaining redundant copies of your data to protect against accidental loss—and for similar reasons, often a file you try to remove from the cloud is merely transferred to a "recently deleted" folder for a period of a few days to a few weeks before it is actually destroyed. And even beyond that, some cloud systems (e.g., Dropbox) keep not just your current file but also a history of all the recent changes made to that file, creating different versions of it on the server.

A special case of that last concern—versioning—involves *version control systems*, most commonly used to track changes in software code but also useful for maintaining a history of changes to important documents, such as system documentation. One of the most popular version control systems at the present time is known as Git, and the most popular cloud-based storage of Git-controlled file sets (repositories) is GitHub (https://github.com). Since GitHub has been gaining popularity both for software development and for more creative uses such as document versioning, you should be aware of one important security pitfall if you're going to use it for library applications. Git is intended to preserve a history of all the changes ever made to a particular file. This can trip people up when it comes to sensitive information being put into a Git-versioned document. If you're creating a new software app, for example, it's very tempting to cut corners by hard-coding database credentials or login information—typing them directly into your code—while prototyping or debugging your work. If you forget that you've done this and add the file to your Git repository, then those private credentials become a permanent part of the document history. Even if you realize your mistake and edit the file to remove the sensitive information, it *won't* be erased from the history; instead, Git will simply create a new version in which the information is no longer present. With special software or careful use of Git's built-in tools, it is possible to remove all traces of particular information from the entire repository history—but it's not necessarily easy, and it's not something you want to do unless you have to.

Two final points to consider are how a particular cloud provider makes its money and what its relationship is with advertisers. Everybody wants to find a service provider that's idealistic and altruistic, hosting your cloud backups and synchronizations with complete privacy and at little or no cost to you. But of course, businesses have to be profitable. Many choose to use some form of advertising to make money (Google being one of the biggest examples). In itself, this is fine; but inserting ads into modern systems often entails a loss of customer privacy and anonymity. For this reason, many expert users prefer to subscribe to paid services rather than use free, ad-supported ones.

TEXTBOX 8.1

IMPLICATIONS OF USING CLOUD SERVICES IN LIBRARIES

These days, it's difficult to *not* use cloud services because so many modern computing paradigms assume the existence of an omnipresent, cloud-like back end to power the functionality and conveniences we've come to expect from our computers, phones, and tablets. Library professionals, though, should be very careful to understand all the implications of using a particular cloud service in a library environment. Just as important is the need to understand exactly where and how your library websites and online systems are coupled to the outside world. It's all too easy to install a new widget on your website as an experiment and then incorporate the widget as a must-have feature without really considering what information is being transferred from each user's session on your website to the widget provider's server logs. A classic example is Google Analytics, a very popular website analytics package. Its ease of installation and user-friendly visualization of activity on your site make it nearly irresistible if you're in the market for a good analysis of how visitors are utilizing your library website. But the obvious dark lining to this silver cloud is the fact that every visitor's activities on your site are being transmitted back to Google's servers. That's potentially quite a bit of data that you're entrusting to Google's privacy and data protection policies. At least Google *has* such policies—but did you stop to read them before installing the Analytics tracking scripts on your pages? And what about something as innocent as catalog cover images? If your OPAC uses an API to pull in book-cover images from a provider like Amazon or Google, then you're passing it data about the items your visitors are searching for and viewing. You might have to do a bit of detective work to figure out just how much data is being sent over, though. Library technologist Eric Hellman (2016) gives detailed instructions for doing this with Amazon links, and you can use the same concepts to investigate other services.

Encryption in the Cloud

Without a doubt, encryption is the best way to ensure that your private data remains private once you leave it in the hands of an external service. Whether you are considering offering encryption utilities on public computers in the library or searching for a cloud storage solution for the library's own data, you should try to use encryption whenever possible. There are two basic approaches you can take to cloud encryption: you can use a service that encrypts your data for you automatically when you upload it, or you can encrypt your data yourself before uploading it to a service provider.

Using Cloud-Provided Encryption

A trustworthy, encrypted cloud file service can be a good choice if your primary concerns are ease of use and data security. Using a service that encrypts your files for you simplifies the problem, and the better services arrange things so that the keys used for encryption are only known to you; not even the service provider itself can read your data when it's uploaded. (This approach is referred to as "zero knowledge.") The encryption process is carried out on your local machine when uploading files. The disadvantage is a loss of compatibility with apps or other services that require you to have an account with a particular cloud provider. One of the most common of these is Dropbox (https://dropbox.com). Dropbox does *not* encrypt your data, but it has become a popular back-end service for use with any number of third-party apps for file storage and syncing of preferences. Services that emphasize encryption are still a nascent subset of cloud providers, so they have much less third-party support than some of their well-established competitors. Since general members of the public are unlikely to be using these services, providing them on public computers or library-lending devices may be of limited benefit. However, they're worth considering if you're looking for a way to do cloud backups of sensitive library data or if you would like to implement a more secure method of synchronizing folder contents à la Dropbox.

SpiderOak One (https://spideroak.com/solutions/spideroak-one) is a popular choice for this type of app. SpiderOak is a company that focuses on encrypted chat and file-sharing systems for enterprise as well as home users. The One product is positioned as a securely encrypted file backup tool. With its desktop or mobile apps, you can select specific folders or file types on your devices to be backed up to their cloud storage; this also enables you to sync folders across devices in a manner akin to Dropbox (but with more flexibility). SpiderOak offers a free trial for the service, but you will have to get a paid subscription to continue using it. To use SpiderOak One to encrypt and back up your data, do the following:

1. Download and install the One app for your device at https://spideroak.com/opendownload.
2. Launch the app. The first view that appears will be an account setup page. Enter an email address, name, password, and password hint, then click Create Account. You will automatically be given a trial account with full access for twenty-two days.
3. Enter a name for the computer you're backing up, then click Next. The app will take a few seconds to finish its setup.
4. You should see the main backup interface (see figure 8.1). Select the Backup tab if you're not already there.
5. From the Backup tab, you can select documents, folders, or types of content to back up to SpiderOak. Note that there are two primary interfaces for doing this: a list of categories (content types or locations) on the left and a folder/file browser on the right. Selecting a category (e.g., Pictures) will back up all the media of that type that the app finds on your computer. Some of the choices in the list also represent significant folders on your computer; checking Documents, for example, will back up all the contents of your Documents folder. The file browser on the right allows you to select other folders for backup or, if you prefer, individual files. Select a few files or folders now, then click the Save button. The backup process should occur automatically, and encryption is performed transparently.
6. Click into the Home tab. From here you can see or adjust the backup schedule, which by default is handled automatically by the app.

You can also use SpiderOak One to synchronize the contents of folders across devices. This mimics the functionality of the more popular Dropbox with the added benefit of strong encryption. Follow these steps to enable this behavior:

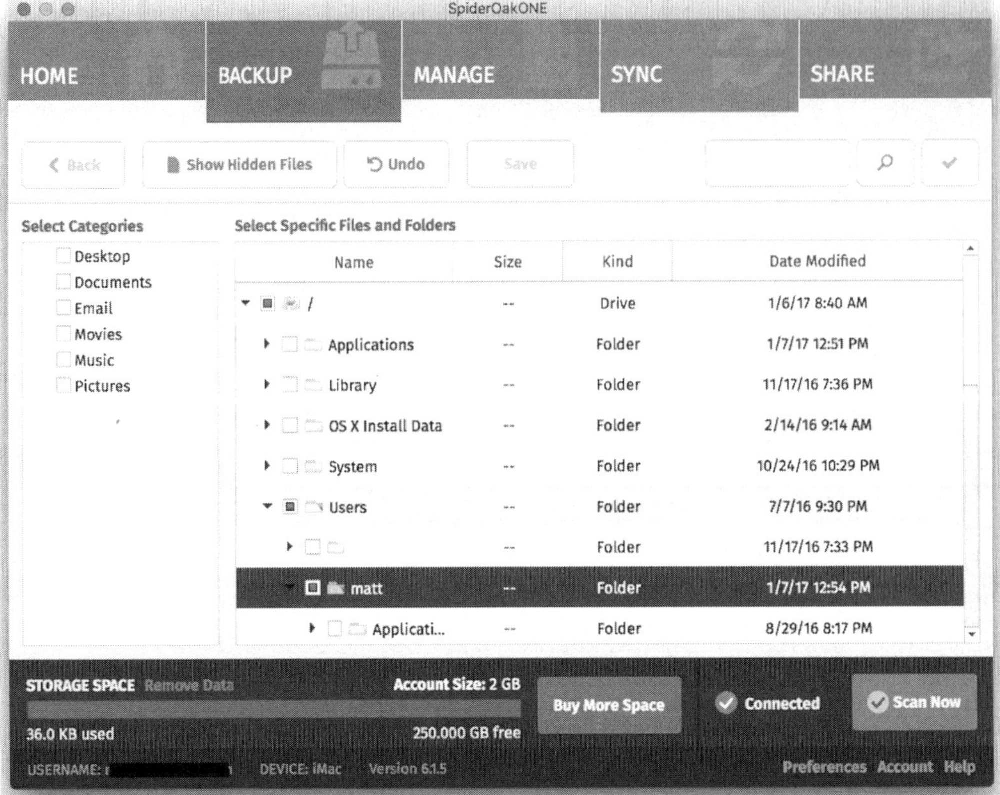

Figure 8.1. The SpiderOak One user interface. Screenshot of SpiderOak's One app.

1. Use the instructions above to create a SpiderOak account and choose some folders for backup.
2. Note that the creation process also created a special folder on your system called SpiderOak Hive. On the Mac, this folder is located in your top-level user folder; on Windows, it's placed within your Documents directory. In either case, there should also be a shortcut to it on your desktop. The Hive folder is a default sync folder akin to the Dropbox folder that is used by that service. Any files you place within the Hive folder will be replicated across every device where you're using SpiderOak. For example, you could install a SpiderOak client on each of your library's public computers, then use the Hive folder that appears to dynamically add or remove public resources for your users. If that's all you need, you can stop here.
3. If you'd like a little more control over what content or folders get synchronized, you can create your own "syncs." To do so, click into the Sync tab in the app.
4. In order to sync custom folders (individual files can't be synced, only folders), each folder that you want to use must be backed up to SpiderOak. Use the Backup tab to make sure they're selected. Usually, you'll want to use two folders on different devices; for demonstration purposes, though, you can use any two that you want. Create two folders on your desktop, maybe "test 1" and "test 2," and add them to Backup.
5. Back in the Sync tab, click New to set up a new sync. Give it a name and description, then click Next.
6. You must now select the source and destination folder or folders (you can sync one source folder to multiple destination folders). The file browser that ap-

pears for each line only shows the devices and folders that are currently registered with Backup. Choose the appropriate folders—test 1 for the source, test 2 for the destination—and click Next.

7. The third step is optional; it lets you exclude certain file types from the sync. Enter some values (e.g., "*.zip") if you want to, then click Next once more.
8. Review the information you've entered. If it's correct, click Start Sync.
9. To test that things are working as expected, drop a file into the test 1 folder. Click the Scan Now button in the lower right corner of the SpiderOak One window. Wait a few minutes (depending on the size of the file you're using), then look inside the test 2 folder. You should see a copy of the same file reproduced there.

The SpiderOak One interface is a bit rough in places, but the functionality it provides can be very handy if you're looking for a thoroughly secure cloud backup service.

Encrypting Personal Files

But if you don't want to use a specialized encrypted cloud service, your other choice is to use a system that works in conjunction with more popular cloud services like Dropbox, handling the encryption and decryption process as an intermediary between your own computer and the cloud provider. One popular example of this category of app is Boxcryptor (https://boxcryptor.com). Boxcryptor boasts that it works with all cloud storage providers, but it's at least safe to say that it works with many of the major ones (Dropbox, Google, Amazon, Box, iCloud, etc.). It's another zero knowledge service, so your encryption credentials are kept safely in your hands and are unknown even to Boxcryptor itself. You can get a free subscription if you only want to work with one cloud provider and up to two devices. To start using Boxcryptor, do the following:

1. Download and install the app from the Boxcryptor website (www.boxcryptor.com/en/download) or an app store.
2. Launch the app. On the first screen, click Create an Account. Enter a name, email address, and password; check off the checkboxes to agree to the Boxcryptor terms of use and privacy policy; and click Next.
3. The next screen that appears is a warning about remembering your password. Check the box and click Create Account.
4. On the next screen, select the free plan and click Next.
5. If all goes well, you should see a congratulatory message. Click Finish.
6. Use your new credentials to sign in to the app.
7. The first time you sign in, you will be taken through a series of pages explaining the features of the Boxcryptor system. When finished, click the checkmark to continue. Don't be disconcerted if the app seems to disappear!
8. Boxcryptor normally appears as a menu bar item. To configure it, click on the Boxcryptor icon in the menu bar and choose Preferences... .
9. The basic preferences window is shown in figure 8.2. Boxcryptor will identify cloud services that you are already using on your computer and display them in a list within the Locations tab, so yours may look a little different. Since you're using a free account, you will only be able to select one provider at a time. This example will use Dropbox.

10. Note that the Dropbox source has a small Link button next to it. That can be used to sign in to your Dropbox account to enable additional features, but it's not required for basic operation.
11. Locate the Boxcryptor folder on your system. This is usually mounted as a top-level volume. If you can't locate it, click on the Boxcryptor icon in your menu bar and choose Open. The Boxcryptor folder should open for you.
12. With the Boxcryptor folder open, select Dropbox in the locations list in the Preferences. Note that a Dropbox folder immediately appears inside the Boxcryptor folder. Open it; you should see an exact copy of your Dropbox folder contents.
13. Using the Boxcryptor folder, you can encrypt individual files or entire folders in Dropbox. To do so, select any item within the Boxcryptor Dropbox folder (*not* the original Dropbox folder), right-click, and choose Boxcryptor > Encrypt. The file or folder will be encrypted immediately. Within the Boxcryptor folder, this will be indicated by a small green lock icon next to the item in a directory list or on the file or folder icon itself in an icon view. Within the original Dropbox folder, encrypted files will be given a .bc extension (e.g., a file originally called secrets.txt will appear as secrets.txt.bc in Dropbox).
14. Test that encryption is working. Choose the file that you encrypted in the *Dropbox* folder and try to open it. Since it has a .bc extension, your computer probably will not know how to open it. Simply drag it into an appropriate app—e.g.,

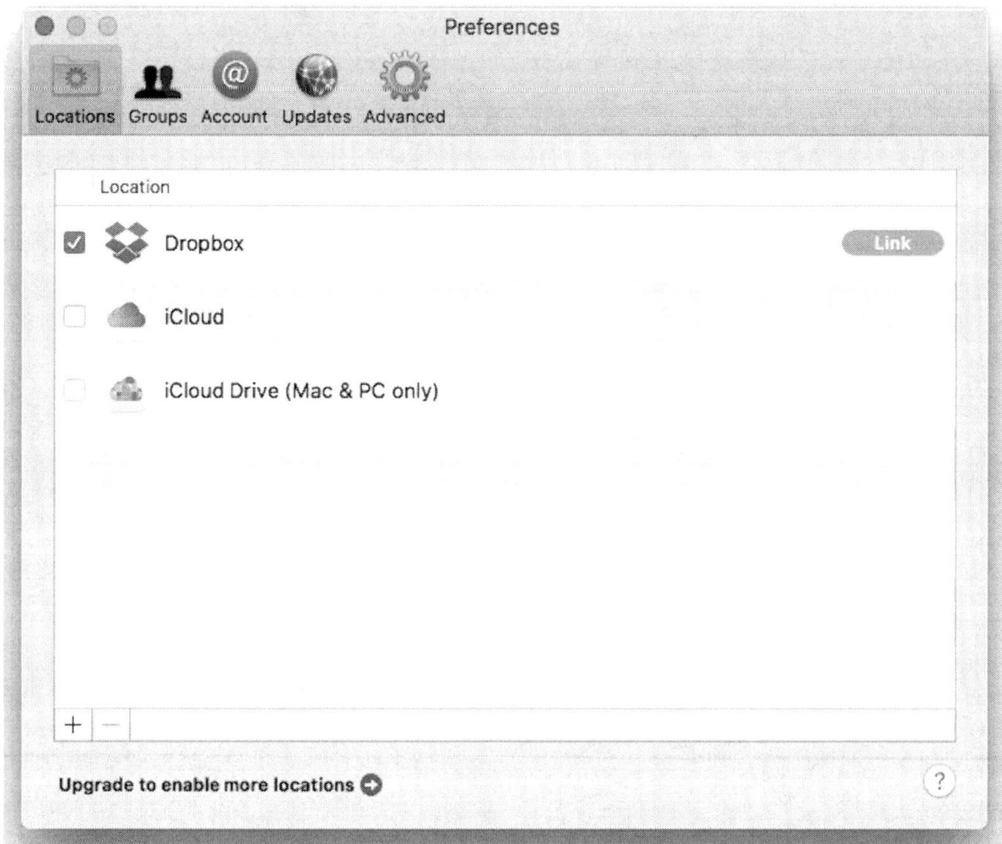

Figure 8.2. Boxcryptor being linked with a Dropbox account. Screenshot of Secomba's Box-Cryptor app.

TextEdit on the Mac for a plain-text file. The contents should look like gibberish. Your secrets are safe!

15. Experiment a bit with the two folders—the original Dropbox folder and the Boxcryptor Dropbox folder—side by side until you understand the behavior. If you drop a folder or file into the Dropbox folder, it will immediately appear in the Boxcryptor folder as well, but it will not be encrypted. On the other hand, if you drop a folder or file into the Boxcryptor folder, it will immediately appear in Dropbox as well *and* will be encrypted. Encryption can be removed from files or folders in the Boxcryptor view by right-clicking and choosing Boxcryptor > Decrypt. Also note that when you drop a file into Dropbox, it is moved from its original location; when you drop a file into Boxcryptor, a copy is made—a duplicate file remains in its original location.
16. Remember that Boxcryptor (the service) has no idea what your username and password are. If you forget your login credentials, you will not be able to decrypt your files!

That's all you need to get up and running with Boxcryptor. Once you've configured your account, it is a very simple and straightforward way to encrypt data even if your cloud provider doesn't offer its own encryption.

Cloud Providers and Law Enforcement

Cloud service providers, especially the more reputable ones, are all vulnerable to one particular type of security breach: an official request for information (in the form of a warrant, court order, or subpoena) from government or law enforcement. This can be an area of concern for libraries, which are generally more protective of user privacy than the average commercial business. More and more frequently, it seems, the interests of users are made antithetical to the demands of law enforcement. Service providers are placed in an awkward position: even if they wish to respect and protect the privacy of their customers' private data, the cost of opposing such official requests can be high both from a legal and a public relations perspective. A company that refuses to comply with a request for a user's data in conjunction with a legitimate police or FBI investigation may be portrayed as colluding with or abetting criminals. This problem has been amplified in the age of terrorism, where the stakes are framed as being that much greater. Complicating the issue is the use of gag orders. Companies that are subpoenaed for user information are often legally barred from even mentioning the fact that the request has been made. This has led to fears that governments are overreaching their authority—with both the requests they make for information and the gag orders that accompany the requests—and also to claims that such orders violate both the First and Fourth Amendments to the U.S. Constitution.

Privacy Laws

The laws governing individuals' privacy and how a government or law enforcement agency can access personal information are complex and confusing. Often they rely on legislation passed decades ago before the advent of the Internet and modern cloud storage concepts. In countries like the United States, they are an entanglement of both federal and state laws. And of course, such laws vary significantly from country to country. In the United States, the most significant federal laws concerning access to cloud-stored information make a general distinction between information that is stored and information that is in transit—the former being susceptible to the 1986 Stored Communications Act, the latter to the 1968 Wiretap Act. The Wiretap Act was subsequently updated and amended by the Electronic Communications Privacy Act (ECPA), also of 1986 (Gilbert, 2013). The ECPA makes the further distinction of content data versus noncontent data (i.e., metadata). Under the ECPA, both types of data can be legitimately requested by use of a warrant, court order, or subpoena, but the release of content data is complicated by the question of how long it has been in storage! If the data has been there for less than 180 days, it can only be requested by a warrant. After 180 days, options open up to include subpoenas and court orders. Yet another wrinkle concerns provisions in the US PATRIOT Act that enable the use of "national security letters" to demand information from cloud providers without having to worry about obtaining permission from a court (Broas and Saxon, 2013).

Since every business is subject to the applicable laws of its region, such requests are an unavoidable possibility if you entrust your data to a cloud storage provider. All that you can do to ensure the safety of your personal information is to shop around and try to find the providers that handle legal requests in the best way possible by only responding to legitimate requests, resisting overreach, and being as informative and transparent as possible about the requests they receive. An exemplar of that final point, transparency, is Apple. Apple maintains a dedicated page on their website with information about the information requests made to it (www.apple.com/privacy/government-information-requests). Assuring visitors that they "believe security shouldn't come at the expense of individual privacy," the company lays out in detail the types of requests it has received, the types of content requested, and even the approximate number of national security orders it receives (being legally barred from revealing the exact number). Other providers have begun to offer similar reports (e.g., Tumblr, www.tumblr.com/transparency). Providing this level of detail increases user trust and provides evidence that a cloud provider is serious about protecting user privacy.

Warrant Canaries

The most onerous of the various legal devices surrounding information requests to cloud providers is the use of gag orders to prevent even the revelation that a company has received such a request. In an attempt to straddle the line—to remain compliant with the law while preserving corporate transparency to users—some companies and organizations have adopted the use of a technique called a "warrant canary." The principle is very simple. A warrant canary is just a statement on a company's website to the effect that it has received no such secret requests for user data as of such-and-such a date. A failure to update the notice in a timely fashion, or its removal, can then be interpreted as a sign that the company now *has* received at least one request. There is no set wording or appearance for a canary; it can appear in many different forms. One example of an active warrant canary is provided by the Medium site (https://blog.medium.com/medium-s-2015-transparency-report-5c6205c48afe) in its annual Transparency Report, which most recently states that "as of December 31, 2015, we received no National Security Letters or FISC orders." If that were ever to change, then the following year's Transparency Report would presumably omit that statement altogether.

The legality and utility of warrant canaries have been debated within the online privacy community. In 2015, the Electronic Frontier Foundation (EFF) launched an initiative, Canary Watch (https://canarywatch.org), to list and monitor warrant canaries across the web. The EFF discontinued its project in 2016, observing that canaries in general give watchers "interesting, but not definitive information" about a site's encounter with information requests (Quintin, 2016). The very nature of a warrant canary means that a change in its presence and appearance can only lead to speculation, not concrete information, about what caused the alteration—whether it was a true "hit" or just a false alarm. Nonetheless, you may want to consider adding one to your library's website. Canaries are imperfect tools but one of the few ways that information providers have of combating threats to their own transparency. Libraries are natural allies to organizations like the EFF that are working to protect individual privacy online. And implementing a warrant canary couldn't be simpler:

1. If you haven't done so already, create a page on your library website with information about privacy policies and the protection that your library offers its patrons.
2. In a section by itself, add your warrant canary. It can be a very brief statement, akin to the text Medium uses. Be sure to include a date.
3. Keep the date current. If you don't want to update it manually (or you're afraid you'll forget), a little bit of JavaScript can be used to increment it on, say, a monthly basis. But it's important to update it—otherwise the canary will appear to be invalid.
4. If the library ever does receive a secretive data request, then the canary becomes invalid. You can handle this by simply removing the canary statement from the page altogether. If you want to let visitors know that there *was* a valid canary at one point, though, you'll have to leave some trace of it. One option is to let the date fall behind. You can also choose to alter the text to say that you *have* received some requests. Be aware, though, that U.S. law does not allow providers to state exactly how many requests they have received, but only a range in blocks of 250; for example, 0–249, 250–499, 500–749, and so forth.

Hosting Your Own Cloud Services

If you're wary of entrusting sensitive library data to a third-party cloud storage service, one alternative to consider is hosting your own cloud storage solution. Despite the hazy, far-away connotations of the word "cloud," there's no requirement that your stored data be hosted at a distance. In fact, cloud storage can be more accurately thought of as *server-based* storage. And a server can be located anywhere from the opposite side of the world to your own office. Furthermore, unlike certain other do-it-yourself solutions (see the warnings against building your own library apps in the previous chapter), hosting your own cloud storage is a fairly safe and straightforward process. There are options available for "cloudifying" your own server hardware or for acquiring a complete hardware and software package. Choices abound for hardware in particular, as storage manufacturers have sensed a growing market. There are other advantages too. If you are working with especially large files or large numbers of files (e.g., high-definition video or a collection of raw camera images), then using your own cloud hardware can be considerably cheaper, gigabyte for gigabyte, than subscribing to a commercial service—to say nothing of the bandwidth costs you'll save if you're only moving files around your local network! Personal cloud storage is also easier to back up and to expand if you need more space later on. On the downside, you're on the hook for keeping your data safe from accidents; without the redundant servers and storage of a commercial provider, you have to be careful to maintain your own backups.

Working with Your Own Hardware

If you already have a spare server lying around (or yes, even an old desktop computer can work in a pinch, but *please* don't push it beyond its means), then you've already got the hardware for your own cloud system. All you need is appropriate software to tell it how to be a cloud. One of the most popular packages for doing so is ownCloud (https://owncloud.org). OwnCloud is an open-source package of server software intended not only to enable cloud storage wherever you install it, but also to create a whole ecosystem of useful cloud apps. At a basic level, it offers file storing, viewing, sharing, versioning, and syncing across devices (there are client apps for both desktop/laptop computers and mobile devices). Once you start browsing ownCloud's catalog of apps, however, many more possibilities open up. There are apps for creating photo galleries, editing text documents, storing calendar data, syncing passwords or bookmarks, streaming media, taking notes, and much more. Several online resources detail plans for creating an ownCloud-based ebook management service using the open-source Calibre (https://calibre-ebook.com) to manage the actual books and metadata. There's even an ebook reader app available for the platform.

Unfortunately, the ownCloud platform has become a little complicated recently. In 2016, in a surprise move, one of the original creators of ownCloud abruptly left the organization, made a fork of the code, and announced the creation of an alternative project called Nextcloud (https://nextcloud.com). This was a highly controversial move, with significant consequences for the business side of ownCloud—and, perhaps, for the future health of the entire project. Once the dust settled, though, users were left with a choice of two fairly similar and fully operational projects (although the similarities will probably fade over time as their codebases diverge). You can, therefore, choose to install either ownCloud or Nextcloud and make a cogent argument defending your choice. If you're making a bet on the future, though, Nextcloud might be the better choice; many of the core developers of ownCloud followed their founder to Nextcloud, and so far the Nextcloud development cycle seems to be the more vigorous and relevant to users.

Both ownCloud and Nextcloud are offered and installed as packaged directories of PHP files intended to be placed within the documents directory of a web server like Apache and configured to work with a database. You'll need some basic knowledge of web administration to get things up and running (namely, an understanding of how to configure a basic LAMP—Linux, Apache, MySQL, and PHP—or LAMP-like technology stack). If you don't have that knowledge, you may want to consider using Nextcloud on a hosted server. There are a number of web hosts that will take care of the installation and support of a Nextcloud system for you (see the Nextcloud website for details). This simplifies things considerably, although using a third-party provider and server for your personal cloud does somewhat invalidate the point of using your own cloud in the first place!

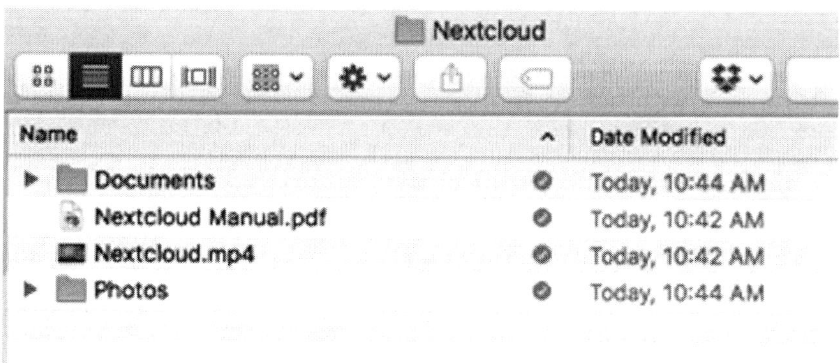

Figure 8.3. The default Nextcloud folder as it appears on a Mac. Screenshot of Nextcloud's Nextcloud app.

Once you have Nextcloud installed, you've got the server component of your cloud in place. What you'll probably need next are some clients for your devices—the desktops, laptops, or mobile devices that you want to connect to your cloud. It's the same basic procedure that you'd use to set up a service like Dropbox. Clients can be downloaded either from the Nextcloud website or through the appropriate app store for your mobile devices. The only tricky part is telling your client where to find your server; you will have to have an accessible URL set up for external connections (e.g., littlelibrary.edu/owncloud). Once you install a desktop client, you should see a special folder appear in your user directory, akin to the Dropbox folder that's installed if you use that service. If you open it, you'll see something like what appears in figure 8.3.

This folder looks and behaves much like a Dropbox folder too. It even has little checkmark icons that indicate the sync status of each file, à la Dropbox! More importantly, it provides the same synchronization behavior. Any file that you drop into your client Nextcloud folder will be quickly synced with your back-end server and any other clients you've installed on other devices. If you log in to the web interface on your Nextcloud server, you'll again see a very familiar environment (see figure 8.4). From this interface, you can tag files, create links to share them with others, access different versions of files, recover recently deleted files, and engage with different Nextcloud apps that you install (like the ebook reader). There's just something freshly magical about seeing familiar cloud services all working in your own little cloud, insulated from the outside world!

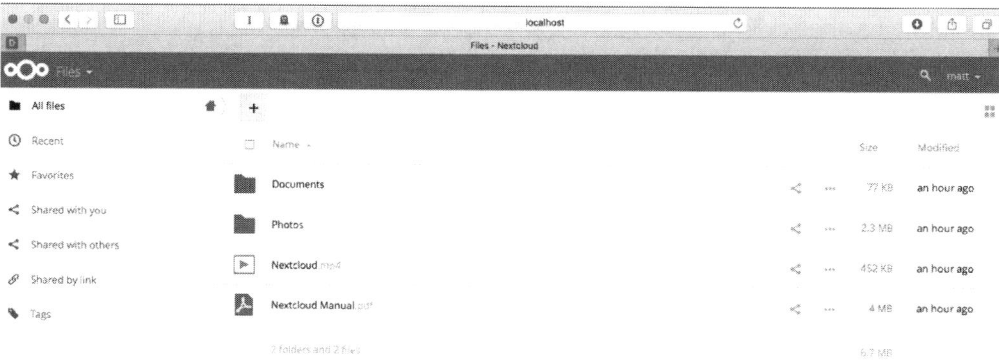

Figure 8.4. The Nextcloud web interface. Screenshot of Nextcloud's website.

Working with Cloud Hardware

As convenient and enjoyable as ownCloud or Nextcloud is to use if your circumstances and resources permit, it does come with some pitfalls—namely, having to fiddle with the finicky details of server administration, network setup, and PHP app installation. If you don't want those potential headaches and don't care to use a third-party provider to take care of your cloud for you, then consider purchasing some dedicated cloud hardware instead.

Cloud hardware is really just a selection of network-attached storage (NAS) devices. And in essence, an NAS device is just a hard drive or flash drive that you hook up to your network with its own on-board software that permits it to function as an independent device. An NAS device can communicate with other devices on the same network or even clients from across the Internet. In terms of hardware and software features, they run the gamut from single drives that function only as file storage units all the way up to sophisticated, hot-swappable, multi-drive bays that offer antivirus software, firewalling and encryption, mail and communication software, and even multimedia management and presentation apps. In theory, getting started is as simple as connecting your hardware to your network—usually directly to your router or hub—and following the setup instructions to make sure that the NAS is accessible from your local network and beyond. The exact procedure will vary with each device, however.

Many companies now produce NAS devices appropriate for personal cloud systems. Western Digital, Seagate, LaCie—big drive manufacturers all—offer entry-level cloud solutions like the My Cloud (http://mycloud.com), CloudBox (www.lacie.com/products/network-storage/cloudbox), and Seagate Central (www.seagate.com/external-hard-drives/home-entertainment/media-sharing-devices/seagate-central). A popular choice for more high-end solutions is a drive setup from Synology, whose high-end hardware and comprehensive NAS software apps make for a reliable and user-friendly (albeit pricey) package that probably hits the sweet spot for an advanced personal cloud setup.

Physical Devices and the Cloud

Multifactor Authentication

Any time you place your personal data in the hands of a third party, which most people do every day when they're online, you want to have a high degree of confidence that your information will be reasonably secure. Most such systems require you to create an account that you can use to connect to them via an app or a website. Commonly you simply have to enter a username and password.

These days, however, a simple username and password system and a "Forgot your password?" link beneath the login box simply don't cut it when you're considering security. Malicious hackers have long since figured out how to socially engineer ways to reset your password and take control of your account, sometimes by calling a customer service representative at the cloud provider and impersonating you by using private information gleaned from social media or other sources to authorize the changes to your account. Now, more and more service providers are turning to multifactor authentication (MFA) to try to prevent this type of account hijacking. MFA simply means that you have to prove your identity more than once before a site or service will give you access to your account. The exact nature of this proof varies, but the most common scenario is a traditional password-based login on a website combined with a second authentication technique—usually a text message or phone call sent to a mobile device that you control (thus the term "two-factor authentication" is a little more common than the acronym "MFA"). The assumption is that even if a malicious hacker is able to crack your login credentials for a particular site, he or she won't be able to do anything with that information without physical access to your phone or tablet. Of course, if someone does gain access to the same device that you're using for authentication, MFA's protection is nullified—especially if you use password autofills in your web browser. That's one reason why it's important to secure your mobile devices with a passcode.

Most libraries probably don't have a need to protect their public-facing systems and sites with MFA. If, though, your library is affiliated with a larger entity (like a college or university), then you might have to interact with it in order to access data or functionality belonging to that organization. For example, if you use a VPN to connect to your university's campus network, then MFA might appear as a login option—or a requirement. Although it is a minor inconvenience to have to wait for an SMS message and type it in on your computer every time you want to log in, it's a small price to pay for a big increase in security and peace of mind. Many major cloud service providers are adopting MFA, so you should consider activating it wherever it's offered. You can check whether it's available on a particular site at the Two Factor Auth website (https://twofactorauth.org).

Always-On Assistants

A new but rapidly expanding branch of consumer technology today is the use of voice-activated computer assistants. Computer speech recognition, which has existed as a field of research and development for decades, has finally started to come into its own over the past few years as the convergence of improved microphones, sophisticated software algorithms, and raw processing power has allowed machines to begin interpreting *natural* speech in useful ways (as opposed to restricting users to the careful enunciation of a precise and limited vocabulary). Apple popularized the new wave of speech recognition technology with its Siri voice assistant, but there's a big push now to market assistants in the form of dedicated hardware devices. Chief among these are Amazon's family of Echo devices, which act as a portal to an assistant called Alexa, and the Google Home smart speaker, which interfaces with the unimaginatively named Google Assistant. Although every smart, voice-controlled assistant is still incredibly stupid in its own idiosyncratic ways, these devices can be surprisingly useful if you happen to ask them things they understand. And they're fun! It's easy to imagine some of these new hardware items finding their way into libraries as components of creative projects or innovation labs. One middle school library is already using an Amazon Echo as a rudimentary substitute reference librarian when the human librarian is unavailable (Scardilli, 2015)!

There is a catch to using these technologies, though. In order to enable the magic of allowing you to speak into the air and immediately receive an answer from an invisible, omniscient genie, tools like the Amazon Echo and Google Home often default to "always-on listening." Everything you say in their presence is picked up by their speakers and run through their local processors. In theory, nothing will be done with that audio until you speak the correct trigger phrase: "Alexa" or "OK, Google" or "Hey, Siri" (yes, the newest generations of iPhones are also constantly listening to you by default). Once you do, the next couple of sentences you speak are carefully picked apart, analyzed, and in many cases sent out as queries to cloud services. For some people, this is an uncomfortable thought. The concept of a computer always listening to what you're saying, and possibly transmitting it back to headquarters, is a bridge too far for them. As always, though, it boils down to a question of convenience versus privacy. Study the implications of a particular company's privacy policies surrounding its always-on assistant: what data the assistant transmits to the company servers; how that data is protected and used; and if the data's retained, for how long. If your library policy is to warn users when their search queries on your website are being sent to an outside service like Google Analytics, shouldn't you also post a sign with a similar warning in an area where you have a Google Home or Amazon Echo device set up?

Consider too that there may be legal implications to using voice assistants like the Echo or Siri. At least one legal scholar, Joel Reidenberg, suggests that the very use of an always-listening assistant that communicates with a back-end cloud service waives your legal right to privacy (Weise, 2016). And the end of 2016 saw a first-of-its-kind warrant issued in Arkansas requiring Amazon to turn over audio data from a personal Echo device that may have "witnessed" a murder (Steele, 2016). The Internet of Things (IoT) is a new frontier in personal technology that's akin to the Wild West in its danger and insecurity—at least from a privacy perspective. But that's beyond the scope of this book.

Key Points

Cloud computing has become ubiquitous. However, it's important to evaluate your use of each cloud service you connect to—how your data is being kept secure, safe, and private. Remember these points as you work with cloud services:

- Thanks to the growth of interconnected systems and online subscription services, libraries may be using a large number of cloud services (e.g., Google Analytics) without realizing it or thinking through the implications.
- If you are storing sensitive or personal data in the cloud, don't trust the security of unencrypted systems. Instead, use a privacy-focused service like SpiderOak or a local encryption tool like Boxcryptor.
- Even cloud service providers with the best of intentions may be vulnerable to legal requests for their customer's data. You can't really avoid this possibility, but you can shop around for providers that will fight for their users' rights. Further, warrant canaries can alert your users if you've been issued with a gag order pertaining to a government request for data.
- If you don't want to deal with third-party services, it's possible to host your own cloud storage and apps. This can be done by adding special software to an existing server (e.g., Nextcloud) or by purchasing and installing a network-attached storage device like a Synology drive bay.
- If possible, use multifactor authentication to sign in to the cloud services you use. This will reduce the risk of an unscrupulous hacker gaining access to your data.
- Always-on voice assistants are growing in popularity, yet they bring with them significant, unfamiliar security concerns.

This chapter concludes our tour of security and privacy at various tiers of networked tech. It started way back in chapter 3 at the network level then gradually narrowed in focus from public computers to web browsers to mobile devices to individual apps before expanding once more to the cloud level. Hopefully, you have some idea now of the vulnerabilities and protections that exist at each of these levels. In the next chapter, you'll learn all about a general-purpose, tough-as-nails privacy technology that you can deploy in your library, the Tor system, along with strategies for outreach and some thoughts about the future of privacy.

References

Broas, Timothy, and Matthew Saxon. 2013. "E-Discovery in the Cloud: Who Can Get Your Data?" Law360. May 9. www.law360.com/articles/439600/e-discovery-in-the-cloud-who-can-get-your-data.

Evans, Will. 2016. "Uber Said It Protects You from Spying. Security Sources Say Otherwise." Reveal. December 12. www.revealnews.org/article/uber-said-it-protects-you-from-spying-security-sources-say-otherwise.

Gilbert, Françoise. 2013. "What Rules Regulate Government Access to Data Held by US Cloud Service Providers." Cloud Security Alliance. https://cloudsecurityalliance.org/wp-content/uploads/2013/02/CLIC-Govt-access-to-data-20130221.pdf.

Hellman, Eric. 2016. "How to Check If Your Library Is Leaking Catalog Searches to Amazon." Hellman Blog. December 22. https://go-to-hellman.blogspot.co.uk/2016/12/how-to-check-if-your-library-is-leaking.html.

Quintin, Cooper. 2016. "Canary Watch—One Year Later." Electronic Frontier Foundation. May 25. www.eff.org/deeplinks/2016/05/canary-watch-one-year-later.

Scardilli, Brandi. 2015. "Alexa and Siri at the Library: How Librarians Are Tapping Into the Internet of Things." Information Today. September 1. http://newsbreaks.infotoday.com/NewsBreaks/Alexa-and-Siri-at-the-Library-How-Librarians-Are-Tapping-Into-the-Internet-of-Things-106059.asp.

Steele, Billy. 2016. "Police Seek Amazon Echo Data in Murder Case (Updated)." Engadget. December 27. www.engadget.com/2016/12/27/amazon-echo-audio-data-murder-case.

Weise, Elizabeth. 2016. "Hey, Siri and Alexa: Let's Talk Privacy Practices." *USA Today*. March 2. www.usatoday.com/story/tech/news/2016/03/02/voice-privacy-computers-listening-rsa-echo-siri-hey-google-cortana/81134864.

CHAPTER 9

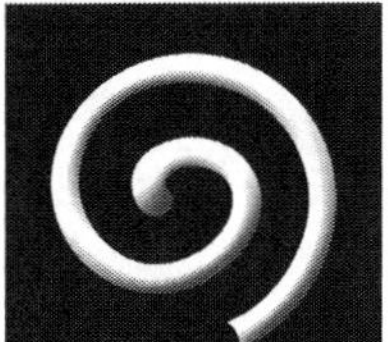

Tor, Privacy Outreach, and the Future of Privacy

IN THIS CHAPTER

- ▷ Understanding the Tor network
- ▷ Installing and using the Tor Browser and Tor service
- ▷ Creating a Tor workstation for the library
- ▷ Configuring and running a Tor relay
- ▷ Learning about Tor on other platforms
- ▷ Running a privacy outreach program
- ▷ Predicting the future of privacy protection

Libraries and Advocacy

MOST OF THE CONTENT OF THIS BOOK HAS FOCUSED on protecting the private data of library users from access or misuse by third parties that have no business accessing or misusing it, be they criminal hackers or government agencies. "Data" is used in a broad sense, meaning not only electronic records or identity information but also browsing history, communication (text, voice, or video), and more. The view taken has largely been one of this personal data as a passive thing—a treasure to be defended by those it is entrusted to (e.g., libraries) and a target to be captured by those seeking to take it for themselves. This chapter, however, explores the library's role in protecting user *activity*.

Libraries have a more than passing interest in protecting free speech and expression. Historically, they have been regarded as treasuries of human knowledge and understanding, usually with the corollary that anything that limits the transmission of that knowledge or access to it, such as censorship, is anathema. Individuals, in order to be able to contribute to these treasuries of knowledge, must be able to express their thoughts and opinions freely and openly, regardless of how unpopular their ideas might be, without fear of reprisal from government or society. Libraries understand that the existence of a free society is dependent upon the protection of these principles, and librarians and library workers have (usually) defended them with passion. And in a time when fear, uncertainty, and doubt about society and government are on the rise, the defense of free expression of thought and open discourse may be more important than ever.

The role of libraries in this defense may be to stretch their definition of "user" or "patron" to encompass a much larger community than their traditional constituency. Modern technology offers a potentially worldwide stage to those who have something to say—but many who wish to say something to the world must do so at the risk of ridicule, assault, imprisonment, or even death. And many such people must speak out in places where they not only face such threats but must also depend on modern communication technology to get their message out to the world. If your passion for privacy protection extends beyond your library's official user base—if you want to take the fight for privacy to the next level—then it's time to start thinking about what your library can do to protect privacy for *everyone*. In this chapter, you'll learn about an important modern tool for doing just that: the Tor system, which can help both your local users and others scattered around the world. Then you'll consider how to share everything you've learned about privacy protection with your users in workshops or outreach programs.

The Tor System

What Is Tor?

For the privacy-conscious, there is a basic problem with Internet communication traffic. This issue can be referred to as the "envelope problem." Consider what happens when you send a physical letter through the postal system: you write out the contents of your message on a piece of paper, fold it, and seal it inside an opaque envelope. Then, on the front of the envelope, you write out your own name and address (the return address) and the name and address of the intended recipient. Then you drop it into a mailbox and let someone else deal with the problem of picking it up, figuring out where to send it, and actually conveying it through the mail network until it reaches its destination. In theory, your message remains private for as long as it's in transit (provided that your envelope isn't torn or tampered with), and only your recipient will ever read it. On the other hand, anyone handling the mail along the way can easily determine where the message came from and where it's going.

This real-world analogy maps very neatly onto the domain of Internet communication—assuming that you've heeded the advice of this book and are carefully using encrypted SSL/HTTPS connections wherever possible. Encryption acts as a sealed envelope around your message (which, of course, could be not only an actual text message but also a voice recording, video, file upload, website request, password reset, or just about anything else), protecting it from prying eyes as it's relayed from server to server across the network. But anyone monitoring those servers along the route your message takes can easily see who sent it and who will receive it. The content of your communication may remain private, but the *fact* of your communication, with an identifiable party, may not.

The envelope problem is easy to explain but very difficult to solve in a reliable way. The Internet, after all, is premised on the concept of addressability. Not only is your message sent out across the network with an identifiable address and return address (in the form of IP addresses)—it's even broken down into dozens or hundreds of smaller packets of data for transmission, and each of those packets has its own copy of your addresses! Obfuscating or withholding part of the address on a packet renders it useless: your message simply won't get where it's going.

Previous chapters of this book have discussed certain technologies and techniques that can be used to partly conceal your sending location. One of the more common ways of doing this is to use a proxy. By its very nature, a proxy serves as a remote, apparent point of origin for all your network traffic. Thus, *once your messages get past the proxy*, they will appear to have originated from that proxy, not from your personal IP address. But this isn't really a very good solution if you're looking for real anonymity. For one thing, you're not fooling anyone; most of the proxies that you'll end up using are known to the world. Someone with access to your Internet service provider (ISP), then, could see that you were using a proxy. There's nothing wrong with proxying your communications in most cases. In theory, though, someone who was able to monitor both your outgoing traffic (through your ISP) and the outgoing traffic of your proxy service could compare the timing of the messages and link you to the sites or servers you're talking to. The proxy, then, becomes a single point of failure. Your limited anonymity depends entirely upon the proxy owner's trustworthiness and ability to fend off legal or illegal attempts to monitor your traffic. Furthermore, governments desirous of restricting their citizens' free access to the Internet can target and block known proxies, making it more difficult for dissidents or activists—or indeed anyone—to circumvent censorship. Ultimately, relying on a proxy to conceal your online activities is a bad choice when the stakes are high.

A more sophisticated solution to the envelope problem originated in the 1990s with the concept of "onion routing." Again, the concept involved is very simple, and the name is evocative. Onion routing proposes the following: rather than sealing your message inside a single envelope with the source and destination visible to the world, wrap it within several layers of envelopes, nested like a set of matryoshka dolls (or, indeed, like an onion), each of which bears on its outside only the address of the next node in the network to which it should be transmitted. This principle is illustrated in figure 9.1. Each layer is encrypted separately and can only be decrypted by the network node for which it's intended. Only the first node in the network knows where the message originated (i.e., your IP address), and only the last node in the network knows where the message is going (the intended destination). Thus, by ensuring that a message passes through at least three nodes—i.e., that it is wrapped in three layers of the onion—the user of such a system can be reasonably assured that his or her identity as the sender of that message can't be associated with the recipient of the message because the middle node is ignorant of both the message's point of origin and its ultimate destination. That user can't be *perfectly* assured of anonymity—just assume that there's no such thing as perfect anonymity online—because it's still theoretically possible to make inferences about a particular user's online activities if a snooper is able to monitor the traffic at both the source and the destination. That's pretty unlikely in most cases, though.

The most widespread practical implementation of the onion routing concept is a system called Tor (originally an acronym for "The Onion Router'). The term "Tor" can be used to refer to several related concepts, but it's most instructive to think of it as a network. The Tor network, first established in 2003, today consists of thousands of servers (aka relays or nodes) used by millions of individuals on a daily basis. The software that makes the Tor network possible is an open-source system that is maintained by the nonprofit Tor Project

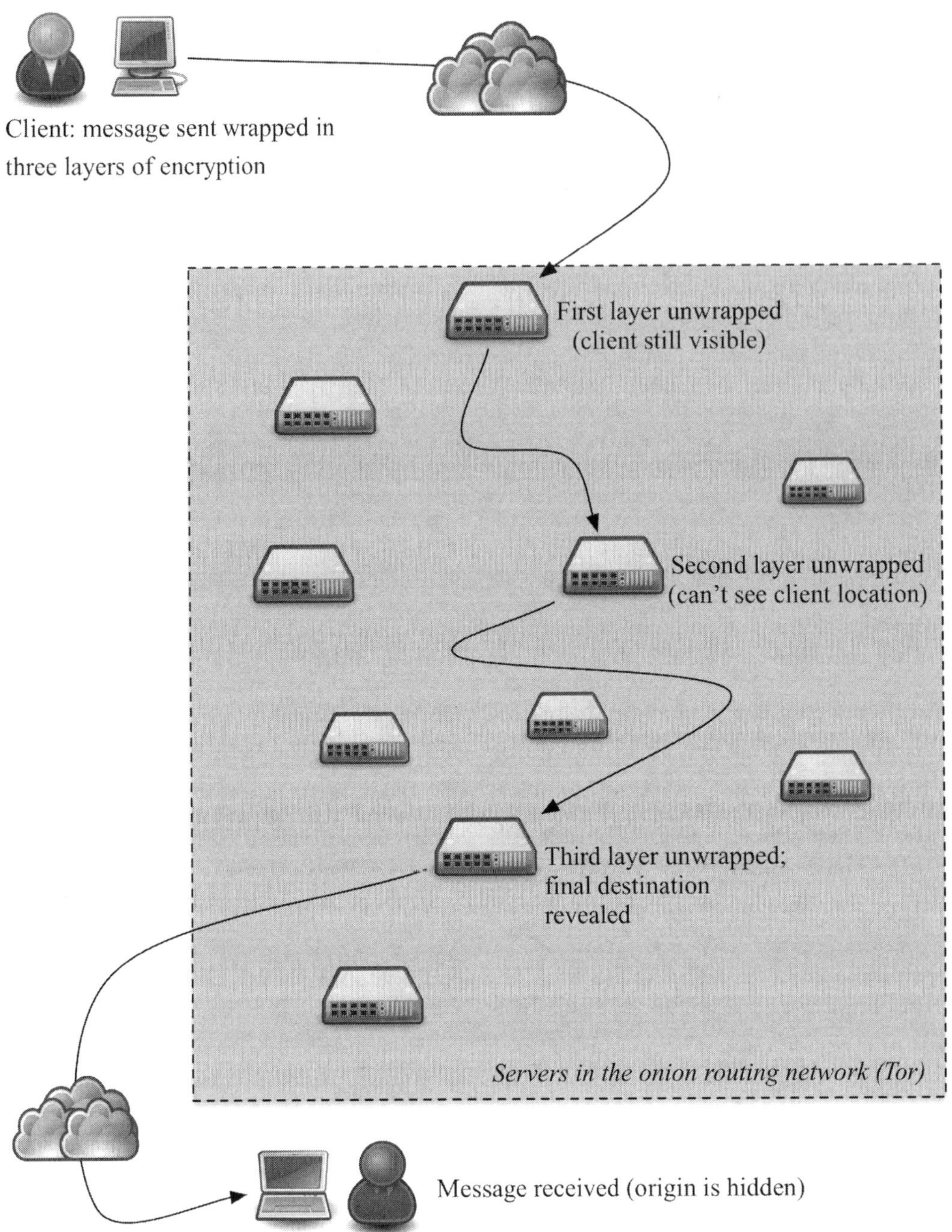

Figure 9.1. Sending a message through a network using "onion routing."

(https://torproject.org). The individual servers that compose the network are maintained by volunteers, often individuals operating a single node. Thus the system is decentralized, and decentralization usually makes a network robust. This stands in contrast to proxies, which provide a single point of failure. Take a proxy server offline and it becomes impossible to proxy your network traffic. Take a Tor node relay offline, or even a few dozen relays, and not much happens—traffic is merely rerouted through different relays.

In theory, any piece of software that communicates over the Internet (e.g., your favorite messaging app) can be adapted to use Tor. In practice, though, ensuring that you haven't accidentally left any security holes in your implementation of the protocol can be a tricky business. For that reason, the developers behind the Tor Project itself strongly recommend that you make use of Tor by means of a special web browser: the Tor Browser. The Tor Browser is actually a modified version of Firefox with a few extra security features built in. Besides using the Tor network to send and receive data, the browser comes prepackaged with security-conscious plugins such as HTTPS Everywhere (https://addons.mozilla.org/en-US/firefox/addon/https-everywhere) and NoScript (https://addons.mozilla.org/en-US/firefox/addon/noscript). The inclusion of these tools points to potential flaws—not flaws in the implementation of Tor itself, but flaws in how people use it. HTTPS Everywhere forces the browser to use the secure HTTPS protocol whenever possible. This is important to do when using the Tor Browser because Tor itself does nothing to hide the contents of your message once it exits the network; the final Tor relay that handles your data will be able to read it if you're not using HTTPS. NoScript, as its name implies, stops JavaScript from executing on the webpages you visit. Recall that hidden scripts are a favorite device of advertisers and tracking systems to discover all sorts of information about you and your online activities. Allowing JavaScript to run defeats the whole point of using Tor. For the same reason, it's important that you do not use any plugins when running the Tor Browser, particularly the notoriously buggy Adobe Flash. You'll also notice that the browser's search engine defaults to the privacy-friendly DuckDuckGo.

Once you're comfortable using the Tor Browser and want to try protecting more of your Internet communications with Tor, you may want to consider installing Tor as a system service—a program that runs in the background on your computer, often continuously—that can be used to route *all* of your Internet traffic through the Tor network. For more information about doing this, see the instructions for setting up Tor as a service later in this chapter.

Getting Started with Tor

The makers of the Tor Browser have conveniently packaged it to be downloaded and installed on various operating systems just as other standard apps are. Most of the procedure to get up and running with the browser should therefore seem very familiar.

1. Download the appropriate installer from the Tor downloads page (www.torproject.org/download/).
2. When the download is complete, double-click the installer and follow the usual procedure for your platform to install and launch the browser.
3. The first time you launch the browser, you will be presented with a network settings pane and asked whether you want to connect to Tor directly or via a bridge or proxy. As the instructions suggest, a direct connection will be the right answer in most cases. Click the Connect button.
4. You should see a small dialog box with a progress bar and the instruction "Please wait while we establish a connection to the Tor network." Although the network settings only appear the first time you use the Tor Browser, you will see this connection dialog each time you launch the app.
5. If all goes well, you should see a browser window showing a welcome message and the pale-green gradient of the Tor Browser's landing page (see figure 9.2). It's tempting to just start typing URLs into the address bar and get moving. But you're not done yet!
6. Before browsing anywhere with Tor, it's important to check to see whether your system is really secure. First, click the "Test Tor Network Settings" link. On the

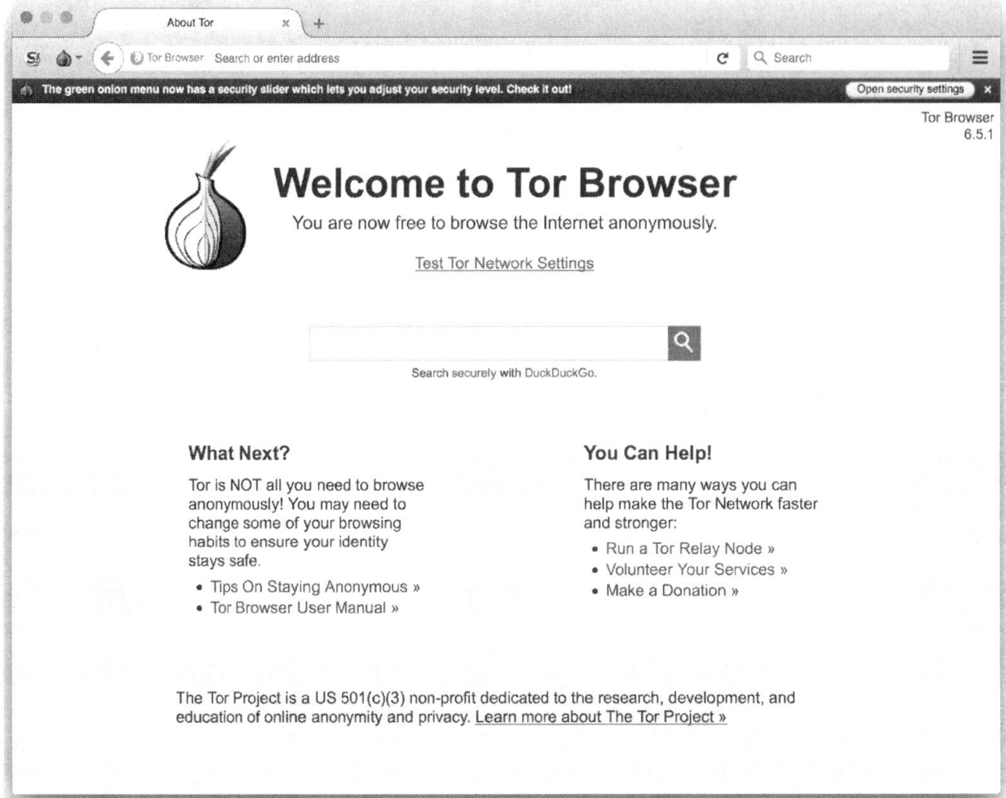

Figure 9.2. Home page of the Tor browser. Screenshot of the Tor Project's Tor browser.

next page, you should again see a congratulatory message, this time reassuring you that your browser "is configured to use Tor." You should also see your *apparent* IP address. This should not be the same as your actual IP address! The address listed on this page is where the world perceives you to be. In fact, it's the IP address of the last Tor node in the chain, the one right before you're connected to your destination website (these final nodes are designated "exit nodes"). It can be fun to search this address on an IP lookup service and see where in the world your exit node is located; it can easily be on the other side of the planet from you.

7. Go back to the home page. Look for a little *S* icon in the left corner of the browser toolbar. This is the NoScript plugin interface. By default, it doesn't block any scripts, but you definitely want it to do so. Mouse over the icon to make a menu appear, and select Forbid Scripts Globally. (If you want, you can get much more sophisticated about blocking particular scripts or sites by looking through the Options further down the menu. A global block, though, is much easier to manage.)
8. Finally, find the little onion icon next to the NoScript icon. Click on it and choose Security Settings... from the menu that appears. The security settings that appear are reduced to sets of rules marked Low (the default), Medium, and High. Selecting Medium or High brings up information explaining what additional settings are in effect at those levels—and what the tradeoffs are between security and convenience. For now, you can keep it on Low. Bear in mind, though, that the higher settings do exist if you need them.

At this point, you should be ready to start exploring the Internet with Tor! This will probably not be as exciting as it sounds. Go ahead, give it a try: go to a few of your favorite sites and see how it works. You'll most likely find the browsing experience familiar (it is essentially Firefox, after all) except somewhat slower than usual and more inconvenient due to your indiscriminate banning of JavaScript, which is used *everywhere* these days. (There's not much that you can do about the speed issue in the short term; its a natural consequence of routing all of your network traffic through a minimum of three random relays that may be somewhat bandwidth-constrained. In the long run, though, the developers of the Tor Project hope that more volunteers will add more nodes to the network, reducing the load on each individual server and speeding up the transfer of data.) But you can take solace in the knowledge that your browsing is anonymous—if you're careful!

Whenever you fire up the Tor Browser, take a moment to read the message that appears on the home page. If the browser is out of date, it will tell you so. Do not ignore this warning! The browser is frequently updated with various changes, many of which are security-related. If you use an older version containing known security holes, you compromise the anonymity that Tor gives you.

The .Onion Domain

As you've seen, you can use the Tor Browser to browse the web in more or less the same fashion as if you were using a standard web browser. Apart from the slower performance, navigating the Tor network is a transparent operation for end users. If you type https://loc.gov, you will get to the Library of Congress. However, the Tor Browser is also capable of interpreting a very different sort of URL.

Try entering the following into the address bar in your Tor Browser: https://3g2up l4pq6kufc4m.onion. If all goes well, you should see the DuckDuckGo search page. Now try entering the same thing into a standard web browser—Safari or Firefox, say. All you'll get is an error message. What's going on? The .onion at the end of the URL is not a standard top-level domain like .com or .edu; instead, it alerts the Tor Browser to the fact that this is a special type of URL that points to a website that is part of the dark web. The dark web is a portion of the Internet (or, more properly, of the web) that is not accessible by normal means or through standard browsers. The apparently random string of letters and numbers that creates the URL itself is mathematically derived from the site's signature. Since it uses Tor, the dark web site itself can remain as anonymous as its users if it chooses to. DuckDuckGo's main presence is on the open web, of course (https://duckduckgo.com), but the company also maintains an onion site at the aforementioned address.

As you might imagine, anonymous websites are attractive to all kinds of people with all kinds of motivations—some good, some not so good. In fact, the dark web can be a very rough neighborhood. Tread carefully. Although it serves as a forum for many legitimate and laudable activities, such as political activism, it is also populated by sites and people engaged in various unsavory and downright illegal activities (such as the infamous Silk Road drug market).

Using Tor in Libraries

For many privacy-conscious Internet users today, a method of becoming wholly anonymous when browsing the web or sending messages is the Holy Grail. You should understand that

Tor does not achieve that lofty standard—there are still weaknesses in its implementation that can be exploited, and you can be sure that government agencies like the NSA are working hard to exploit them—but still, it does a really good job of protecting your privacy. And that fact makes it an immensely useful tool in all sorts of situations where privacy may be not just desirable but essential. As a library employee desirous of protecting your users' privacy, your brain is probably already firing with ideas and possibilities. The Tor Project itself suggests that some of the uses of the network include circumventing censorship, allowing "socially sensitive communication" for victims of abuse or illness, talking to "whistleblowers and dissidents," "maintaining civil liberties online," and helping workers in non-government organizations (NGOs) operating in foreign countries access their organization's website without alerting local governments to the fact that they're working for the groups (see www.torproject.org/about/overview.html.en). If your library is affiliated with a school or college, another scenario might be students or staff members who want to report inappropriate behavior by a teacher or professor. Although your institution should already provide means for them to do so anonymously, not everyone trusts an online form just because it *says* there's no personally identifying information in a submission. A Tor session might put those reporters more at ease. And what about local immigrants who want to talk to their families left behind but, because of their country of origin, incur unwanted attention from the government when they try to do so?

Creating a Dedicated Tor Workstation

Providing one or more specially configured Tor workstations in your public computing area might be a way to put some of those ideas into action. By providing a dedicated public computer for using Tor, you can control the software configuration and keep users from doing other things that might negate the anonymizing effects of the Tor browser (e.g., signing into GMail using both Tor and a regular browser at the same time). Be sure to provide clear instructions explaining what Tor is, what it does and does not do to protect the user, and how to use it.

If you want to take this concept a step further, you can create a dedicated workstation on which *all* network traffic is routed through Tor—not just when using the custom Tor Browser but when using other browsers as well as email clients, messaging apps, etc. To do so, you'll need to install Tor as a service—a program that can run in the background on the computer, often full-time—and then configure the computer's network settings to use the connection to Tor instead of the "clear" Internet. This is a more advanced set of instructions than most in this book. If you're not comfortable poking around on the command line or installing service-level software on your machine, consult your nearest systems administrator for help. (As an alternative, consider installing the Tails operating system—described in a later section of this chapter.)

1. Install the Tor service on your computer or server. The procedure for doing this will vary depending on your platform and operating system. On the Mac, which will be used as an example here, the most straightforward approach is to use the Homebrew package manager (https://brew.sh). If you have Homebrew installed, simply open a Terminal window and enter "brew install tor." It may take a few minutes for the package manager to download, install, and configure the Tor service.
2. Assuming there are no problems with the installation, you can start running Tor by typing "tor." You should see some status messages appear as Tor does some

self-configuration and attempts to open a Tor circuit. If successful, somewhere near the bottom of the text you should see a message akin to "[notice] Tor has successfully opened a circuit. Looks like client functionality is working." Note that although the Tor service is up and running, you are not routing any of your usual network traffic (web browsing, email, etc.) through it.

3. Read through the status messages until you find one that says something akin to "Opening Socks listener on 127.0.0.1:9050." The number after the colon—9050 in this case—is the port on which Tor is listening. You'll need that number in a bit.
4. Now that Tor is available, you'll have to tell the computer to use it for its network connections instead of connecting through the outside world in the usual way. Again, instructions for doing this will vary with the platform and operating system. Continuing with the Mac example, the best way to go about this is to create a new network location to separate your Tor sessions from your default network connection:
   a. Go to System Preferences > Network. A list of locations is shown in a drop-down menu at the top of the Network pane. Click the list, choose Edit Locations..., and click the plus sign to add a new location.
   b. Give the location a name (e.g., "Tor") and click the Done button. This brings you back to the main Network pane, now with your new Tor location selected. (At this point, all the network settings on your computer are still the same as they were before; you've only given them a new name.)
   c. In the left-hand list of network connections, pick the ones your computer is using to connect to the Internet (these are most likely Wi-Fi and/or Ethernet). For each one, highlight the connection, then click the Advanced... button.
   d. In the Advanced pane that appears, click the Proxies tab. Then, in the list of protocols on the left, check the SOCKS Proxy box. Finally, under "SOCKS Proxy Server," enter "localhost" in the large text box and "9050" (or whatever port number you found in step 3) in the smaller one. This configuration is shown in figure 9.3.
   e. Click the OK button to close the advanced settings, then click Apply in the main Network window to apply your changes. Wait a minute. Then try browsing to a regular webpage using your normal browser. If that works, check to make sure that you're actually using Tor by visiting https://check.torproject.org. If you've configured things correctly, you should see "Congratulations. This browser is configured to use Tor."

The steps listed above are somewhat complex, but the principle of what you've just done is pretty simple. You installed Tor as a service on your computer that can be stopped and started at will. When the Tor service is running, it will patiently listen for any network traffic on its designated port. Next, you told the computer to send all of its network traffic to that same port. Easy! As a final experiment, switch back to your original Location in the Network settings pane (this will probably be "Automatic" unless you've changed it) and click the Apply button again. Wait a minute, then refresh the Tor confirmation page. This time, you should see the message: "Sorry. You are not using Tor." This is because the computer is now ignoring the Tor service and sending all its network traffic out through its usual channels again. Any time you want to use Tor again, just switch your network location and fire up the Tor service.

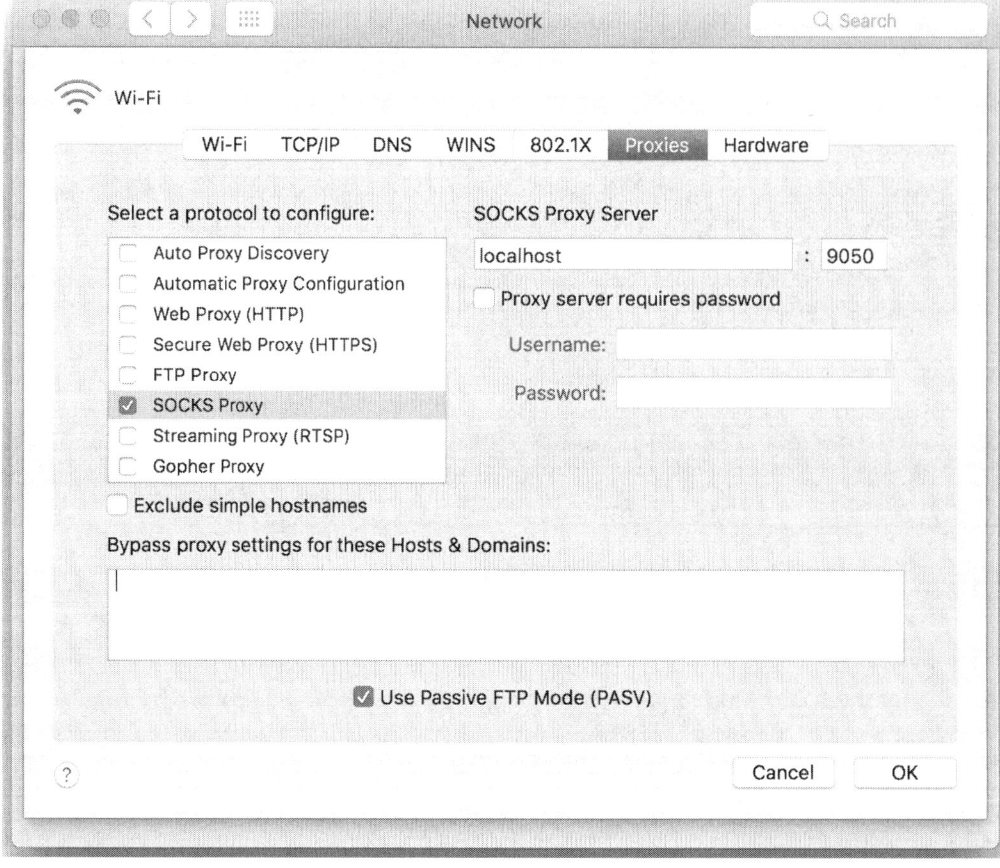

Figure 9.3. Configuring the Mac network settings to use the Tor proxy. Screenshot from Apple macOS.

Running a Tor Relay

Making Tor available to your library users can be an effective way of empowering them. Recall, though, that you can also contribute to the Tor effort in ways that will help all of its users. Usually, doing so will mean understanding a little more about Tor relays. (A relay is simply a server, but the term "relay" conveys more of its purpose. The term "node" is also used interchangeably.) A Tor relay is a server running special software configured to handle Tor transmissions. As described earlier, a message sent through the Tor network passes through a minimum of three relays before reaching its destination. Each relay is responsible for decrypting one layer of the onion wrapped around the message, figuring out what its next stop should be, and then sending the package to it. The final relay in the chain is called an "exit node."

The more relays there are, the better Tor's robustness, speed, and anonymity will be. That's why the people behind the Tor Project are eager for new volunteers to run additional relays in the network—and they make it simple to do so.

There are actually three different types of nodes used in the Tor network. The most common variety is a "middle relay" (or "internal" or "intermediate" relay) that acts as node within the internal part of the network. Unlike exit nodes, internal nodes never appear to be a source of traffic to the outside world. The third type of node, the "bridge relay," is distinguished from the other types primarily by not being openly published in Tor's master list of nodes (which is used by Tor itself to identify routes for traffic). They are functionally equivalent to other nodes, however. Bridge nodes were introduced as a way of circumventing attempts to block the Tor network. Since nodes of other types are easily identified, they can be individually blocked by an ISP or a government that wants to shut off Tor traffic. However, the availability of semi-hidden bridge nodes makes it that much more difficult to censor the network.

Because of the limited sight within the Tor system—a node is only aware of two nodes, one on either side of it, in the route being used by the client—internal nodes are pretty well protected from any scrutiny that a Tor server might otherwise be subject to. Running an intermediate relay is therefore a relatively safe choice. Tor makes it easy to get started hosting a node too (see below); only a few lines of configuration code entered into a file will get you off the ground and running.

Running an exit node, on the other hand, takes a bit more bravery—and, most likely, a great deal more negotiating with library administration and soothing of fears. The problem is that an exit node becomes a de facto "face" of Tor to the outside world. For all intents and purposes, it looks like the exit node *is* the source of the traffic using it. (This can be a particular problem with people and organizations who simply don't understand the difference between the Tor network and ordinary Internet traffic.) Unfortunately, if anyone wants to go after a Tor user for his or her activities, whether to pursue criminal activity, serve a DCMA takedown notice for alleged copyright violations, or persecute a dissident trying to speak to the world, an exit node is the likeliest target. If the system is working, after all, then both the originator of the activity and most of the Tor relays involved in the circuit are hidden behind an opaque wall; only the exit node is visible. Fortunately, the Tor Project offers a number of resources for both minimizing the risks involved and coping with any problems that may arise as a result of the traffic passing through your node. The most important of these is the involvement of the Electronic Frontier Foundation (EFF; https://eff.org). The EFF, whose motto is "Defending Your Rights in the Digital World," is a staunch supporter of the Tor system and has written a number of assistive documents, such as a legal FAQ (https://torproject.org/eff/tor-legal-faq.html.en) and a sample response letter to a DCMA takedown request (https://torproject.org/eff/tor-dmca-response.html.en). The EFF clearly believes that running a Tor relay, even an exit relay, is both altruistic and legal and that the host of a relay (e.g., your ISP) is exempt from liability for the content that passes through it. The Library Freedom Project is also urging libraries to consider hosting exit nodes and has set up a page (https://libraryfreedomproject.org/torexits) with resources to support that initiative.

There are other special considerations to running an exit node. While it's probably okay to run a middle node from your personal network and even a personal computer, that's not a very good idea for an exit node; if someone does go after your node due to some activity that runs through it, your home or library might become the focus of some very unwanted attention or harassment. The preferred approach for running an exit node is to place it on a server run by a Tor-friendly ISP and then make sure that the ISP knows exactly what you're doing with it so they won't be surprised if they receive queries about it. Some ISPs that allow Tor relays have special requirements for them such as rules that you have to respond to any abuse queries or takedown notices within a certain time frame.

With all that in mind, here are the basic steps to hosting your very own Tor relay. The only real requirement is that you are able to provide an adequately fast network connection. As of early 2017, the Tor Project was requesting a minimum bandwidth of 250 kBps in each direction. You will also have to decide whether to run a relay using the Tor software embedded in the Tor Browser or through a separate Tor service running on your server. Using the Browser's Tor is good for experimentation or occasional use. If you're going to maintain an ongoing relay, though, you'll probably want to install the separate service, as covered in the instructions above. The following directions assume that you have installed Tor as a service.

1. If the Tor service is running, stop it by typing Ctrl-C in the Terminal window where it's running.
2. Locate the Tor configuration file, named "torrc". You might have to hunt around to figure out where this file has landed. If you're on a Mac and used the Homebrew installation procedure, you will find a sample torrc file at /usr/local/etc/tor/torrc.sample. Make a copy of that file in the same directory with the name "torrc".
3. Open the torrc configuration file in a text editor. If you've ever poked around a configuration file for a system like the Apache web server, this should look pretty familiar: copious amounts of comments explaining the purpose of each section of the file, accompanied by inactive config parameters that can be switched on by removing the comment symbol ("#") from the front of the appropriate line. You can learn a lot about how Tor is set up by studying the comments in this file.
4. Edit the configuration file to enable your relay. This isn't too difficult:
   a. Find the line that reads "# ORPort 9001". This specifies the port on your computer used for incoming Tor traffic. Uncomment the line (remove the "#"); if you wish, you can also change the port number. Note, however, that whatever port you open must be accessible from the Internet (i.e., you have to ensure that it isn't blocked by your network or computer firewall). Enabling this single line is enough to turn your computer into a Tor relay, but it's good to make a few more adjustments, as below.
   b. Look for lines containing "ExitPolicy"; these govern the exit node behavior of your relay. Unless you want to run an exit relay, uncomment the line that reads "ExitPolicy reject *:*". As a note in the file indicates, this means "no exits allowed."
   c. Not essential, but a good idea: Find the lines containing "Nickname" and "ContactInfo." These help users of Tor refer to your relay (by its nickname) and figure out whom to contact if there's a problem with it (via ContactInfo).
5. Save the file and restart the Tor service. The first time you do this, it will take a little while for Tor to consult its directory of relays and build up enough information to start a network circuit (the Tor Project's own documentation advises that this can take up to twenty minutes). Be patient. Once it's finished, you should see a success message somewhere in the system output. And then you're up and running, relaying anonymous messages from the outside world!

For much more documentation about using Tor and running relays, consult the Tor Project website.

Special Configurations of Tor

The usual approach to using Tor is to install the Tor Browser bundle or the Tor service on a desktop computer, laptop, or server. It's a flexible system, though, and Tor has been adapted into a number of different forms. Some of the more notable examples include the following:

- Orwall, Orbot, Orfox, and related apps (https://guardianproject.info/apps/orfox, Android only) can route all of your Internet traffic through Tor on your phone or tablet. Orwall blocks non-Tor network connections; Orbot lets apps connect to Tor; and Orfox is the Android equivalent of the Tor Browser for desktops and laptops.
- iCepa (https://github.com/iCepa/iCepa) is the iOS equivalent of Orwall, intended to be a system-wide Tor connector. Still under development, it requires some manual configuration and installation—you won't find it available in the iTunes App Store (yet). There are a number of other browsers that *are* available in the App Store that purport to use Tor. Pick carefully, though; the impregnability of the Tor connection depends on the skill of the browser's developer.
- The single-board Raspberry Pi computer has grown steadily more powerful and capable, and now it makes a fine platform for a Tor relay too. There are a number of ways to get Tor up and running on the Pi, but perhaps one of the simplest is to use the tor-box command-line scripts (https://github.com/CMoncur/tor_box). This project includes detailed instructions for configuring Tor on a Raspberry Pi, most of which is done with the aid of a single executable script that sets things up to act as either a Tor client or a Tor relay.
- Tails (https://tails.boum.org) is a complete, self-contained, Tor-enabling operating system made to fit on a USB thumb drive. It can be used as a means of temporarily making any computer a safe system for anonymous Internet usage and all the other protections that Tor affords you. In order to do this, Tails is installed on a USB drive as a bootable system. When you use Tails, you boot your computer from the USB thumb drive instead of from its usual hard disk or flash drive. While using the Tails OS, the system works hard to ensure that no trace of your activities is left on the host computer. This extends even to preventing apps in Tails from using swap space (a section of a hard drive used as temporary memory storage) on the computer's hard drive. Tails can be downloaded for free and installed on an unlimited number of USB thumb drives. Consequently, it seems tailor-made for a library privacy workshop. Buy a batch of inexpensive thumb drives (4 GB minimum capacity) or have users bring their own; teach attendees how to use Tails correctly; and then send them on their way with their own, portable anonymity tool.

Privacy Outreach

The earlier chapters in this book focused on defense—strengthening your privacy policies and the barriers around your library's networked systems to protect them from incursion or surveillance. This chapter is about going on the offensive. With the Tor system, you have an opportunity to contribute to a worldwide effort to bring anonymous, surveillance-free Internet usage to everyone. And the final piece of the puzzle is to take what you've learned from this book and disseminate the information to your library users. How you go about this is up to you. A series of educational pamphlets is one option, with each one going into detail on one aspect of practical privacy protection (e.g., using good passwords). Frequently, though, people have so many questions and misconceptions about how security and privacy work online that it's useful to have knowledgeable library staff who can talk about these questions directly. A great way to do this is to offer a series of privacy workshops in the library. Doing a series, rather than several offerings of the same workshop, is recommended: it's likely that you won't get very far in a single session before getting bogged down in a Q&A about one or two of the particular topics that you're trying to teach. Start with the basics, then offer intermediate and advanced workshops to follow up on more specialized topics. If you can get your users to change just a few of their insecure computing practices, you'll be ahead of the game.

The specific topics that you cover are your choice. Size up your audience and their needs, and program accordingly. Here, though, are a few suggestions that you might want to incorporate in your planning:

- The beginning of this chapter talked about the important role that libraries play in defending the privacy of at-risk groups on the global stage. Remember, though, that in today's world, at-risk groups might not be that far away. Look at your constituency, think about what's going on in your corner of the world, and make a special effort to reach out to any advocacy or protest groups that might be under threat (or might be considered a threat by others). They may be grateful to have some guidance on how to protect themselves.
- Reassure your users that librarians are pro-privacy and on their side. The ALA makes the point that "while we librarians don't often think of ourselves as government bureaucrats, members of the public may see us as authorities just like a uniformed police officer or a robed judge" (ALA, 2014). Make sure there are no misconceptions about what your library teaches and upholds about user privacy.
- Try hosting a CryptoParty. CryptoParties (www.cryptoparty.in) are hosted all over the world as a way of educating the public about privacy and security. The intent and curriculum of a CryptoParty are similar to a traditional workshop, but the format is a little different. The event opens with a short introductory talk, but then people break up into small groups based on what they want to learn about. Usually tables or smaller meeting rooms are set up where members of the audience can go to hear about a specific topic—and, preferably, to actually implement the privacy protection in question while they're sitting there. For example, at one table, users could learn about using encryption to protect their laptop's hard drive, while at another table, users could do a privacy audit of the apps on their smartphones and revoke the permissions of any apps that they aren't still using. The CryptoParty website has more information about suggested formats and topics for parties as well as links to relevant resources and a list of upcoming events.
- Observe Choose Privacy Week (https://chooseprivacyweek.org). This event, another initiative of the ALA, is observed annually from May 1 to May 7 as a way of both promoting privacy protection and acknowledging the special relationship to privacy that libraries have. What you do to celebrate Choose Privacy Week is up to you and your colleagues, but the website provides suggestions and resources for planning your event.

Looking Ahead

The battle over online privacy is not going to end any time soon—the forces that are antagonistic to user privacy protection are simply too large to overcome completely. If nothing else, criminals and malicious hackers will continue trying to defeat online security for their own personal gain; new forms of malware will be introduced into the "wild" of the

Internet; new bugs will expose accidental vulnerabilities in security systems; and for the foreseeable future, governments and agencies preoccupied with the spread of terrorism will conclude that sacrificing the privacy of citizens is an acceptable price to pay for the chance to avert attacks. None of that is likely to change.

There is some good news, though. It's possible that the third major outside threat to privacy, online advertising and marketing systems, may prove to be a tractable problem. For the time being, ad blockers are doing a pretty good job of holding their own against intrusive advertising and tracking scripts. Developers at the ad firms are naturally working on solutions to this "problem," but unlike purveyors of pure malware, they have to abide by certain constraints placed on them by the technical architecture of web browsers and websites. Ad systems can't do just *anything* to track you, in other words. Makers of web browsers are becoming increasingly sensitive to the violations of privacy that online advertising and third-party scripts enable, and they are taking steps to curtail their activities. For now, the fight favors the browser makers and users.

Emboldened by Apple's resistance to FBI overreach and the general buzz about privacy, more and more tech companies are implementing encryption and other security features in their devices and apps by default. This will not eradicate malware attacks or unauthorized online surveillance, but it will make life more difficult for the third parties attempting them—and that's a good thing.

Library users are also awakening to the threats that are out there, and that fact is the greatest hope for the future of privacy protection. Librarians and library staff have a crucial role to play in protecting the privacy of their users, but they can only do so much to guard and educate. Once users are aware not only of the threats but of the existence of tools and countermeasures they can use to combat those threats, then they can join the fight on their own behalf. And isn't user empowerment what libraries are all about?

Key Points

This chapter has covered a lot of ground. Here are some main thoughts to take away:

- Libraries have a natural affinity for free-speech advocates, activists, and the voices of threatened minorities. Participating in large-scale privacy protection efforts is a natural outgrowth of this affinity.
- The Tor system is a robust network that enables users to browse the Internet and communicate while remaining (theoretically) anonymous. It relies on onion routing, a method of wrapping a message in multiple layers of encryption and relaying it from node to node through a network.
- The Tor Browser is a modified version of Firefox that enables web browsing through Tor in an easy-to-install and easy-to-use package.
- Tor is also the system used to access the .onion domain of the dark web, which consists of anonymously run websites that are used for both laudable activities (e.g., advocacy and free speech) and illegal ones (e.g., drug sales).
- Libraries can help the Tor network grow by hosting the nodes that compose the network. Individuals or organizations can host middle nodes, exit nodes, or bridge nodes with varying degrees of risk.
- Tor is expanding to other platforms, including mobile devices and single-board computers like the Raspberry Pi.

- The Tails operating system can be placed on a USB thumb drive and used as a mobile, temporary system for working with sensitive materials on any host computer without leaving "fingerprints."
- Privacy outreach and education are important components in a library privacy protection program. Workshops and CryptoParties are good ways of teaching your users about the basics and the details of keeping their private data safe online.
- While the outlook for privacy protection in the near future is not altogether good, there are signs of hope: good technical solutions to limit the impact of tracking by advertisers; more proactive work by tech companies to build secure devices and apps; and a growing awareness among users of the importance and feasibility of protecting their own privacy.

References

ALA (American Library Association). 2014. "Questions and Answers on Privacy and Confidentiality." American Library Association. July 1. www.ala.org/advocacy/privacy/FAQ.

Index

About the Author

Matthew Connolly is an application and web programmer at Cornell University Library, where he has worked for more than ten years on a variety of library services and tools for the public and library staff. He holds a master's in engineering from Cornell, specializing in systems engineering. He has published articles in both popular and peer-reviewed journals and coauthored *Using iPhones, iPads, and iPods: A Practical Guide for Librarians*. A longtime technology enthusiast and professional, Matthew has watched recent privacy-related developments in the tech, government, and legal sectors with growing interest and concern.